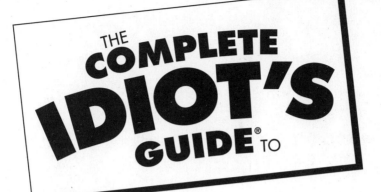

THE
COMPLETE IDIOT'S GUIDE® TO

Changing Old Habits for Good

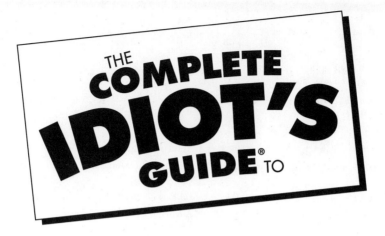

THE
COMPLETE
IDIOT'S
GUIDE® TO

Changing Old Habits for Good

by G. Alan Marlatt, Ph.D.,
and Deborah S. Romaine

ALPHA

A member of Penguin Group (USA) Inc.

ALPHA BOOKS

Published by the Penguin Group

Penguin Group (USA) Inc., 375 Hudson Street, New York, New York 10014, USA

Penguin Group (Canada), 90 Eglinton Avenue East, Suite 700, Toronto, Ontario M4P 2Y3, Canada (a division of Pearson Penguin Canada Inc.)

Penguin Books Ltd., 80 Strand, London WC2R 0RL, England

Penguin Ireland, 25 St. Stephen's Green, Dublin 2, Ireland (a division of Penguin Books Ltd.)

Penguin Group (Australia), 250 Camberwell Road, Camberwell, Victoria 3124, Australia (a division of Pearson Australia Group Pty. Ltd.)

Penguin Books India Pvt. Ltd., 11 Community Centre, Panchsheel Park, New Delhi—110 017, India

Penguin Group (NZ), 67 Apollo Drive, Rosedale, North Shore, Auckland 1311, New Zealand (a division of Pearson New Zealand Ltd.)

Penguin Books (South Africa) (Pty.) Ltd., 24 Sturdee Avenue, Rosebank, Johannesburg 2196, South Africa

Penguin Books Ltd., Registered Offices: 80 Strand, London WC2R 0RL, England

Copyright © 2008 by Amaranth IlluminAre

International Standard Book Number: 978-1-59257-780-4
Library of Congress Catalog Card Number: 2008929021

10 09 08   8 7 6 5 4 3 2 1

Interpretation of the printing code: The rightmost number of the first series of numbers is the year of the book's printing; the rightmost number of the second series of numbers is the number of the book's printing. For example, a printing code of 08-1 shows that the first printing occurred in 2008.

Printed in the United States of America

Note: This publication contains the opinions and ideas of its authors. It is intended to provide helpful and informative material on the subject matter covered. It is sold with the understanding that the authors, book producer, and publisher are not engaged in rendering professional services in the book. If the reader requires personal assistance or advice, a competent professional should be consulted.

The authors, book producer, and publisher specifically disclaim any responsibility for any liability, loss, or risk, personal or otherwise, which is incurred as a consequence, directly or indirectly, of the use and application of any of the contents of this book.

Most Alpha books are available at special quantity discounts for bulk purchases for sales promotions, premiums, fund-raising, or educational use. Special books, or book excerpts, can also be created to fit specific needs.

For details, write: Special Markets, Alpha Books, 375 Hudson Street, New York, NY 10014.

Publisher: *Marie Butler-Knight*
Editorial Director: *Mike Sanders*
Senior Managing Editor: *Billy Fields*
Executive Editor: *Randy Ladenheim-Gil*
Book Producer: *Lee Ann Chearney/Amaranth IlluminAre*
Development Editor: *Lynn Northrup*
Production Editor: *Kayla Dugger*

Copy Editor: *Nancy Wagner*
Cartoonist: *Steve Barr*
Cover Designer: *Bill Thomas*
Book Designer: *Trina Wurst*
Indexer: *Joan Green*
Layout: *Brian Massey*
Proofreader: *Mary Hunt*

Contents at a Glance

Contents

Introduction

It takes effort and focus to change, and it helps when you have a support team to cheer you on when you're going strong and to pick you up and get you going again when you stumble. We'd like this book to be part of your support team.

Our old habits run the gamut from annoying to disruptive or damaging. It doesn't matter what your habits are; the processes for change are the same. Though we take a lighthearted tone in our writing, we know the problems your habits create for you in your life are serious.

The information we present in this book reflects what's known in clinical jargon as "evidence-based" knowledge and methods—objectively studied, tested, and demonstrated to be reliable. It's not foolproof and not absolute—nothing is. But it is scientifically sound. And so you can apply all of this to your personal circumstances and intentions, we've included opportunities for you to craft your own map for change.

Although the stories of people and their habits that appear throughout this book reflect real issues, circumstances, and struggles, they are composites we've created to illustrate key points we want to make. You know, it's the picture's-worth-a-thousand-words approach, only we've painted our pictures with words. That you might say to yourself, "I know someone just like that!" or "Who told you about this?!" is testament to just how common, and predictable, the behaviors of habit truly are.

How to Use This Book

We've organized the chapters of this book into six sections, each of which explores a different aspect of habits and the processes of changing them.

Part 1, "It's Not Over Till It's Over," looks at the habits we have and how they came to be. You'll read about your brain's cravings for pleasure and how you develop habits—good and bad—to satisfy those cravings. You'll discover how your brain establishes pathways to make the tasks of daily life easier. And you'll learn why relapse is a normal part of the change process.

Part 2, "Giving Up, Getting Out, and Letting Go," explores the journey of change, from quitting the bad habit to developing new (and more satisfying) habits. You'll learn what researchers know about what happens in your brain and your body when you quit a habit. You'll see how your brain's desire to get the old habit back—relapse—distorts your perception. And you'll begin to plan your personal change itinerary.

Part 3, "Wanting and Needing," pulls back the curtain on what really drives our desires and the behaviors we use to try to meet them. You'll discover how these motivations cloud your view of yourself and your life and learn techniques to clear the haze so you can see things for what they really are. And you'll begin to explore the role of your personal environment—the people, places, and events of your daily life—in your habits and behaviors.

Part 4, "You Can't Do It Alone," investigates the roles other people play in your efforts to change. You'll gain new insights into who helps and who hinders and learn how to find the support you need from those who are closest to you as well as within the greater community. You'll see how you can help others who are also making changes.

Part 5, "Out with the Old, In with the New," examines what it means to you in your daily life to be this different person. You'll uncover your old habit's final hiding places and learn how to separate yourself from their pull on you. And you'll learn ways to manage pressures and stress in your life to keep your perspective and your well-being intact.

Part 6, "What Does Recovery Mean?" celebrates the new you! There's no looking back—these chapters take you into your future, into the life you've always believed you could enjoy. No longer does your old habit define you. Believing is what it's all about, and in these final chapters you'll learn more ways to keep the faith in yourself and your changes.

By the Way

We have a lot to say about habits and change, and sometimes what we want to tell you doesn't quite fit the main flow of information. When we've got something extra to tell you, you'll see it in a special box:

 Be Mindful

These boxes offer tips and suggestions for making the changes in your life that you desire.

 **Steer Clear**

These boxes warn you of pitfalls and challenges you might encounter along your journey of change.

def•i•ni•tion

These boxes define words and terms that may be unfamiliar to you or that have a particular context in this book.

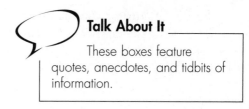

Talk About It

These boxes feature quotes, anecdotes, and tidbits of information.

Trademarks

All terms mentioned in this book that are known to be or are suspected of being trademarks or service marks have been appropriately capitalized. Alpha Books and Penguin Group (USA) Inc. cannot attest to the accuracy of this information. Use of a term in this book should not be regarded as affecting the validity of any trademark or service mark.

Part 1

It's Not Over Till It's Over

We know how to stop these bad habits of ours. We've had lots of practice. One minute we're sitting pretty, confident that *this* time we've beaten that old habit. Then before we know what happened, we're in the middle of it again. What we need are ways to make our changes stick for good.

The chapters in Part 1 explore the realities of our habits. Chapter 1 looks at the habits we have, good and not so good. Chapter 2 turns the spotlight on relapse—that all-too-familiar and oh-so-human slide back to the old habit. Chapter 3 uncovers the ways relapse pushes us even deeper into those old habits.

Everybody's Got at Least One Bad Habit

In This Chapter

◆ Defining a habit

◆ Looking at change through a different lens

◆ How much do your habits run (or ruin) your life? A self-quiz

◆ Other factors that might be at play

We all have habits we want to change. Maybe you can't resist the QVC special of the day, or never miss an episode of *The Biggest Loser*, even in reruns. Maybe you always need five more minutes (that stretch into hours) to finish a project or like this book's coauthor, Deb, can't start the day without a mug of coffee strong enough that the smell alone carries a caffeine buzz. Perhaps you nibble your fingernails to the quick, chew the ends of your pens, twirl your hair, or tug at your eyebrows.

Or perhaps you turn to your stash of candy bars when the day turns stressful—and anymore, *every* day is stressful. Maybe you can't resist the clatter of chips at the poker table, a last drink (make it a double) before last call, or a secret cigarette. Maybe you swear a blue streak whenever you're upset, belittle yourself when you make mistakes, or take on responsibilities that would overflow a 36-hour day. Oh, the habits we can have! The list is endless.

And odds are, you've changed some of those habits that cause you the greatest grief. Indeed, you've likely changed them over and over again. Experts tell us that 9 out of 10 of us fall back into old habits within a year of changing them, no matter what those habits are. It's not that we can't change our habits; we're actually quite good at it. What we don't handle quite so well is making the change stick.

The Thing About Habits

When it comes to habits, we just can't seem to help ourselves. It's as though we're on autopilot—and we are. We act without even thinking about what we're doing or why and how we're doing it. A *habit* is a pattern of *behavior* we learn over time; a particular situation causes us to engage in a specific behavior. That is, we do, think, or feel something which generates a result that somehow meets a need.

def•i•ni•tion

A **habit** is a pattern of behavior learned through repetition and reinforcement that results in automatic, or unconscious, thought, emotion, or action. A **behavior** is a thought, emotion, or action. A **trigger** is the circumstance—which may be a person, place, event, experience, stressor, or other factor—that activates a habit.

The next time the same circumstance arises, the behavior comes to us more quickly. The next time, even more quickly. And so on, until the *trigger* and the behavior blend into one, and we don't think about either. Before we know it, a habit is born. And like every product of creation from kids to ideas, a habit soon takes on a life of its own.

We rag on habits, but the truth is, without them we'd have a tough time making it through the day. Imagine if we had to consciously consider every little move and action we make. We'd never get out of bed! Habits are the brain's shortcuts for handling routine activities—thoughts, emotions, and behaviors. We engage in habitual behaviors, beneficial and not so beneficial, mostly without giving them a second thought. Our brains already know what to do and what to expect; habits are easy and efficient.

Most habits start out as helpful behaviors, like brushing our teeth and putting the milk back into the fridge after pouring some on our cereal, and many remain so. But some habits become unhelpful, undesirable, and even harmful over time. And some habits aren't good for us right from the get-go.

Because habits are automatic, we're often unaware that we engage in them. (Deb can brew a pot of coffee in the morning and not even realize she was in the kitchen.) Then comes that moment of truth when we realize—or someone points out to us—certain habits don't serve us so well anymore. They've become behaviors that cost us time, money, sleep, health, happiness—and sometimes relationships, jobs, and even freedom.

How Habits Come to Be

Though habits themselves come easy, the process of learning and perfecting them typically takes years, and we make many mistakes along the way. Look back to when you learned to drive a car, for example. Remember how overwhelming it seemed simply to back the car out of the garage and onto the street? Turn the key; start the engine; buckle up; look in the side mirrors; look in the rearview mirror; put your foot on the brake; put the shifter in reverse; look back over your shoulder; move your foot from the brake to the gas—*WHOA!* Open the garage door first! Whew.

Yet today you can go from your morning coffee to the office and not even remember your commute, let alone opening the garage door and backing out onto the street. Why? Habits. Learned patterns of behavior help you easily accomplish repetitious tasks. Though you no doubt have room for improvement in your driving habits, as do we all, these are nonetheless habits we generally accept as "good." We need such habits, and they benefit us. All habits start this way: they fulfill a need and provide a benefit.

 Be Mindful _____

Just for fun, pay attention to your thoughts, emotions, and actions the next time you head off on your regular commute to work or to the store. How much do you usually tune out? Does it take you longer to get there when you're paying such attention to detail? If you're driving, do you feel you're a better driver on this test trip? Does the extent of your automated behavior surprise you?

Often, and especially with the habits we want to change, the need and the benefit have an emotional component—the habit makes us feel good in some way. Identifying the need is like turning off the cruise control. Suddenly the road is actually beneath our wheels, and it takes attention and effort to keep those wheels on the road.

The Good and the Bad of It

"Good" and "bad" are such judgmental words, but we use them all the time to talk about our habits. So let's agree that here, in this book, these terms are shorthand for "works to support me" and "works against me." This gives us leeway to allow that sometimes a habit that's good for one person might be bad for another person. It's all in how the habit affects your life. And of course, some habits are bad for everyone … more on that in later chapters.

But I Like My Habits!

What's not to like about habits? They're comfortable and they make life easier. Like a pair of beat-up shoes or threadbare jeans, habits fit just right. But when we take them off and hold them up to the light, they often aren't what they were when they were new or what we think they are now.

Some habits, like waiting until the last minute to leave for the airport or to gather receipts to prepare the tax return, are more annoying for other people than for us. Oh, sure, there's the price of frenzy and anxiety. But a friend might have to pay for a taxi, or the accountant may have to work into the night.

Other habits have more serious consequences for us as well as others. A glass of wine with dinner may be the perfect complement to a lovely meal, but a bottle (or two … or three) is hazardous. You may not even recognize you drink as much as you do … or smoke, or engage in other habits that put your health and the safety of others at risk.

When it comes to the habits that make us uneasy, the habits we want to change, these are at the top of the list:

- Cigarette smoking
- Drinking alcohol
- Drug use/abuse
- Overeating/unhealthy eating habits/perpetual dieting
- Procrastination/chronic lateness
- Working too much
- Self-doubt/self-criticism/self-sabotage
- Gambling

- Shopping/exorbitant spending

- Web surfing/online activities

If yours is not on this list, that's okay. What matters is that it's important to *you*. Habits, like the people who have them, are widely diverse.

Often it's others in our lives—family, friends, coworkers, health-care providers—who first draw attention to the negative effects of our bad habits. Sometimes awakening comes in the form of a DUI arrest, bounced checks, or other situations that leave us little choice but to sit up and take notice.

Talk About It

Carlos started playing an online role-playing game at a friend's house but soon downloaded the free 30-day trial onto his own computer. He played through the first levels, acquiring assets and characters. By the end of the free trial, he had a screen identity and regular exchanges with other players, so he subscribed to the game. The moment he rushed through the door after work, he signed on and often played until 3 or 4 in the morning. He talked about the characters as though they were real people. Carlos started getting to work late and leaving early. The third time he didn't show up at all, his boss put him on probation and fired him after he missed three days in a row.

Your habits aren't really that bad, you say? You make it through the day just fine. Well, you can tell yourself that, for now. You can even tell yourself you're reading this book to prove to yourself (or whomever gave you the book) your habits aren't all that bad. But you *are* reading this book, and that's the first step in the right direction. And who knows, maybe your habits really aren't that bad. But changing them might make your life amazingly better!

Great Expectations

Wouldn't it be great to wake up tomorrow morning with a whole new slate of habits? To have the slate wiped clean of all the old, counterproductive, destructive, flat-out bad habits we've accumulated? And in their place, have all new, productive, affirming, enviable *good* habits?

The problem isn't that we don't know what to do when it comes to changing our habits. We know all too well how to change, as our numerous excursions into success demonstrate. The challenge is turning those side trips into lifelong journeys.

When we're first forming habits, we don't know that's what we're doing. We may have enough insight to know we're learning something new, especially when it's something we've chosen to do such as driving or typing or pitching a curve ball. Even bad habits like cigarette smoking have a conscious learning curve, a period of time when we're figuring out how to do things like, with smoking, for example, to inhale without having a seizure.

When we learn new behaviors—including patterns of thought and emotion—we usually have some level of conscious desire or intent. We expect—or should expect—to make mistakes along the way. And we expect to eventually reach a point, through focus and practice, where the behavior becomes automatic and its results predictable: a habit.

But when we're trying to change habits we already have, forget process—we want instant results! We forget that we are again learning new behaviors. We forget that this learning takes focus, time, and practice. And we don't recognize that we're at the same time _un_learning old behaviors. Change requires conscious preparation, concentration, and practice.

A New Model for Change

If so many of us are back in the ruts of our old habits within a year of working so hard to break free, is the problem with us or with our approaches to change? Until the 1990s, health experts and regular people alike presumed _relapse_ was a flaw of some sort in the individual. With the right amount of focus, commitment, and willpower,

according to the prevailing wisdom, permanent change was not only possible but also inevitable. Therefore, according to the prevailing wisdom, inability to change or to maintain a change reflected an inability of the individual to put forth enough focus, commitment, and willpower.

Then along came a new wave of researchers, among them Alan, our own expert coauthor, who decided to look at the problem through a more practical lens. It was curious, these researchers reasoned, that the approach was right, yet 90 percent of people who used it failed. Could it be—gasp!—that the approach to change was flawed?

Twenty-five years of research have since demonstrated that, while perhaps not really flawed, many long-held ideas about changing habits were at least incomplete. The foundational belief that change is an event gave way to the understanding that change is fluid and dynamic. Focus, commitment, and willpower remain the cornerstones of change. But within this triangle lies an entire landscape of process with predictable challenges and outcomes. The better we understand this landscape, the more successfully we can navigate it.

Habit ... Or Something More?

Until recently, health experts viewed *addiction* as a physical or biochemical state in which the body experienced a change in function with and without the source of the addiction, such as alcohol, narcotic drugs, or the nicotine in cigarettes. Boom—you're hooked. Research into the functioning of the brain with high-tech help, such as PET (positron-emission tomography) scans that let scientists peek into the inner workings of the brain, shows that addictive habits are really a complex intermingling of physiology, chemistry, and behavior.

Today most health experts use the term *addictive behaviors*. This gives focus to the importance of the behavioral aspects and the intertwining of physiological, psychological, and social factors. Addictive behavior often involves substances such as drugs, alcohol, and nicotine. Such substances do alter the way our bodies function, establishing *dependence*.

def•i•ni•tion

> **Addiction** or **addictive behavior** is a pattern of behavior in which you continue to engage even when the result is harmful to you in some way. **Dependence** occurs when one has a physical or emotional need for a substance or behavior.

However, eating disorders, compulsive gambling, workaholism, impulsive shopping, endless web surfing, and other intense habits—even those that are otherwise good for us, such as exercise—may also cross the border into addictive behaviors. Some experts call these habits "soft addictions" when they reach the level of interfering with everyday life. Your brain on a shopping high might look very much like your brain on drugs—the same kinds of biochemical changes take place. We discuss this idea in more detail in Chapter 2.

Addictive behaviors have layers and complexities that often require the aid of a professional, such as a physician or psychologist, to help you unravel. Until you uncover the key factors that drive an addiction, your efforts to change your habits are not likely to succeed over the long term. It's worthwhile to take a closer look at your habits to see whether other factors are at play.

Walking the Line ... Or Over It: A Self-Quiz

Are your personal habits simply counterproductive, or are they truly disruptive? Even when you know some of your habits do you no good, you may not realize how much they affect your daily life. This short self-quiz will help you get a better idea. Select one habit, then choose the answer—a, b, c, or d—that best fits each question. You can come back to repeat the self-quiz for as many habits as you like.

1. Are you late for or do you miss work because of your habit?

    a. No, never

    b. Every now and then

    c. Yes, but not often enough for anyone to notice

    d. Yes, but they've come to expect this from me, so it's not really a problem

2. Are you late for or do you miss family or social commitments because of your habit?

    a. No, never

    b. Every now and then

    c. Yes, but I can usually appease them with treats or gifts

    d. Yes, but they've come to expect this from me so they should know to go ahead without me

3. Do you get into arguments with family members, coworkers, friends, or others about your habit?

    a. No, never

    b. Every now and then

    c. Yes, but only because they don't understand

    d. Yes, at least once a week

4. Do you experience unpleasant or adverse physical effects as a result of your habit?

    a. No, never

    b. Every now and then

    c. Yes, but not often or severe enough for anyone to notice

    d. Yes, at least once a week

5. Do other people worry about your behavior or warn you to control yourself?

    a. No, never

    b. Hmmm … I've never noticed

    c. I hear rumors, but no one says anything to me

    d. Pretty much all the time

6. Do you take extraordinary risks to indulge your habit?

    a. No, never

    b. What do you mean by extraordinary?

    c. Yes, but I'm very good at covering my tracks

    d. Yes, at least once a week

7. Do you hide your habit from others?

    a. No, never

    b. I just happen to be alone; I don't plan it that way

    c. Only from those who don't approve

    d. Always

Fill in the number of responses for each letter choice:

a = _____

b = _____

c = _____

d = _____

If you got all a's, then yes! Advance directly to Go, and collect $200! (Monopoly money, of course.) Your habits are of the ordinary kind, which is not to make less of them ... we know they cause you discomfort and disruption in your life, and you want to make long-lasting changes.

If your answers are a mix of a's and b's, take a close look at your behaviors. It's likely your habit is walking the line, and you may benefit from professional help. If most of your answers are c's, you're back-stroking down Denial River. And mostly d's ... you already know you have an addiction, even if you don't admit it to others. When substances drive your habits—eating, smoking, drinking, doing drugs—your chances of success in changing your habits are likely to improve when you seek professional help.

> **Steer Clear** _____
>
> It isn't always *what* you do but the extent to which it affects your life that flirts with—or crosses—the line between habit and addiction. Breaking the hold of an addiction often requires help from a qualified professional such as a physician or psychologist. Treatment approaches may include cognitive-behavioral therapy (CBT), medication (pharmacotherapy), meditation, hypnosis, and acupuncture, among others.

No matter whether your habits are ordinary or are influenced by other factors, the information and suggestions in this book are relevant for you. When substances such as drugs—including illicit drugs, prescription drugs, alcohol, and nicotine—are involved, however, the complexity of issues may mean you need additional help. The insights and methods we present come from Alan's decades of research and work teaching people how to use relapse prevention methods across the spectrum of addictive habits.

A Matter of Mental Health

The hallmark of habit is a repeated, automatic pattern of behavior. However, when the pattern becomes extreme, the circumstance may include—and sometimes instead be—a mental-health condition that requires treatment from a psychiatrist or psychologist.

For example, it's one thing to wash your hands throughout the day as a matter of personal hygiene. This is a good habit. But when you wash your hands 17 times—no more, no less, and start over if you lose count—every time you touch a doorknob, you might instead have *obsessive-compulsive disorder* (*OCD*).

The hallmark of OCD is excessive repetition of certain thoughts and actions—from the outside, looking for all the world like habits. But the thoughts and actions fill the conscious mind to the exclusion of all else (the obsessive part), and there is no conscious control over the behaviors that follow (the compulsive part). The person may recognize the thoughts and behaviors are not productive but is powerless to pull out. Though habit is a factor, the underlying issue is the disorder.

def•i•ni•tion

Obsessive-compulsive disorder (OCD) is a mental health condition in which a person has uncontrolled, repeated unpleasant thoughts or feelings (obsessions) and engages in uncontrolled, repeated behaviors (compulsions) to try to make the thoughts or feelings go away.

Steer Clear

David Hyde Pierce's character Dr. Niles Crane on the long-running TV sitcom *Frasier* (a role for which Pierce won four Emmy awards) and Jack Nicholson's character Melvin Udall in the 1998 movie *As Good As It Gets* (for which Nicholson won an Oscar) are among the memorable portrayals of life on the fringes of OCD. Though we see much humor in the struggles of these fictional characters, in real life, OCD often prevents those who have it from functioning in their daily lives.

Sometimes the addictive habit is a misguided attempt to self-medicate. For example, depression and excessive alcohol consumption often go hand-in-hand. The "buzz" from a few drinks takes the edge off; a few drinks more make for a fuzzy euphoria. With enough to drink, there's numbness. Some people use food in a similar way, though the effects on the body are different.

Other mental health conditions in which habits take on increased significance include depression, generalized anxiety disorder (GAD), self-injury (cutting), eating disorders (anorexia nervosa, bulimia, binge eating), and bipolar disorder. Some experts believe that mental-health conditions often underlie addictive habits. Although the methods we discuss throughout this book are commonly part of the overall treatment approach for many mental-health conditions, appropriate diagnosis and medical treatment are essential.

Stop the Merry-Go-Round, I Want to Get Off!

People change in steps, one step at a time. Some people appear to leap into new habits, but they're only putting the pieces together faster. We all learn new behaviors one step at a time.

Whether our habits are out there for all the world to see or we keep them to ourselves (so we convince ourselves, anyway), those that prevent us from living as we desire can be especially painful. It's no easy task, changing a habit. But with a strong support structure—within yourself as well as in your personal environment—you can change any habit … for good.

The Least You Need to Know

- Although we perceive them as automatic, habits are patterns of learned behavior.

- Many habits are beneficial, and we need habits to function in our daily lives.

- The formation of a habit is a dynamic, though predictable, process, rather than a defined event.

- Changing a habit requires conscious, persistent focus to develop new behaviors that replace old ones.

Relapse Happens

In This Chapter

- ◆ Wired for action: your brain on habits
- ◆ Forget the stairway to heaven; hop on the pathway to pleasure
- ◆ You can only change when you're ready … really!
- ◆ Change is a moving target

For as long as we've known about habits, we've known about relapse. Indeed, relapse is the most predictable component of the effort to change. The diet industry banks on it, knowing we'll drop pounds in the short term and then pack them back on plus more before we even know what happened. But relapse isn't failure. It's human, it's predictable, and it's not the end of the world—it's part of the process of change.

We tend to focus efforts to change on the end results of complex sequences of events that take place deep within the most mysterious structure of the human body: the brain. We want to stop smoking; we throw away the cigarettes and resolve that ne'er again shall even one—not *one!*—touch our lips. This is like purging the dandelions from our lawn by mowing their dancing yellow heads. Of course we'll have new blooms budding in a few days, we left the roots!

Changing our bad habits means getting to their roots. To change the way we behave, we need to change the way our brains function. Change starts at the cellular level. So let's get started with a little Brainology 101. Don't worry, there are no tests!

Your Wired Brain

In Chapter 1, we touched on the formation of habits as the laying down of patterns that the brain remembers and follows without so much as a conscious thought. This happens because brain cells develop a form of chemical shorthand that makes communication among them incredibly efficient.

Neurons—the brain cells that transmit information in the form of electrical impulses—don't actually touch each other. If they did, they'd be "on" all the time. Imagine what chaos that would be—you'd never have a clear thought or snap your fingers, let alone walk. So instead tiny channels, called synapses or synaptic clefts, separate brain neurons from one another.

A neuron looks like a life form from the far side of the galaxy, though you need a high-tech microscope to see it. And to look at it, you wouldn't think it was capable of doing all that much. It has a blobby, roundish body with a single "eye"—its nucleus, which directs the neuron's activity.

Like a bad haircut from the '70s, dendrites stick out around the cell body. These branchlike filaments pull in information; they are like the neuron's antennae poised in the synapse. The axon extends from the neuron's body like a stalk or stem. Most neurons have a single axon with one or more frills at the end; axons send out information.

def•i•ni•tion

A **neurotransmitter** is a chemical messenger that enables communication among neurons (nerve cells). A **neuroreceptor** is a specialized molecule on a neuron's axon that receives (binds with) the neurotransmitter.

When one neuron wants to communicate, it releases a messenger molecule called a *neurotransmitter* from a dendrite. The neurotransmitter floats into the synapse until it makes contact with a *neuroreceptor* on another neuron's axon. The neurotransmitter docks, or binds, with the neuroreceptor, transferring its message.

When brain neurons receive the same messages over and over, they align themselves into pathways that speed the messages along. It's like your brain on autopilot. These pathways are both physical and functional. The brain neurons extend and shift their dendrites and axons to narrow the gaps between them. And the neurons may acquire extra neuroreceptors so they can accept a higher volume of neurotransmitter molecules—like the post office brings on extra staff to handle holiday package shipping.

In Chapter 1, we established that habits form to help the brain handle repetitious behaviors. How that happens at the cellular level is like the old-fashioned fire brigade line that winds its way from the river to the house on fire. It's faster and more efficient for people to line up and pass buckets of water up the line than for each person to fill a bucket, run to pour it on the fire, and run back to the water for the next bucketful.

Of course, your brain's pathways are incredibly intricate and complex. And unlike the fire brigade line, they remain in place after they develop. Your brain, after all, is all about efficiency. It sees no point in reinventing the wheel … or the pathway. And plenty of other neurons—millions and millions—build more pathways. Your brain has nearly unlimited capacity for such projects. This is great news for you and your new habits—think of the possibilities!

Yeah, Baby, Let's Have More of That!

One of the largest and most highly developed pathways in your brain is the pleasure pathway, also called the reward pathway. Its primary neurotransmitter is *dopamine*, the fairy godmother of all "feel good" sensations we experience. (Dopamine also is essential for voluntary movement, like walking, but through different pathways in other neighborhoods of your brain.)

def•i•ni•tion

Dopamine is a key neurotransmitter in the brain associated with perceptions of pleasure, desire, elevated mood, and motivation.

When you do something your brain perceives as pleasurable—say, like eating chocolate or having sex—the neurons along the pleasure pathway get so excited they flood dopamine molecules into the synapses. There are only so many neuroreceptors for dopamine docking, though, so all those molecules crowd and jostle in the gaps. Wow, what a rush! The frenzy sends your brain's pleasure meter off the scale.

Some behaviors are naturally pleasurable, and you learn to repeat them to experience their pleasure. Among them are life's basics when it comes to feeling good: food, sex, and intense physical activity, such as sports. Your brain even learns to link pleasure with the experiences that result in it and react in anticipation of them. How about that lovely dinner out before a romantic evening in?

Oh, but you say that intense physical activity is not as satisfying as food or sex? This may be because the experience of food or sex provides more of an instant gratification; to experience the benefits and pleasures of intense physical activity requires establishing a core fitness level and working out from there to improve health and strength. If you embark on a fitness program, be sure to consult your doctor and a good personal trainer to get you properly started. Then you're more likely to stick with it, and reap those pleasure rewards (and all the other rewards that come with being fit)!

Talk About It

A PET (positron-emission tomography) scan uses a harmless and rapidly deteriorating radioisotope that piggybacks onto glucose molecules. Glucose, or sugar, is the brain's energy source. Active brain cells gobble glucose, so they really light up on the scan. PET scans can show researchers how substances such as cocaine and behaviors such as gambling activate and alter the brain's pleasure pathways. PET scans also can show the long-term, and perhaps permanent, changes in the brains of people who have addictions compared to the brains of those who don't.

The pleasure pathway links numerous areas of the brain, though not necessarily in direct fashion. And not, new research suggests, in the same ways in all brains. Some nerve impulses may shoot straight to a specific destination while others dart off on side trips. The pleasure pathway also interacts with other brain pathways, some of which aim to dampen the pleasure effect. Even in your brain, there are party-poopers.

Here are some of the main stops along the pleasure pathway:

♦ The ventral tegmental area (VTA), a collective of specialized neurons near the base of your brain, just above the brainstem, which produces significant amounts of the feel-good neurotransmitter dopamine

♦ The nucleus accumbens, which determines how many dopamine receptors brain neurons have (and thus how good those neurons can make you feel) and is believed to be the bridge between emotion and reason, playing a key role in motivation

♦ The amygdala, an almond-shaped structure in the core of your brain that receives and decodes primal emotions, such as fear and desire, and establishes a *conditioned response* to them

♦ The hippocampus, not a college for huge water beasts but rather your brain's gallery of intense, pleasurable memories

♦ The hypothalamus, which sits at the top of your brainstem and regulates the nerve and chemical signals from your brain to your body that tell you to eat, drink, have sex, and otherwise be merry

♦ The prefrontal cortex, a segment of the front of your brain—your thinking brain—that's responsible for *selective attention*, learning, motivation, planning, intellect, short-term memory, and interpreting mood and emotion

def•i•ni•tion

A **conditioned response** is a learned association between a cue and a behavior that have no natural connection—for example, feeling hungry (the behavior) when you hear a clock chime five o'clock (the cue) because when you were a child dinner was served promptly at 5 P.M., by the chime of the mantle clock (the learned association).

Selective attention is the ability to choose to focus on specific details at the exclusion of others—for example, listening to one person in a crowded room. Selective attention is crucial to learning and making reasoned decisions.

Your brain enjoys pleasure—and what's not to enjoy about pleasure?—so much that it can even override its own protective processes. You might even say your brain's hooked on pleasure. Your bad habits are living proof.

Rewired: Compulsive Behavior

With persistent exposure to substances and experiences that activate the pleasure pathway, the brain neurons along the route further change. Their dendrites and axons enlarge and expand, even becoming distorted and misshapen. Neuron cell bodies change to respond more quickly to the impulses that reach them.

Your amygdala, charged with protecting your nervous system, responds by reducing the numbers of neuroreceptors. With less neurotransmitter docking, you get less effect. So it takes more of whatever you're doing to get the same thrill. Your brain builds *tolerance*. You escalate your habit; you're compelled to seek that which gives you pleasure. And so the cycle continues.

def•i•ni•tion

Tolerance is the brain's diminished response to persistent stimulation.

Many researchers believe these changes are permanent or, at the least, are very long term, though the technology to study them is still too new for clear answers. But it appears that the brain essentially rewires itself to get more of what it craves, those *goo-oo-ood* feelings. And your brain will literally stop at nothing in its pursuit of bliss and happiness, even if it kills you.

You, however, can step in to break the chain and change the habit. Because also built into your brain's amazing design is the ability to think, reason, and plan—the foundation of learned behaviors through which you can plot new brain pathways.

Dancing the Limbic Limbo

The brain's pleasure pathway closely intertwines with the limbic system, a network of structures deep within the brain. Among them are some of the key stops along the pleasure pathway: the amygdala, the hippocampus, and the hypothalamus. The limbic system integrates memory, emotion, learning, and motivation.

Though many of the brain's pathways intersect with the pleasure pathway, none does so with such intensity as the limbic system. Habit pathways also intersect with the limbic system, giving them direct access to the pleasure pathway. Your brain is wired for pleasure, and not much gets in the way of it getting what it wants.

The Path of Your Long-Standing Habits

Dealing with a long-standing habit is like living in a house on the corner where everyone cuts across your lawn because it's shorter and faster than walking all the way around on the sidewalk. Before long a wide and distinct path diagonals the corner, and you've got more people traipsing through your yard than taking the sidewalk. Some wave and greet you by name and pick up your newspaper and put it on your porch. Maybe you should invite everyone in for breakfast!

At first you don't mind; it's kind of fun to know so many of your neighbors. But after a while you don't much like the look of this swathe through your lawn, like a scar. And each day you have more trash to clean up. It's not so much fun anymore.

So you throw some grass seed on the path, cover it with topsoil, and put up a few "please stay off the grass" signs. For a few days people stop, look at the signs, and stay on the sidewalk. Then one morning, here comes Phil from the brown house in the middle of the block. He's running late, and the bus is already at the stop. He doesn't look at the signs, just dashes across on the path. Later in the day Maria comes by.

She's on her way to the library and carries two bags of books. She notices the footprints in the dirt, turns, and takes the path; the books are heavy and it's shorter. By week's end the new topsoil is hard-packed. And Bette Sue's Chihuahua is leaving you presents again, daily.

In your frustration, you plant a hedge around the edge of your lawn and cut off access to the path. Over time, grass grows over the path and, for the most part, it blends into the rest of the lawn. People walk around on the sidewalk, but those who remember still slow and look over the hedge. The path is still there even though no one uses it now.

Steer Clear

The longer your habit thrives, the more ingrained in your brain it becomes. Literally. Scientists have long known that substances such as narcotics, alcohol, and nicotine physically change the way the brain functions. New research demonstrates that activities which generate a thrill—ranging from base jumping to high-stakes gambling—do the same.

Unraveling the Riddle of Relapse

In the late 1970s and early 1980s, faced with the knowledge that at least three-fourths of those who completed alcohol treatment would drink again within three months, Alan and his colleagues decided to add a psychology component to the treatment mix with their alcohol treatment clients. They conducted a session of classes to teach these clients to identify, anticipate, and cope with their individual triggers for drinking.

The novelty of this approach was that it applied a conventional psychotherapy method—*cognitive-behavioral therapy (CBT)*—in an unconventional setting. The approach dulled a key feature of relapse: the risk of surprise. Preparation and practice could trump temptation. Over the next decade, relapse prevention became a staple across the spectrum of behavior modification. (See Appendix B for further reading about the research and writings of Dr. G. Alan Marlatt and colleagues.)

def•i•ni•tion

Cognitive-behavioral therapy (CBT) is a treatment approach within psychology based on learning to recognize your personal high-risk situations and developing behaviors to respond to them.

Stutter Step: The Lapse

So you sat in your car after work and ate five candy bars, one after the other. It's been three months since you've indulged this old habit, but you had a really rough day. The boss was on your back about every little thing. The network was down for most of the morning, so you couldn't print the report that was due for your 11 A.M. meeting. Coworkers and customers alike were snippy and demanding. The call from school checking to make sure your daughter truly was home with the flu for the fourth day in a row pushed you over the edge. You didn't even think about it; you simply bought five candy bars—the limit of your cash supply—from the vending machine in the lobby. And now scattered around you are the empty wrappers, stark evidence of your *lapse.*

As distressed as you feel when you recognize what you've done, it's not the end of the world. More important, it's not the end of your efforts to change your ways. And it's not necessarily the first step on the path back to your old habit—unless you keep walking toward it.

def•i•ni•tion

A **lapse** is a single episode of the old habit. **Coping skills** are behaviors that you learn and practice so you can make choices in high-risk situations that prevent lapsing or relapsing.

We all lapse in the process of changing habits, often when we least expect to do so. We're unprepared for or unsuspecting of a situation in which we're especially vulnerable, and the old habit surges to the front of the line. This is the pivot point of relapse prevention, and it's where the *coping skills* you learn can help you turn your back on the siren call of your old habit.

I Hate Myself! I'm Such an Idiot!

Alan and other addiction psychologists know the very idea that you've taken a step sideways is enough to send you swirling into an emotional downspout. You feel you've failed, and nothing you say or do can redeem you. So you might as well keep right on sliding.

Okay, hold it right there! That's a nice little melodrama you've got going there, but it's oh so predictable. Yep. Predictable. It's like water from ice. You see, in the psych world the phenomenon you're experiencing even has an official name: *abstinence-violation effect* (*AVE*). You feel guilty and ashamed because you let everybody down, including yourself. You feel helpless, hopeless, and doomed to return to the path of your old habit.

This is a mind game your own brain plays with you. But these are *your* rules, now, and this is *your* game of change. Your brain pathways have hijacked you. So step back onto the platform and let this train leave without you. (And by the way, you're not an idiot. You're perfectly normal. You'll learn from this and be stronger for it. Next time, you'll be ready for this particular hazard!)

def•i•ni•tion

> The **abstinence-violation effect (AVE)** is a predictable and common reaction to a return to an old habit. Hallmarks of this reaction include feelings of guilt, shame, and hopelessness.

At the Very Least, Do Less Harm

Needle exchange programs, when they first surfaced in the 1980s, polarized health experts. While none could legitimately dispute their value in the context of reducing the spread of infectious diseases (namely, at the time, HIV/AIDS and hepatitis), some challenged the perceived encouragement for illicit intravenous drug use. Now, twenty-some years later, needle exchange programs are fundamental to infection control efforts around the world.

There's a fine line between encouraging a habit and acknowledging that people are going to engage in the habit no matter the danger to themselves and others. *Harm reduction* efforts attempt to walk that line to minimize the risks and the damage done. If you can't get your mind around something like needle exchange programs, try this one: designated driver. Need we say more?

def•i•ni•tion

> **Harm reduction** is a structured approach to minimizing the risks of potentially dangerous habits, such as drinking or substance abuse. Common examples of harm reduction efforts include needle exchange programs, moderate drinking, designated driver practices, and condom distribution. Harm reduction views risk as a continuum (scale from most risk to least risk) rather than a dichotomy (either/or).

The Stages of Change

About the same time Alan and his colleagues were reconfiguring perceptions and understanding about relapse, two other young psychologists—Carlo DiClemente, Ph.D., and James Prochaska, Ph.D.—were redrawing the big picture. What if, they proposed, change is a fluid process, not an event?

DiClemente and Prochaska called their approach the "Transtheoretical Model of Change," and by the late 1990s it had revolutionized substance abuse treatment programs. (See Appendix B for further reading about the work of DiClemente and Prochaska.) Psychologists also realized the concepts and steps in the model—now commonly called the Stages of Change model—apply broadly to the process of behavioral change, no matter what the change.

The Stages of Change

1. **Precontemplation**

2. **Contemplation**

3. **Preparation**

4. **Action**

5. **Maintenance OR**

6. **Relapse**

Though for the most part these stages are linear—that is, we move from one stage to the next in sequence—there also may be considerable overlap between stages, or one might go back and forth before finally moving to the next stage. Each stage, or the sequence overall, takes no set length of time. The one clear "rule" is that an individual can only deal with what's happening within the stage where he is. He can't do what he's not ready to do.

Many people move back and forth between stage 5, Maintenance, and stage 6, Relapse. These two stages represent a "fork in the road." The choices we make determine the fork we take. Neither is a journey set in stone. Some people stay in stage 5 for years or decades. Other people sometimes visit stage 6. With conscious awareness (mindfulness), these visits become less frequent and shorter over time.

Stage 1, Precontemplation: Not *My* Problem

You don't know it yet, but you have a habit that's not doing you any good and may be doing you harm. Odds are, you're alone in your secret; family, friends, and coworkers do know. But they aren't saying much to you because you're not listening. Your habit is not that bad; you're doing just fine, thank you very much. And who are they to say you've even got a habit, anyway?

For most people, precontemplation is the longest stage and can span years. In other models of change, such as the *12-step programs*, this is the stage of denial.

def•i•ni•tion

The **12-step programs** are recovery programs that require participants to follow specific procedures to remain "clean" from addictive behaviors. The original 12-step program was Alcoholics Anonymous, founded in 1935. The 12-step program concept views risk as a dichotomy (either/or) rather than a continuum.

Stage 2, Contemplation: Well, Maybe

The light's beginning to shine for you … often because someone else is shining it *on* you. Maybe your boss put you on probation; the highway patrol stopped you for DUI; your doctor told you your blood sugar's borderline for diabetes; or you've realized that for what you spent on cigarettes last year, you could've gone to Paris for two weeks. But … is the light really that bright? Maybe, maybe not.

You're starting to watch other people who you believe have problems because of similar habits and behaviors, and what you see is uncomfortably familiar. This is an interior stage; you're spending a lot of energy to think about your habit and how it affects your life, but no one else would know it because you're still very much engaged in the behaviors of the habit.

Stage 3, Preparation: Pondering Pros and Cons

Okay, you've decided maybe there is something to all of this, so you cruise the web in search of information about how other people have tackled this same habit. You might talk, in a roundabout way, to people at the gym or in the lunchroom who seem to share your habit. You might even call a few substance or alcohol treatment clinics, fitness centers, or smoking cessation programs. And maybe you've already started to make small changes, just to see whether you can and how it feels.

Because this is a stage of transition, most people stay in it for a fairly short time— a few weeks to a few months is typical. Being able to find encouraging, supportive information is crucial. Fortunately your budding desire to change is steering you toward resources that can help.

Stage 4, Action: Get Out of My Way!

You're convinced. Your habit is responsible for all that's wrong in your life. So you're gonna charge right through it and put it to rest once and for all. You're strong; you're in control; and you're winning. In your head, you might already be across the finish line, and you feel great.

For many people, this is the most public stage of change. You've come out, so to speak. Of course this is no surprise to those who are in your everyday life, but everyone's relieved to have it in the open. Friends and family—and even the strangers waiting in line at the grocery store with whom you spontaneously and exuberantly share your efforts—are supporting you and rooting for you.

This is also a goal-driven stage, so it's easy to measure—and celebrate—your success.

Stage 5, Maintenance: Staying the Course

Everyday life is not quite as thrilling as the chase, but it's where habits live. And who knew habits lived such lavish, complicated lifestyles! Every time you turn around, you find another temptation, another challenge. Little wonder you developed the habit in the first place; it's everywhere.

Be Mindful _____

A recent study suggests the easiest way to change one habit is to change several habits that are related. The study looked at people who had three lifestyle risk factors for heart disease: smoking, high blood pressure, and lack of physical exercise. Those who concentrated on stopping or reducing their smoking, reducing the amount of salt in their diets, and taking daily walks were more successful in making measurable improvement in at least one habit than were those who tackled only one of the three habits.

In the minds of everyone else, you've done it. The support team's moved on, either to cheer for someone else or back to their own lives. But how are you supposed to do this all by yourself? And for some people, the excitement of making changes becomes as much a habit as the habit itself (more about this in Chapter 3).

Maintaining your new habits and behaviors requires a different focus than changing them did and encompasses a new set of challenges. Relapse prevention moves to front and center.

Stage 6, Relapse: On the Old Trail Again

What happened? After all that hard work, even you don't quite know how or why, but here you are, back in the rut of the old habit. You've relapsed. Not defensively, but matter-of-factly, you need to say to yourself, "Okay, now what?" because change is a process, not an event—and relapse is part of the process.

The pull of habit is intensely strong, and the old habit's been around a lot longer than the new habit. The challenge of relapse is to identify the factors—those pesky, persistent triggers—that conspired to pull you back.

Chronic Relapse Disease

Like the path in the lawn that never quite goes away even when people stop using it, once formed, your habits don't truly disappear. Or, if you're not the lawn-care type—like erasing data from your computer hard drive. The illusion that troublesome habits are gone may be strong, but there really isn't anywhere for them to go. Some may forever remain dormant after you replace them with good, supportive habits, and you never know of them again. Others break through now and again, like corrupted files.

In light of new understanding about how the brain functions, health experts are moving away from the perception of addictive behavior as a contained event that, like an inflamed appendix, is cured by removing its apparent cause. Instead, we're now looking at the full gamut of habits—from substance abuse to cutting to procrastination to nail-biting—collectively as chronic conditions. And, like some chronic health conditions, such as high blood pressure or diabetes, they require diligent, ongoing care and maintenance. Plus, like other chronic conditions, they feature periods of remission and periods of relapse.

More and more, we're hearing the term *chronic relapse disease.* The condition (the addictive habit) is chronic (always present with symptoms that wax and wane). The element of relapse (returning to the ways of the old habit) is simply part of the sequence. This is the "addiction as a brain disease" model in which there is no cure.

Now, had it been left to us, we'd have taken the glass half-full perspective and gone with "chronic remission disease" because most people spend far more time in remission (following the path of new, good habits) than in relapse. And because the best way to get where you want to go is to look in that direction, you can spend even more time there when you focus attention and effort on the new habit rather than worrying about falling back into the old. But first, we do need to explore what goes wrong when we slip off track. So let's move on to Chapter 3 and take a closer look at where our habits take us.

The Least You Need to Know

- Your brain establishes pathways among neurons (brain cells) to make communication efficient.

- Your brain has numerous pleasure centers that direct your behaviors.

- A sidestep or a slip—a lapse—is not necessarily a strong cause for alarm and need not be the first step to relapse.

- Successful change requires both time and timing.

The Best of Times, the Worst of Times

In This Chapter

- ◆ Why do we ride the rollercoaster of our habits?

- ◆ Relapse can be its own kind of thrill

- ◆ Look where you want to go

- ◆ Small changes, huge effects

Up, down, high, low, fast curves, and jolting stops—what a rollercoaster, these bad habits of ours are! Our habits mess with our bodies, our heads, and our hopes. So why do we keep going back for another ride?

Some of us, whether we admit it or not, thrive on the excitement all the havoc causes us. When we're on the roll of a bad habit, all we feel is the thrill. What's wrong with everybody else, that they don't get it? This is what life's all about!

Bad Habits in the Spotlight

Celebrities who lapse—and relapse—make headlines almost daily. From astronauts to senators, actors to rock stars, the excesses of bad habits become increasingly spectacular. And the media frenzy that follows ends up generating more publicity than had the excess never occurred.

> ### Talk About It
>
> It's [addiction's] not caused by anything, it's just there. It waits. It lays in wait for the time when you think, "It's fine now, I'm okay." Then, the next thing you know, it's not okay.
>
> —Robin Williams, American actor, *Good Morning America* interview with Diane Sawyer

Actor Robert Downey Jr. made nearly as much of a career from his addictions as his acting, even to the extent of drawing across the lines of both when playing roles that cast him as an addict. Singer Britney Spears monopolized the tabloids with her after-hours escapades. The fallout from their bad habits got jail time for celebs Lindsay Lohan, Paris Hilton, Nicole Richie, Kiefer Sutherland, and Tom Sizemore, among a slew of others.

Golf pro John Daly wrote in his 2006 autobiography that he was able to give up drinking but "has a plan" for managing the gambling habit that once had him $4 million in debt to casinos and has cost him some $60 million since the 1990s. And pro basketball Hall of Famer Charles Barkley said on an ESPN broadcast that he, too, needs only to get his gambling under control so he loses thousands instead of millions of dollars at the blackjack table.

On the other end of the spectrum, actress Kirstie Alley turned her yo-yo struggle with weight into career success with her Showtime sitcom *Fat Actress* … then turned the tables and channeled her efforts to change her habits for good into commercial success as a spokesperson for Jenny Craig weight loss programs. As did Sarah Ferguson, the Duchess of York, with rival Weight Watchers.

> ### Steer Clear
>
> One of the biggest television hits of mid-2000s was the weight-loss reality show *The Biggest Loser*, which sequestered teams of contestants in a boot camp setting where every activity targeted losing weight. The over-the-top nature of the show riveted and motivated millions of viewers. A key highlight was the weekly challenge, an apparently Herculean task designed to push contestants to the edges of their determination. Somewhere in the middle was the greatest challenge of all and one viewers knew all too well—time in the real world, dealing with the pressures and stresses of everyday temptations. This challenge became the moment of truth for staying on the path of new behaviors.

Similar dramas unfold in our own lives, albeit on a much, much smaller stage. But *we* get to take center stage because it's our life. Our family and friends rally to our support, cheering and pushing to get us through our relapse and back on track with our changed habits. We become, after a fashion, a celebrity in our own universe. And after the struggle of walking the straight and narrow path of our changed habit, being the center of attention feels kind of good.

However, neither celebrities nor we slip back into old habits simply for the attention it gains us (at least not intentionally). But it's hard, and often lonely, to keep going. Whether the whole world recognizes our face or our boss doesn't even know our name, the issues are the same. Once the thrill is gone, we're more vulnerable.

The Recovery Rush

In the beginning, changing a habit is kind of exhilarating. There's the deep breath of "the last one." Often there's the relief of coming out about our habit, even though odds are the only one who's thought of it as a secret is *you*. Most of us spend months to years hanging out in the precontemplation stage of change (see Chapter 2), convinced that our bad habits aren't really that bad. It's not necessarily that we're denying them; we simply don't believe they're hurting us.

When we move to planning and then into action, we can't believe we didn't see the problem sooner, and we can't fix it fast enough. We head into the mechanisms of change like we're pushing through the turnstile at Disneyland. Family and friends are excited, too; they've been waiting even longer than we have for this time to come. We're front and center—everyone else focuses on us. Recovery can be the same kind of rush/relief we experience from our bad habits.

When the Thrill Is Gone

It's easier to stay the course when others are cheering us on. We want to do our best when we have an encouraging audience. We don't want to let them down, even when we might feel that it's all far too much work.

At first, our supporters cheer even the smallest of successes. But when we get closer to our goals, the gallery saves itself for the bigger achievements. It's not that they care less. It's that they're more confident about our resolve and our ability to remain focused. We've grown and changed, and they've watched, so they know. And as we make it to each new level of success, the bar raises.

It's much harder, and some days feels impossible, to push the extra effort all on your own. Yet that's what we all must do to maintain the changes we make in our lifestyles. It's exciting to finally be on the path we want to follow, but it's not always easy to do the following.

The Path Formerly Traveled

The trail of the old habit, no matter how cold it turns, still lurks. Sometimes even the mere thought of traveling it, just once, is too exciting to bear. That the thrill is illicit—one we've chosen not to indulge—makes it all the more enticing.

Temptation to travel a former path starts with a *craving*, like when all you can think about is chocolate. An *urge* follows—you head off to the kitchen to scout around for chocolate, any kind of chocolate. The lapse comes when you find—and devour—an entire bag of chocolate chips. And for a while, you feel content, you'd say you were happy. (Though maybe a tad nauseated—that's a lot of chocolate, even though the chips seemed so tiny and inconsequential at the time you ate them ….) Dopamine floods your pleasure pathway, and for the moment life is good.

def•i•ni•tion

A **craving** is a feeling of desire for an experience. An **urge** is the intent to act on the craving.

But then you realize what you've done, and the abstinence-violation effect kicks in—all those feelings of self-doubt and helplessness. You hate yourself for your transgression and see no hope for redemption. Though succumbing to cravings and urges is only a lapse—a single, isolated event—you feel you're now axle-deep in the muck of the old habit. You are, but you still have enough traction to pull yourself out.

The craving that calls to you might be a martini, the slot machines, a one-day-only clearance sale, a new *World of Warcraft* expansion pack. Whatever your habit, if you answer the call of the craving you're likely to do so in a big way. You might as well, your faulty reasoning tells you. One step or a long walk, what's the difference?

Who's at the Controls?

Your brain's laid down quite a network of pathways to support your habits, such that you may feel like there's a Wizard of Oz kind of thing going on in there. If you could pull back the curtain on your mind, you'd see an odd little man standing on a stool, pulling levers, flipping switches, and punching buttons.

Over time, it takes more of your habit to give you the rush or relief you crave. This is a huge part of why your habits get away from you. And it's a huge part of why it can take a bigger slip to jolt you into recognizing you've relapsed. The road back feels longer and bumpier each time.

But like the odd little man behind the curtain, this perception is a fantasy. *You* are in control … or can be. Your courage, your determination, and your desire come from within you. The brain cells that make the difference, when it comes to making changes, are the ones in your brain that think. These are the brain cells that can evaluate your feelings—emotional and cravings—and select new ways to respond.

We all can learn to recognize the subtle shifts that mean those feel-good cells are drifting back toward the old pathway, and we can consciously block their way. Sometimes the awareness itself is enough to redirect the behavior; sometimes we need to take more decisive and tangible action.

Talk About It

> And this is the Noble Truth of the arising of sorrow. It arises from craving, which leads to rebirth, which brings delight and passion …. And this is the Noble Truth of the stopping of sorrow. It is the complete stopping of that craving … being emancipated from it … being released from it, giving no place to it.
> —The Second Noble Truth and the Third Noble Truth, *The Pali Canon: Samyutta Nikaya* (the teachings of Buddha)

Can we prevent lapses and relapses? Well, probably not entirely, at least not right away and perhaps not ever, depending on the nature of our habit. Relapse is not a battle of willpower; it's a stage in an ongoing process. But we can reduce the effects that our slips and sidesteps have on our lives and on our sense of who we are.

Move *To*, Not From

It's easy to focus on the bad habits we want to drive from existence. After all, they cause us problems, and who wants that? Such a focus gives short shrift the "change" part of giving up old habits. Sure, we want to stop the destructive behaviors. But more important, we want to establish new, positive, supportive behaviors to replace them. Otherwise we'll always be looking back instead of ahead. For example, stop smoking and start exercising.

Remember the self-quiz you took in Chapter 1? Think now about the habit you focused on when you answered the questions. When you think about this habit, what could you do instead? Feel free to be creative, though keep it real. Think in terms of the short term (to fill the time you otherwise would spend on the habit) as well as the long term (ways the new behavior or activity might improve or enhance your life). Make this your focus.

It's a key shift in momentum to focus on a purpose in your life beyond the habit you want to leave behind. Suddenly there's something out there that's actually enticing, something you want to do as much—and even more—than what you're doing now.

Be Mindful

Because our habits have become the fabric of our lives, we're often unaware of their costs, especially in terms of time. For example, the cost of a pack of cigarettes averages about $5 in the United States or 35 cents a cigarette. It takes about six minutes to smoke a cigarette. So that $5 you spend on a pack of cigarettes also costs you half an hour of time. Smoke two packs a day, and you're looking at $70 a week—and seven hours. When you think about the time you spend indulging your habits, whatever they are, you'll be surprised how much it all adds up.

Habits are a lot about attitude, even down to whether we consider them good or bad (which can be a variable judgment, depending on the circumstances). When we focus on what we want to stop—stop drinking, stop taking drugs, stop spending, stop gambling—it's all about giving up something that, despite the trouble it causes us, we purport to enjoy. The idea of not doing this habit is about as inviting as going to afternoon tea at Great-Aunt Mildred's house. We do it because we should, but we know it won't be any fun.

So here's a different stop message for you: stop thinking this way! Ask yourself, right now, *why am I making this change?* Forget all the politically correct answers and blah-blah babble. When it comes right down to it, you want to make this change for only one reason: *because you want a better life.*

Isn't that truly the bottom line? Sure, there's more to it than that. But your bad habits wreak havoc in your life—with your job, your family, your romantic partnership, and your friendships. It isn't so much that you want the pandemonium to end. It's fun and exciting, in its way, like a never-ending party. And maybe, in your heart of hearts, you'd love to have the chaos without the consequences.

But you want a job you enjoy and a boss who appreciates your work—and a regular paycheck. You want a family that can't wait for you to come through the door. You want a significant other who loves being with you, whether you're staying in or going out. You want friends who have you on speed dial and IM. You want a life that satisfies you. Your bad habits, in the end, are a poor substitute for this satisfaction.

Mind Your Triggers and Cues

Robert hadn't had a cigarette for three years. Then one day he left work early to buy tickets for a Seattle Mariners game. A line snaked along the street to the outdoor ticket windows. Though the sun was out, the day was cool. The woman in front of Robert lit a cigarette. A swirl of smoke wafted back. Robert coughed.

The woman turned to look at him, and another drift of smoke, this one mixed with the unmistakable fragrance of *Chanel COCO*, encircled him. The woman smiled and offered Robert a cigarette. He took in a deep breath. Marlboro Lights. He accepted and even bummed a second when the woman turned to leave the window with her tickets.

On his way to work the next morning, Robert stopped at a convenience store and bought three packs of Marlboro Reds, the brand he'd smoked when he'd first started. By week's end Robert was smoking a pack and a half a day.

> **Be Mindful**
>
> In an ironic twist, perhaps one of the most significant indicators of our ability to change even the most challenging of habits is the success of advertising campaigns for low-tar/low-nicotine cigarettes. Though these ads do not encourage people to stop smoking, they do quite effectively convince people to change the way they smoke above and beyond normal brand loyalty.

Though Robert didn't recognize it at the time, his cough signaled the reawakening of a habit he'd developed when he was a smoker: it was what he did right before lighting up. Every time. Though his friends teased him about it, he didn't recognize, most of the time, when he was doing it. He didn't recognize most of what he was doing when he was smoking.

The *Chanel COCO* might as well have been *Dior Addict* for the effect it had on Robert. His former girlfriend, the one he was with during his heaviest smoking, used this scent. She was also a smoker, and his break-up with her was one of the motivating factors in his decision to quit.

Robert hadn't really had health concerns or any of the usual worries about smoking; he simply wanted to distance himself from her and the relationship as much as was possible. Quitting smoking, in Robert's mind, wasn't all that hard. He didn't want anything in his life to remind him of his ex, and smoking was part of the ex.

> **Steer Clear**
>
> Long-term, heavy abuse of drugs and alcohol causes permanent damage to areas of the brain responsible for cognition (thinking and logical reasoning), memory, inhibition control, and motor skills (movement and coordination). These changes may require additional treatment approaches similar to those used to help people recover from stroke and traumatic brain injury.

Our brains are quite adept at responding to cues without our conscious awareness, just like television talk show hosts who read from cue cards only they can see. All we notice, as the viewer, is the smooth, effortless banter and dialogue. When the cue cards are in our own mind, we don't notice them at all.

I Didn't Mean To

We all have the best of intentions. But when cues for the old habit pile up, intentions are not good enough. Cues are more like the odd little man behind the curtain; they flip switches in our brain that fast-track our slide from new habit to old pathway. Unless we're prepared for the cues of our old habits, we won't know our brain's encountered them until suddenly we look up and ask, "How did I end up back *here*?"

Increasing your awareness about your triggers and cues (the circumstances that set off your cravings) helps you to prepare a plan to divert your actions to stay on the path of your new behaviors. Methods that work include mindful meditation and cognitive learning therapy, which we'll discuss in later chapters.

Dangerous Liaisons

Some people bring out the best in one another, and others ... well, others don't. Friends and family members, places and events, feelings and experiences all play roles in the habits we develop and nurture. Some are easy enough to change, while others remain unavoidable (or irresistible) cues to old behaviors. In psychologist-speak, this is the sometimes touchy balance between social pressure and social support.

Who—or where—are your personal dangerous liaisons? They may lurk in the workplace, at home, or within your favorite forms of entertainment. For most of us, there are risks in nearly every relationship and environment. Short of running away to a deserted island, sticking with our new habits means we have to learn how to deal with familiar threats in new ways. We'll come back to this in greater depth in Chapter 17.

Shared Delusions

Carla and Daniel had already been through a bankruptcy. After five years of real-time payment for items they needed and wanted, they decided to accept an offer that came in the mail for a credit card. They agreed it was for emergencies only, like flying to Boston should Carla's elderly father have a health crisis or for handling unexpected car repairs.

The arrangement worked fine for a while. Then one afternoon Carla was at lunch with a group of friends who decided on a visit to the spa instead of dessert. Short on cash, Carla pulled out the plastic. When she later told Daniel, he was unfazed. "Everyone needs a little reward now and then," he told her.

A few weeks later they were out with friends for dinner when the guys started talking about their upcoming weekend golf getaway. Carla was astonished and confused that Daniel was such an animated part of the conversation. On the way home, he admitted he'd booked the trip on the credit card weeks ago when the discussion first came up.

When partners or friends (sometimes entire families) share the same bad habit, they may find themselves in a dance of delusion. Each ignores the other's transgressions because doing so supports his or her own. Psychologists call this *enabling*. It's a slippery slope that more than doubles our risk for sliding back into old habits. In enabling relationships, neither person can see the actions of the other or of himself as lapses.

def•i•ni•tion

Enabling is a pattern of behavior that implicitly or explicitly supports another person's damaging habits.

Dodging the Bullet

Not many of us care to be in trouble for things we've done or not done. For example, lab rats will perform amazingly complex tasks (well, complex for rats) to avoid an electrical shock. Now we know, thanks to technologies such as PET scans that can peek into the brain's biochemistry, that avoiding punishment is its own reward. It activates the brain's pleasure pathway in the same way as does any other reward—such as in the case of our hapless lab rats, a tidbit of food.

In people, this punishment avoidance mechanism correlates to thrill-seeking behaviors like base jumping, skateboard stunts, having sex in public places, and addictive habits such as high-stakes gambling and illicit drug use. Being able to get away with the behavior is as pleasure-provoking as the behavior itself. The anticipation of the good feelings we're about to experience further stimulates the brain's pleasure pathway. We might even think of it as a form of self-medication.

Casinos notoriously take full advantage of this phenomenon, barraging gamblers with flashing lights and ringing bells. But any experience that we know will bring us pleasure or excitement has the same ability to cue us on the behaviors to take us down that pathway.

You're Not in Kansas, Dorothy

Relapse doesn't just happen, swirling out of nowhere like a tornado. The signs of its impending arrival are everywhere. Odds are, everyone around us sees them. Friends and family may even try to warn us. But we're blissfully blind.

> **Talk About It**
>
> You can make miraculous recoveries from seemingly hopeless situations if you put your mind to it and you have enough support.
> —Robert Downey Jr., American actor as well known for his addiction struggles as for his acting talent

Even tornadoes, the genuine weather kind, arise from known and predictable circumstances. The earlier forecasters recognize the gathering forces, the better able they are to anticipate the tornado's strength and course.

So, too, with your lapses. When you know your triggers and cues, you can develop new strategies for responding to them. Over time, you'll become increasingly adept at playing these scripts.

Back to Best

Relapse often pushes your bad habits not just into your life but to their extremes, leaving you reeling. Though your brain at first revels in relapse, your life suffers. In the end, there's no joy in it.

Instead, give yourself a major time-out. Grab a pen and notepad, and go somewhere you can be alone. Working backward from your lapse, list everything that happened, everything you felt and thought. Look for the "aha!" points along the trail; you should recognize several. What should you have noticed at the time that you missed? What did you notice but ignore? Hindsight is 20/20; this is as good a place as any to use it.

Make a mark beside every point at which you made a decision or a choice. These forks in the road are your opportunities to catch yourself next time. Next, reaffirm your commitment to the new habit. Write it on your paper, and speak it out loud.

What was the best you felt when you were on the path of your new habit? Close your eyes and focus your mind on experiencing this feeling now. Any time a sliver of the old habit tries to sneak into the image, mentally brush it away. Hold the focus until you feel calm in the core of your being. This is what you want to retrain your brain to seek.

Changing a bad habit is a big deal! It has enormous consequences and benefits. It's so big that it sometimes seems well beyond reach. But like everything else, the saving grace is in the details. The tiniest of efforts have the most amazing results. Scientists call this "sensitive dependence on initial conditions." The rest of us call it the "butterfly effect," named after the popular presentation of the concept: the flutter of a butterfly's wings sets off a cascade of events that changes weather patterns halfway around the world.

We're not likely to know whether the flight of a butterfly in Brazil truly can cause a tornado in Texas as the title of a 1972 scientific paper on the subject poetically speculated. But we do know that no change takes place in a single leap.

> **Talk About It**
>
> Science fiction author Ray Bradbury popularized the premise of the butterfly effect in his 1952 short story "A Sound of Thunder." In the story, a time traveler unintentionally steps on and kills a butterfly in prehistoric time. The world the time traveler returns to is one of subtle but numerous changes from the one he left.

The Least You Need to Know

- Relapse can become a habit itself, part of the pattern of our behavior.

- Triggers and cues activate responses in you that you often don't realize until your behaviors are those of the old habits.

◆ It's important to focus attention and efforts on new habits, rather than always looking back at old habits.

◆ Though you can't, through sheer willpower, override the biochemistry of your brain, you can establish conscious, planned reactions to circumstances and events that redirect your behaviors.

Part 2

Giving Up, Getting Out, and Letting Go

Our habits run much deeper than we realize—until we attempt to change them. Then we see just how much of our lives center around those habits. Everywhere we go, there's something to remind us. Everything's the same, yet everything's different.

The chapters in Part 2 look at the first part of the journey of change. Chapter 4 investigates what researchers have learned about how our brains and bodies react when we quit old habits. Chapter 5 discusses how relapse blurs perception, our own and that of others. Chapter 6 delves into the short-term challenges and successes of changing our old habits for good. Chapter 7 broadens the view with an exploration of, and solutions for, long-term issues and concerns.

Pause for PAWS: Post Acute Withdrawal Syndrome

In This Chapter

◆ You're not really losing your mind

◆ Forget the keys ... where's the car?

◆ As the mood swings

◆ Treat yourself to some fun

You're not losing your mind. Really. No matter what anyone else says or implies, no matter how discombobulated you feel. You truly are experiencing a wide range of seemingly unrelated symptoms that have a lot to do with ditching those old habits. After all, you're undergoing some major shifts.

Your brain and your body are working to right themselves, and in the process they're doing a lot of off-loading and readjusting. Though the worst of the backlash—physical and emotional—punishes you in the first few days to weeks after you've evicted the old habit, those old pathways in your brain still want traffic.

What's hitting you now is what some people call post acute withdrawal syndrome, or PAWS. These are symptoms, ranging from irritability and restlessness to palpitations and nightmares, that just show up. You're not expecting them, and often they seem unrelated to anything that's going on in your life. But take heart—you can manage your PAWS symptoms. And they're living proof that you truly are changing.

What PAWS Is

PAWS describes a set of experiences—*symptoms*—common during the first months of settling into your new lifestyle. That's the "post *acute*" part, which means "after the immediate" in medicalese. Though PAWS is not a clinical condition, the pattern of these experiences gives it the image of one. Symptoms that occur in a recognizable pattern, as these appear to do, constitute a *syndrome*.

def•i•ni•tion

Symptoms are subjective experiences of feelings and sensations; others are not able to detect them. A sore throat or nausea, for example, is a symptom. In contrast, redness and swelling of the throat or throwing up are signs that others are able to observe. An **acute** symptom or sign is one that arises suddenly, is usually intense, and is of short, predictable duration. A **syndrome** is a set of symptoms and signs that consistently occur together, indicating a health condition.

The symptoms of PAWS are the discomforts and difficulties you experience in your body, your thoughts, and your emotions. Although they tend to ebb and flow without much apparent predictability, for many people they seem tethered to key "anniversaries" like three months, six months, or even two years from the time of giving the old habit the boot.

The good news is that you can learn to recognize feelings related to the changes you're making in your life, and learn ways to manage them that continue to support these changes. And PAWS does go away. Each bout of symptoms feels less severe and lasts a shorter period of time than the one before. Although PAWS seems ultimately to fade away whether or not you do anything about how you feel, you'll definitely feel better if you take steps to ease your symptoms.

Can't Think, Can't Remember

There you are, in the checkout line at the grocery store. "Paper or plastic?" asks the clerk. You stare at her as though she's asked you for the square root of 781. Someone in line behind you snickers. Finally taking your nonresponse as indication that you don't care what kind of bag carries your groceries home, the clerk gives you plastic. You take the bag and stride authoritatively from the store into the parking lot—and freeze. Where is your car? And more important, what did you do with your keys?

Steer Clear

> Though the character and timing of PAWS symptoms vary among individuals and with the nature of the addictive behavior, symptoms may come and go over a period of about two years. It takes this long for your brain to reconfigure its pathways, and, when your habit involved alcohol or drugs, to repair damage these substances cause to brain cells and neural pathways.

It's okay! It's only your brain on overload. You're not usually aware of it, but your brain lives in minutiae of details. It busily routes you through your daily activities, its thousands of neurons firing off messages directing you to think, move, and feel. This industrious bustle all happens in the background, just like with your computer. And like your computer, when there's a glitch, everything stops, at least for the moment.

The circuits of your brain are endlessly more complex and capable than those of your computer. They can accommodate an amazing level of fragmentation, rerouting signals around sluggish brain cells. But even they can reach a point of critical mass at which there's simply a gap in performance. You forget.

What Cognitive and Memory Symptoms of PAWS Feel Like

Cognition and *memory* are essential functions of your brain. They make it possible for you to learn and to use what you've learned. When glitches develop in your brain pathways that handle these functions, you have trouble with cognitive tasks that were once simple for you. You may struggle to find the right word or speak the wrong one. You might be unable to choose the correct bills and coins to pay for your restaurant meal.

def•i•ni•tion

> **Cognition** is the process of logic and reasoning. **Memory** is the storage of learned knowledge and experiences.

Your focus at work may be inconsistent, causing coworkers and your boss (and even you) to question your reliability. You might drive right past the school instead of dropping off the kids, put cat food in the dog's dish, lock the keys in the car, or put the milk in the cupboard and the sugar in the fridge, but only sometimes and with no pattern. Some days you're fine, and other days … well, other days you're not.

To have these kinds of lapses is unsettling and frustrating, to say the least. Because your memory's not what it used to be, you might even be unsure whether you've done something to reactivate your old habit. Did you drink a six-pack, smoke a few cigarettes, order three takeout meals (and eat them all in your car), or lose the night (and your wallet's contents) at the casino? You don't know because you can't remember!

You might fear you're losing your mind. But you're not; it's all right there. It just isn't working quite right at times. Your old habit had your mind trained to function in certain ways, and every now and again your brain neurons get confused about which pathways they're supposed to follow.

Ways You Can Ease Cognitive and Memory Symptoms of PAWS

As hard as it is, try to relax. The agitation that strikes when you can't pull something from your brain that you know is in there only worsens the situation. Take a few minutes to calm and center yourself.

Try this simple and effective relaxation technique:

1. Slowly breathe in over a count of 10.

2. Hold the breath in your lungs for a count of 10.

3. Slowly breathe out over a count of 10.

def•i•ni•tion

A **mantra** is a brief saying or set of sounds you repeat, often in meditation or prayer, to focus your mind and your energy. An **affirmation** is a positive statement of intent or truth.

Focus on your breath, and keep the pace of your count steady. Repeat the sequence until your sense of control begins to return. You might also repeat a *mantra* or an *affirmation* to help you clear your mind and refocus. Often the tension of trying to force the issue is worse than the issue itself.

And remember: *you are in control of the situation, even if you can't, for the moment, handle the task.* You have plenty of time to find what's eluding you. The world won't come to an end because you can't remember your PIN or the accounting formulas for your spreadsheet won't come to you.

Laugh! Use humor to defuse the stress you feel within yourself and the concern or worry other people might feel when they see you're struggling but don't understand why and don't know what to do—or whether they should do anything—to help you. If you can laugh or joke about your "brain bubble," other people will relax and the overall tension level will drop. And they'll laugh, too, because everyone has moments of forgetfulness. Often someone will step forward to help you out … in good humor.

> **Steer Clear**
>
> It's not only substances of habit that can cause withdrawal symptoms. Many medications, prescribed to treat a wide range of health conditions from asthma to seizure disorders, cause the body to develop tolerance and dependence. Read prescription labels and patient information materials carefully before you stop taking any medications, and contact your doctor or pharmacist if you have any questions or concerns.

Melancholy Baby

When PAWS strikes, your moods swing. And we're talking some potential extremes here. First you're so "up" people might wonder if you've relapsed. Then you're so "down" people might wonder if you've relapsed. Even you might wonder if you've relapsed—did you do something you don't remember and now you're back to the old ways? You exhibit all the wild emotions that were so much a part of your expression when your old habit was running the show.

You might have trouble connecting your emotional responses with the events that elicit them. Nightmares may jolt you awake. You might even dream about your old habit. Small stresses overwhelm you, and major stresses … well, major stresses are off the scale. Intense feelings of anger and guilt are also common.

Or you could experience episodes when you feel emotionally numb. No matter what happens, you have no reaction. Other people in your daily life tend to react more strongly when you're at this end of the mood spectrum. Friends and family worry that you've slipped into an emotional black hole. They may also feel betrayed (wrongly, but only you know this) because they've given so much support to you and you seem not to care. You do care—very much. It's just that right now, you're not able to show it. You feel like you have no feelings.

What Emotional Symptoms of PAWS Feel Like

When you're in the eye of an emotional storm, you don't have much ability to see what's whipping up around the edges. Maybe you rant, cry, sing, or dance without recognizing the depth of emotion that underlies these expressions. Or maybe the world truly is flat, from your emotional perspective. Nothing angers you; nothing excites you; nothing even interests you. You may feel empty inside, as though there's no reason to feel emotional. You might also feel dark and depressed. Your struggles to maintain new habits in place of old habits while at the same time keeping up with your regular daily life can make each day seem like an uphill hike.

> **Steer Clear** _____
>
> We all have times when we feel down, unappreciated, and misunderstood. This is normal. When you feel worthless, helpless, hopeless, and like there's just no point to living, this is more serious. If you're feeling so despondent that you're thinking about ending it all, tell someone. 1-800-SUICIDE is a toll-free, 24/7 hotline you can call from anywhere in the United States.

Negative emotional states—especially frustration, anger, and anxiety—are the most significant risk factors for relapse. This is because we're often not aware, in a conscious way, of the reasons for our emotional reactions. Emotional responses are often themselves habits. And if it was your old habit to turn your troubles over to Jack Daniels when you were angry or to eat a box of cookies when you felt helpless and frustrated, the link between the emotion and the habit requires little to activate it. Your brain wants to go straight to that connection whenever it encounters those same emotions. One habit wants to lead to the other, and before you know it, you're on the old path again. Your relapse prevention plan is especially crucial at such junctions, to help you stay true to your journey of change.

Ways You Can Ease Emotional Symptoms of PAWS

Your body holds much of the tension you feel. Your muscles tighten, and your posture stiffens. You look—and feel, if you think about it—rigid. Often, just having fun is enough to relax the tension in your body for at least a little while. The more an activity engages all of you—mind, spirit, and body—the more effectively it reduces your stress and helps you recenter yourself.

What did you do for fun when you were a kid? Many of these same activities are great for lifting your spirits now, too. Here are some activities that are easy to enjoy:

- Go roller skating.

- Take a bike ride.

- Run through a field of tall grass.

- Read a book.

- Toss a baseball up in the air and hit it with a bat.

- Throw a Frisbee so it comes back to you.

- Fly a kite.

- Take a dog for a walk.

Methods such as meditation and visualization are often helpful for the mood swings of PAWS. Meditation is especially calming for the "hyper" end of the scale. Regular meditation can stabilize your moods; "just in time" meditation techniques can help you deal with specific circumstances of stress, anxiety, and other intense emotions. Meditation also increases your awareness of how events and other people affect your moods and emotions.

Body Language

How can it be that you've lived in the same house for the past 10 years, and now you're running into everything? Last night you reached out to put a glass on the counter and entirely missed, dropping the glass onto the floor. And this morning, you even stumbled when you walked across the kitchen—and there was nothing there to trip you up!

PAWS can affect your balance and coordination. Your brain's neuro-networks are changing, and the transition is not always smooth. Think of it as sort of like street repairs: first there's a lot of ripping up the old before laying down the new. For a while, the going is pretty rough.

Physical symptoms are more common, and often more pronounced, when your old habit involved alcohol or drugs, because substance abuse directly affects multiple and diverse brain functions. However, you can experience physical symptoms as part of

PAWS when you're transitioning from any intense behavioral habit like gambling or shopping. Even when your addictive habit does not involve chemical substances, many of the same changes take place in your brain's circuitry.

> **Steer Clear**
>
> Substances most likely to result in physical symptoms when you stop using them include alcohol, nicotine (cigarettes), prescription pain meds, benzodiazepines, illicit narcotics (heroin) and stimulants (cocaine, amphetamine, methamphetamine, ecstasy), and anabolic steroids. Such drugs cause widespread changes in the nerve pathways in your brain and may also affect nerve pathways throughout your body.

What Physical Symptoms of PAWS Feel Like

The physical symptoms of PAWS can be vague. You may not even recognize that's what they are until they've happened enough for you to detect the pattern. Dizziness, coordination problems, and slowed physical reactions also can be PAWS symptoms. You might take a stutter step or two or feel a half-step off. Your reflexes may be slower—you may not duck quite in time to avoid bumping your head or dodge someone who's on a collision course with you. You may feel and look clumsy and might acquire quite an impressive collection of bumps, bruises, scrapes, and other minor injuries.

Like other PAWS symptoms, physical problems come and go. You might feel just fine one minute and then, for no apparent reason, feel queasy, lightheaded, and unsteady on your feet. You may have particular trouble with hand-to-eye coordination—putting your car key in the ignition, for example, or pouring soda into a glass.

> **Talk About It**
>
> You can turn painful situations around through laughter. If you can find humor in anything … you can survive it.
> —Bill Cosby, American comedian

Emotional symptoms can foster or intensify physical symptoms, too. Anxiety can cause you to feel that your heart is racing and even to break out into a sweat. You may feel like you're going to throw up—and sometimes you do just that. Stress tends to make your physical symptoms feel worse than they are.

Having trouble falling or staying asleep, nightmares, and other sleep disturbances are other ways you may experience physical symptoms related to PAWS. You might be unusually tired if you're not getting enough restful sleep, which can contribute to difficulty concentrating and remembering. Lack of sleep also affects your energy level.

You might also have very vivid dreams about your old habit, such that you wake up and believe, for a few moments, that you're really in the dream situation. Your dreams may even be so intense that they activate your physical senses. You might smell and taste alcohol or cigarette smoke, for example, or chocolate chip cookies. Your fingers might tingle as though you've been shuffling poker chips. Rest easy. Though they're eerily realistic in your perceptions of them, all of these sensations are in your head—specifically, in your brain.

Ways You Can Ease Physical Symptoms of PAWS

Be active! Regular physical activity is a great way to calm your physical symptoms. Establish a 30-minute walk outdoors as part of your everyday routine. Take your walk no matter what. It's easy, especially when you're feeling depressed and unenergetic and the weather's less than desirable, to feel it's too much effort to get yourself dressed and get out there.

And don't feel limited to walking. We suggest it because it's something just about everyone can do. If you like other activities, do them. The most important factor is that you stay active and keep your body moving. To move is to live. Whatever you choose to do, keep doing it.

Getting yourself moving stretches and warms your muscles, helping to dissipate the stress that accumulates in them. Investing in an hour or two with a licensed personal trainer can be well worth the cost to help you return to being active in a way that boosts your energy and keeps you from injuries caused by trying to do too much too fast. Take it slow and steady if you're having coordination problems. Your daily walk helps remind your brain how it's supposed to direct your body's activity. And getting out there to work your body every day has the added advantage of helping you maintain your desired weight.

> **Be Mindful**
>
> If you've been a couch potato, be gentle with yourself as you start your return to physical activity. Work up to the things you want to do. Take some lessons or classes to refresh yourself about proper technique and gear. Things change!

What PAWS Is Not

PAWS is not the withdrawal that accompanies separating your body from chemical substances such as alcohol, drugs, and nicotine. PAWS is not chronic (ongoing), and PAWS is not relapse, although the flare-ups of symptoms do put you at increased risk for relapse. And PAWS is not a message from your brain that you should bag the new habit and go back to your old habit.

Sometimes other medical conditions, such as anxiety and *depression*, resurface or develop as your brain and body are realigning themselves to accommodate the end of the old habit and the start of the new habit. When this happens, you experience the symptoms of the condition even when other PAWS symptoms have abated.

def•i•ni•tion

Depression is a clinical disorder in which a person feels intensely sad, hopeless, and worthless. **Generalized anxiety disorder (GAD)** is a clinical disorder in which one feels so intensely fearful and stressed that he's unable to function in his daily life. In both depression and GAD, there are imbalances among brain neurotransmitters.

It's often difficult to tease apart all of what's happening with you. You may need the perspective of a specialist, like a psychologist or physician, to help determine the extent to which what you're feeling relates to your changing habit or to other conditions. You may benefit from medical treatment for *general anxiety disorder* (*GAD*) and depression.

If the habit you're leaving behind is a dependence on medications used to treat either of these conditions (such as *benzodiazepines* or SSRIs), your doctor may understandably be cautious about prescribing such medications for you now. You may need to carefully weigh the benefits and risks and consider alternative treatments. However, if you need medication, you need medication. Don't be afraid to seek and receive the care you need. We talk more about short-term and long-term needs and challenges in Chapters 6 and 7.

def•i•ni•tion

Benzodiazepines are a class of medications to treat anxiety, muscle spasms, and sleep disorders. Common benzodiazepines include valium (diazepam), Xanax (alprazolam), Klonopin (clonazepam), Halcion (triazolam), Ativan (lorazepam), and Dalmane (flurazepam). SSRIs, or selective serotonin reuptake inhibitors, are a class of antidepressants. Commonly prescribed SSRIs include Prozac (fluoxetine), Paxil (paroxetine), Zoloft (sertraline), Celexa (citalopram), and Lexapro (escitalopram).

If possible, see a doctor who specializes in addictions when you seek care for GAD or depression. At the very least, make sure the doctor you're seeing knows your full history—all the substances you've used, how long you've used them, and what efforts you've made to quit. Full disclosure may be uncomfortable for you, but it's the only way to sort through all of what's going on with you.

How PAWS Differs from Relapse

PAWS is how you feel—physically, mentally, and emotionally. Relapse is a return to your old habits. The feelings you experience with PAWS increase your risk for relapse.

For a while, your brain will want to default, in autopilot mode, to the old habit as the solution for whatever causes you stress and discomfort—like your PAWS symptoms. Often, simply knowing this is the case is enough to restore your faith in your new path. You recognize the symptom, and you know its appearance is short-term. Your coping plan has you ready to meet this challenge head-on.

PAWS symptoms do increase your risk for relapse, especially the emotional symptoms. It's hard enough to stay the course just through the ordinary pressures of daily living. When all that stress begins to pile up, your brain wants you to make it stop in whatever way you can. Before, it was your old habit that gave you the illusion of relief. Now, you need to establish other ways to cope with stresses and challenges.

Keep in mind that not all negative moods and emotions have to do with PAWS or your changing lifestyle. Ups and downs are the normal pattern of life.

How to Tell Others What Kinds of Support You Need

Friends and family often want to help you through the rough patches but don't know quite what to do. And you may not quite know what you want them to do, either. If you can, sit down with the people who are important in your life and explain what's happening. Having someone simply listen to you without judgment or commentary can give you a lot of support.

Part of the challenge for others is no different from the challenge that confronts you: knowing that what's going on is PAWS. Because PAWS symptoms tend to be intermittent and sporadic, even when you know what they can look like, it's easy to miss what they are. Often, it's the other people in your life who can say to you, "Hey, things are not quite right with you!" When you and your loved ones are working together to support your efforts to change, such an observation is a good tip-off that PAWS is making an appearance.

It's more effective when you can talk with people in-between bouts of symptoms, so you're clear-headed and undistracted. Let people know what they can do that helps you. Do you want people to wait patiently while you try to find the right word or to suggest words to you? When you're struggling with memory, would it help to have reminder notes for things you're supposed to do or the locations of items you need? Do you want someone to let you know—gently and kindly, of course—that your temper is out of control or you seem disinterested in how school's going for the kids?

After you let people know the ways they can help you, you might need to assure them that you'll accept their offers of help, especially if you've been resistant in the past. Sometimes people are reluctant to intervene because, frankly, they don't want their heads handed to them! Your PAWS symptoms are frustrating for you; it's easy to turn that frustration on others.

How to Know When You Need Medical or Other Care

The symptoms of PAWS can mimic symptoms of other health conditions that need a physician's attention. This is especially a factor to consider with physical symptoms like dizziness and losing your balance. These symptoms may suggest potentially serious conditions such as stroke or irregularities in your heartbeat (particular risks with some drugs of abuse).

After a few rounds of PAWS symptoms you'll have a good sense for what you typically experience, which will help you separate the "oh, yeah, I remember this" from the "I've never had *this* before" kinds of symptoms. When in doubt, have your doctor check it out. Your health is not worth the risk of speculation.

Take care of yourself! Eat nutritious meals, get plenty of sleep, and walk at least 30 minutes a day, every day. When you look at yourself in the mirror, be proud and be happy. Looking back at you is the face of someone who's making some significant changes for the better.

The Least You Need to Know

◆ The variety of physical, mental, and emotional symptoms you experience after stopping an old habit are very real.

◆ PAWS can affect you no matter what your old habit was.

◆ The symptoms of PAWS come and go without much predictability, though they may intensify around anniversary markers.

◆ Although PAWS does eventually go away, you can minimize the discomforts of the symptoms of PAWS in numerous ways.

When No One Understands

In This Chapter

♦ The comfort of familiarity

♦ Do *something!*

♦ The secrets we keep

♦ Beyond willpower

When it comes right down to it, change can be lonely. The old habits that we're leaving behind once sustained us in ways we don't even recognize until they're no longer part of our daily lives. And the new habits we're cultivating are, well, new, stiff, and awkward. Like a new pair of jeans, they haven't yet faded into comfort.

Does *anyone* understand how hard this is, this process of change? It seems that no matter whether we're following the new path or slipping back to the old one, no one else really gets it. Even other people who are making similar changes don't quite seem to understand what we're going through, though we think they certainly should.

What's So Hard to Get?

You'd think everyone who knows you would be overjoyed at your decision to change your ways. After all, your old habit has caused you grief in many areas of your life, affecting many people. But not everyone appreciates and applauds change, especially when your change causes them to think about changes they want—or ought—to make in their own lives.

def•i•ni•tion

Status quo is a Latin term that means "state in which." In common use, we use the phrase to mean the situation as it currently exists.

The *status quo* is familiar. We like it. We're comfortable when events and people in our lives are predictable. This is, of course, a key reason we so love these habits of ours. Change upends things. Our habits define many of our daily activities and relationships with others. When our habits change, our relationships change.

Say, for example, you give up smoking. Now what happens to the smoke-break friendships you've formed over the years? Sure, you only see each other for 10 minutes or so at a time, standing outside in the parking lot or the courtyard or the designated smoking area. But if you go down for a smoke four times a day, five days a week, you're spending more than three and a half hours a week with your circle of smokers! Even if you talk about nothing important while you're together on your smoke breaks, the social interaction is important in the daily lives of all of you.

People whose main connection to you was through your old habit will miss your participation. Some of them will simply lament that you've moved on, as if you've moved to another state (and maybe you have!). Others will feel resentful that your chosen change is (as they see it) cutting them out of your life. They may try to cajole or bully you into joining them anyway and may act like you think you're better than they are. You may even encounter people who try overtly to sabotage your efforts to stay on track with your new habit.

Of course you're making this change in your life—whether to stop smoking or to change whatever your old habit happens to be—for you, not for anyone else. Try to keep this perspective, though you may have to remind yourself of it from time to time. We talk more about the challenges of dealing with other people in Chapters 13 and 17.

Lonely Heart Club

You know you're not the only one who's trying to make this particular change. So why is it that you feel so alone in your efforts? Well, what are you doing when your habit circle heads off without you?

C'mon! Get yourself moving! Use your breaks at work to go out for a walk instead of a smoke. Fill your lungs with fresh air; stretch your legs; swing your arms. See how fast you can get your pulse rate high enough to make you breathe through your mouth. Or maybe it's easier for you to duck into the library to read the latest issue of your favorite magazine or find a quiet place where you can go to meditate.

What you can do, of course, depends on where you are, what options are available to you, and what interests you. The point is, *do something!* It's harder to feel alone when you have a mission, even when it's only to hoof it around the block.

Can't think of anything to do instead of following your old ways? Then let's take a few minutes right now for you to brainstorm some ideas. Identify seven activities or feelings related to your old habit, and think of seven activities or feelings that can support your life without that old habit. Be creative—have fun!

What I Used to Do/Feel

1. _____
2. _____
3. _____
4. _____
5. _____
6. _____
7. _____

What I Can Do Instead

1. _____
2. _____
3. _____
4. _____
5. _____
6. _____
7. _____

Photocopy this page when you're done, so you can stick it up on the fridge, tack it on your bulletin board, or tape it on your dashboard. When you're feeling caught between the old and the new, look at your list to draw from the new instead of turning back to the old. In Chapters 6 and 7, we talk more about putting together a "change itinerary" to keep you busy in your new habit.

People Really Do Want to Help ... Don't They?

Most people in your life want to see you succeed in changing the ways of your old habit. Those who are closest to you know what you're like when you're free from those behaviors. And they like this you much better than the bad habit you because this you is happy, productive, caring, reliable, and fun—and in the driver's seat of your life journey. They want this person back.

But they may not know what to do or say to help. Maybe they've tried before and said or done the wrong things, or they don't really understand why the call of this habit is so hard for you to ignore. Sometimes just sitting down to talk about it—without judgmental response on either side—will let you get to a middle ground of understanding and support. It's worth a shot, and we'll tell you how to do this later in this chapter and in other chapters as well.

Dilemma surfaces when the people who say they want to help you change really want you to stay the same. These might be people who share your habit or have habits of their own that your changes would challenge. When your bad habit is long-standing, as is usually the case with habits we want to change, your behaviors are at least familiar to the people in your daily life. Change is disruptive for them, too; if you change, so, too, must they.

Steer Clear

It's sometimes hard to decide whether you have to give up a friendship to maintain the path of your new life. A good starting point is to think about what you and this friend have in common besides the old habit. Unless you can come up with substantial activities, beliefs, and goals that have nothing to do with the old habit, this is a friendship that will challenge your determination to change and put you at risk for relapse.

Sometimes other people in your life do not want you to change. They may be quite open about this, confronting your decision and the actions you take to bring that decision to reality. You might feel you have to constantly defend your choices, which eventually will cause you to question them yourself.

And sometimes people say they support you but act in ways to undermine or even sabotage your efforts. They may not recognize their own fears and worries about your changes and may feel that once you change, they'll lose their relationships with you. These may be well-founded fears, especially if these are people who share your old habit, like coworkers who smoke or drink.

In any case, you might find you must distance yourself from people who've been present in your daily life, at least until you sort through the feelings you have about their responses and actions about the changes you're making. In Chapter 13 we focus on your relationships with others during your journey of change, and in Chapter 15 we look at ways to help you find and develop other relationships that support your new lifestyle.

Garden of Secrets

Most of us try to keep our addictive behaviors to ourselves, to the extent that is possible, except, of course, for the sharing we do with others who are part of the habit's secret life. When our habits overflow our ability to contain them, then the cover's blown. But until then, it's as though we have two lives, one life with the habit and one life without.

Not only do we have secrets, but we also work so very hard to keep them. We keep secrets about our old habits, our cravings, our lapses, and especially our relapses. It's hard enough to send the old habit packing. So how can we admit we've welcomed it back, especially when much fanfare greeted our efforts to change? Even when other people in our lives know about our troubling habits, we often don't tell them the extent to which those habits cause us anguish.

Others who share the same habits as us are not always understanding about the challenges we face with ours, either. They may be in different stages of change or simply have different approaches or perspectives. They may not want to acknowledge that they share this common circumstance with us, especially beyond the realm of the habit.

Out of the Bag

Wanda's family and friends joked among themselves and even teased Wanda about being a shopaholic. There wasn't a sale she could pass up, they said—and they were right. Even when Wanda had no idea what she'd do with an item, if it was marked "take an additional 30 percent off last ticketed price," she'd buy it. It would be foolish, she reasoned, to pass up such deep discounts. Eventually she'd find a use for it herself or make it the perfect gift for someone else.

And Wanda truly did love shopping. It was the only time she was entirely at peace within herself. No one was wanting anything from her, and she felt a deep satisfaction and sense of comfort when she bought things for her home or for her wardrobe. Wanda could spend hours, even the entire day, shopping her way through store after store in mall after mall.

Talk About It

There are no secrets better kept than the secrets everybody guesses.

—Mrs. Warren's Profession, Act III, George Bernard Shaw

Most people in Wanda's life had no idea how much shopping she actually did. Wanda's closets overflowed with items she'd purchased and stashed away, either because she didn't have an immediate use for them or she didn't want other people to see them.

Sometimes even Wanda herself didn't know the extent of her shopping sprees until her credit card bills arrived. She became as good at shuffling her credit card balances onto new, interest-free cards as she was at finding bargains. But finally came the day when Wanda realized she could not pay even the minimum amounts due on all her credit cards. Nor could she pay any of her other bills.

The friends whose names Wanda had provided as alternate contacts on her credit card applications began getting calls from her creditors. The repo man came to take her car one afternoon while she was at work. Seemingly overnight, *everyone* knew the ugly reality of Wanda's shopping habit. Wanda's house of cards came crashing down, and she could hide no longer.

True Lies

The thing about the secrets of our habits is that they sound and look a lot like lies. And you know the old saying ... if it walks like a duck, quacks like a duck, and looks like a duck, well, then, it must be a duck.

Your secrets may begin as lies of omission—not telling the entire truth or leaving out key information, like Wanda and her shopping. Or you might say you'll be home late, but you don't add you're going out to the tavern after work with a group of coworkers to shoot some pool. Before long, the lies become blatant. You say you're going one place, but you go somewhere else. You're out with one group of friends but say you're with others.

And then you cross into absurdia, that odd place where even you know what you're saying makes no sense but you say it anyway. You come in at 2 A.M. and deny that it's late or you're late. You lash out when others ask legitimate questions like, "What happened to the car?" and "What do you mean, you're not working there anymore?"

What's with the inquisition? You become sullen and defensive. This is the twenty-first century, you're an adult; whose business is it what you do and who you do it with? Your indignation blurs the line between fact and fiction, and even you start to have trouble knowing which is which.

The Betrayal Pit

If you ask the people in your life who've had to deal with the secrets of your old habit, they'll tell you they feel betrayed. You lied to them, and in the beginning (and maybe even until the truth roared straight at them like a runaway truck) they accepted your lies because they wanted to believe you. We all like, and want, to believe the best about others, especially people we love.

So when you say you're giving up the old habit, people want to believe and support you. But they're cautious or even leery; they may have traveled this road with you already, too many times to count. What makes this time different? What are they to believe about you? And more important, what are you to believe about yourself?

Talk About It

Just 'cause you got the monkey off your back doesn't mean the circus left town.

—George Carlin, American comedian

None of us wants to admit, even to ourselves, that we're struggling. We want to believe the best about ourselves, too. When we can't make a change stick, when we relapse, we feel worse about it than anyone else even though we're not likely to show it. There's that secrets thing again. But we feel we've let ourselves down, and the people around us feel let down, too. This whole habits thing has more faces than Batman's Joker.

Road to Redemption

But this road to change is not a dead-end. What looks like the end of the road is really a turning point. You can change, and you can be happy in your life as a result of making the change. You already know you won't be happy staying in the old habit; turning back to it *is* a dead-end.

You can't make other people understand, and you can't make other people support your choices. Not anymore now with your efforts to change, than before with your determination to follow the path of the old habit. (How much effort have you put in, through the years, to justifying the ways of your old habit? How many people tried, without success, to talk you into changing?) But you can demonstrate the changes you're making in ways that they can't help but notice. Seeing, as the cliché goes, is believing.

Once people see you're really serious about this, their perceptions will change. People who want to see you succeed will be better able, by watching what you do and how you act, to say and do things that help and support you. People who don't want to see you succeed will eventually fade from your daily experience because, frankly, they'll find you boring. And this is good!

Can't *Anything* Be Easy?

Who wouldn't want to go to sleep tonight and wake up in the morning a changed person? That would be sort of like living in *The Sims* game! Sorry to say, it doesn't work that way in real life. The best you can do is go to sleep tonight replaying in your thoughts the successes you've had today and wake up strong in your determination to continue on your path of change.

This means learning to recognize the old habit's influence on your thoughts and feelings so you consciously redirect it to support your new lifestyle. Yes, your new *lifestyle*. The new you, living the life you envision free from the chains of the old habits.

Though it's hard to believe right now, things will get easier as your new habits become your regular habits. Sure, the old habits will still call to you at times. But you're learning to look at those old habits in the light of day, and they aren't nearly as imposing as you once thought them to be.

The Myth of Willpower

If only I was a strong enough person …. The myth persists that changing a bad habit is all about willpower. You might even believe it yourself, that because this is so hard, you must be lacking in *something*. Willpower, determination, character, moral fiber—whatever it is, you don't have it.

This is not true. Certainly it takes resolve and effort to make major changes in your life. You have willpower, determination, character, and moral fiber. But habits are not about any of these. Habits are learned behaviors, and you have what it takes to change them. You have the desire, and you have a plan.

A better way to look at willpower is as a blend of your motivation and determination (your will) and the coping skills you learn that help you stay on track (see Chapter 7).

Tell Them What You Need

Who are the people in your daily life that matter when it comes to how you live? These are the people you should consider bringing on board as your support team. It won't always be appropriate to share your plans for change with your coworkers, for example, but your significant other can be a lifeline for you at the times when you struggle the most.

When talking with others about your journey of change, be specific and I-oriented. The more tangible you are, the easier it is for other people to understand what your changes mean both for you and for them. Be reassuring, but be honest. This is not an easy journey, and no one knows that better than those who've watched you embark on it before. Acknowledge that this time might look like all the other times, from the outside.

Ask what settings others have noticed to be risky for you; you can't see everything yourself, especially so early in the change process. In Chapter 6 we encourage you to write a change-commitment contract; give copies of yours to the people closest to you, so they know you're serious about this and can see the measures of change that you've identified for yourself.

With or Without

Sometimes it's tough to decide which is harder, living with or living without the old habit. And sometimes you can feel like both: you're living "with or without" your habit and that is confusing and stressful. That old habit's been with you a long time, and it's natural to see only the good side of it when you're apart—like any relationship that's ended.

Keep your focus on what lies ahead—the path of your future. Let your past provide some of the lessons that guide you, but look beyond for new insights and learning.

The Least You Need to Know

- The secrets we keep to guard our bad habits sometimes make it difficult for others to believe and support our efforts to change.

- Some existing relationships depend on your old habit while others will thrive without it, but it's not always easy to know which is which.

- Many people in your inner circle want to help you succeed but may not know how to best do so.

- Some people who've been part of your daily life are not so thrilled to see your efforts to change and may challenge or even sabotage you.

Chapter 6

Just for Today

In This Chapter

- The many ways to say good-bye to your old (bad) habit
- The open road of your new (destination) habit
- Talk nice to yourself
- If you need more help

You're relieved, and even excited, to be moving in a direction you've long dreamed is where you want to be. For the first time in a long while—and maybe ever—you believe you can really do this. And you can!

The first few weeks of change are a mix of exhilaration, confidence, and fear. You're doing it, and you feel good. Yet despite your resolve, the tracks of your old habit are still fresh in your brain and pull at you. You find yourself thinking about the old habit and missing it. You may even find yourself beginning to engage in the old habit, then suddenly catch yourself and slam on the brakes.

That's okay. Everyone goes through this; it's the landscape of change. These first few weeks require your full awareness and focus, which takes more than a full-time job's worth of effort and energy. Your old habit is now an intruder, although it doesn't yet know that. It wants back into your life in the worst way, and you've got to teach it: that's not going to happen.

Making the Break: The Quit

Even as you focus on the new habit, the new you, you still must face the reality of giving up the old habit. Once you've made the decision, it's time to take the first steps on your journey of change.

You've moved through the first three stages of change—precontemplation, contemplation, and preparation—and now you stand at the threshold of stage four: action. (See Chapter 2 for a review of the Stages of Change model.) You've acknowledged your habit is a problem for you, made the decision to change, and thought about how to make the change. Now you're taking action to make the change.

For some bad habits, *abstinence* is the goal—no further relationship whatsoever with the habit. Conventional wisdom holds that abstinence is essential for habits that cause physical harm to your health and well-being, such as smoking and drug abuse. Many addiction programs, like the 12-step programs (Alcoholics Anonymous being the first and most famous of these), emphasize abstinence as the *only* way to change an addictive habit that involves a chemical substance.

def•i•ni•tion

Abstinence is the complete stopping of a behavior.

However, many addiction specialists now accept that for most of us, abstinence alone isn't enough to hold us when it comes to dropping an old habit. We need to find a new focus that's more enticing, more compelling than the old habit, to shift interest and energy to a new way of living.

There are numerous ways to go about stopping a habit, as you know all too well and we discuss in the following pages. No one way is necessarily better than another, and many people combine two or more methods. We don't mean to sound cliché here, but the best approach is the one that works for you. Your approach to quitting a bad habit must be a good fit with how you think and what you believe, in general and about yourself.

Cold Turkey

Etymologists—the folks who study the origins of words and phrases—believe the term "cold turkey" comes from the early 1900s and originally referred to the ease of preparing a cold turkey meal. Over the century, cold turkey came to mean "without preparation." When you quit your bad habit cold-turkey, you just up and turn your back on it.

You might think of cold turkey as quick and clean, and it can be. But it also can be challenging, even harsh. Remember, those habits have taken years, maybe decades, to entrench themselves into your brain, and now they alter the chemistry and function of your brain. Cutting them off cold may set off a backlash sort of reaction that intensifies your cravings—for the short term. Once your brain recovers from the shock, things will go back to normal. But be prepared for that bump in the middle.

Steer Clear

Quitting an addictive behavior cold turkey may sound ideal if the do-it-now, no-nonsense approach is your usual way. But for many addictive substances—notably benzodiazepines, SSRIs, barbiturates, and prescription pain medications (opiates)—and heavy alcohol use, suddenly stopping the drug has potentially severe risks for your health. In some situations those risks are life-threatening. To safely quit such drugs, it's best to seek treatment from a physician who specializes in addiction medicine.

The advantage of quitting cold turkey is that it's a swift kick in the keister to your bad habit. The risk of quitting cold turkey is that the shock might be so much for your body, thoughts, and emotions that you can't get back to your old habit fast enough. With chemical substances—alcohol, nicotine, caffeine, other drugs—you might experience physical withdrawal symptoms. If this happens, you need to talk with your doctor.

Many people find cold turkey the most effective approach with environment-associated addictive behaviors such as gambling. It's more difficult to apply the approach to habits such as procrastination.

Replace

Replacement is an approach of substituting the undesirable habit with a healthier action. If you're breaking the smoking habit, you might chew gum or suck on hard candies. People working to distance themselves from alcohol may opt for a fruit-flavored soda or soda water instead of a drink. Those who are changing their eating habits might fill the fridge with snack-ready sliced fruits and veggies to replace stores of ice cream and candy. These substitutions give your brain a way to accommodate existing cues without falling into the rut of the old habit.

This is not the same as finding a new habit (a collection of behaviors) to pull your focus away from the old habit, though your replacements can be things you want as part of your new lifestyle. But in this narrow context, replacement is a single, new behavior in response to an old trigger. Replacement is most effective when you're first quitting the old habit. You might choose to recall it to duty as part of your relapse prevention plan, too, to help keep you centered and on track through a particularly challenging time.

Be Mindful _____

Meditation and mindfulness practices are effective methods for diffusing cravings. These mental exercises calm your thoughts and emotions, helping you to observe and experience your feelings without judgment. A very simple mindful meditation practice is to focus your attention, like an objective observer, on what you feel when a craving strikes, without judgment or trying to control your feelings. Attempt to engage all your physical senses in your observations. With practice, you'll be able to allow the craving to exist and then disappear with no intervention from you.

The benefit of replacement is that it lets you respond to cues and cravings, relieving anxiety and giving you a sense of being in control. You're not just sitting there fidgeting and struggling to keep yourself in check. And you're not trying to pretend the craving doesn't exist. Instead, you make a conscious and aware choice to answer the call of your old habit with a different behavior.

The risk of replacement is that you may find yourself exchanging one bad habit for another. Replacement often works well in combination with the cold turkey approach, letting you shift your focus to something else while your brain and body adjust to the absence of your "fix."

Choose your substitutes with care, though, keeping in mind your overall plan for change. Replacements work only when they are as easy as, or easier than, the old habit. If you're going to chew gum instead of smoke, put packs of gum everywhere you used to have packs of cigarettes. If you're changing your eating habits, make it as easy to grab some dried fruit as it was to have a handful of M&Ms.

Taper

If what you're doing is bad for you, then doing less of it is at least better (harm reduction). This is the premise of tapering—gradually cutting back on a bad habit. Some people feel that tapering is like undoing the habit, rolling back its entrenchment until it finally disappears.

The advantage of the taper approach is that it lets you wean yourself from your habit, which may be less stressful than going cold turkey. The risk of tapering is that you may prolong your relationship with your old habit, teasing every last bit from it before finally letting it slip from your fingertips.

The taper approach is most effective when you establish a measurable decline over a set period of time. For example, if you're quitting smoking, first determine how frequently and how many cigarettes you currently smoke. At what rate would you have to cut your smoking to be smoke-free in four weeks? Three weeks? Two weeks? Then stick to your plan, without exception. You might find it helpful to make up a chart so you can keep track or count out each day's cigarettes and put them in a container. Some people combine tapering and substitution.

Aversion

Aversion is creating a negative association or sense of unpleasantness around your old habit, like wearing a rubber band around your wrist and snapping it when you feel yourself on the edge of indulging the habit. The idea is that the pain you then experience is unpleasant enough to turn your attention away from the craving.

> **Steer Clear** _____
>
> One medical variation on the theme of aversion is the medication disulfiram, better known by its trade name, Antabuse. Disulfiram, which a physician must prescribe, works by blocking the liver's ability to metabolize alcohol. Consuming alcohol while taking disulfiram results in many unpleasant physical symptoms.

The downside of aversion is that it's a form of negative reinforcement, which runs counter to the framework of creating positive replacements for your bad habit. It's human nature to avoid that which is uncomfortable or unpleasant. The risk of the aversion method is that we may decide we're stuck choosing the lesser of two evils and the bad habit looks better. If aversion appeals to you, combine it with ways to reward yourself for staying on track.

Avoidance

Avoidance is removing the temptations of your old habit from your environment or removing yourself from the temptations. Donate the coffeemaker to Goodwill, or find a new route home after work that bypasses the tavern where you used to stop for happy hour.

Many addiction specialists recommend adding avoidance to all methods of quitting a bad habit. Change is tough enough without constantly challenging yourself with the same cues and triggers. To move on in your habits, you must move on in your life. And that means distancing yourself from the old in physical and tangible ways.

Sometimes avoidance is itself a major challenge. How do you avoid cigarettes or buckets of fried chicken or a case of Rolling Rock or the Internet if these are features of daily life for others in your family? Some people are able to establish smoke-free or alcohol-free zones in the house or get smoking family members to take their habit outside. Maybe you'll have to fix your own meals and eat at different times than the rest of your family until you are comfortable in your new routine.

Or maybe the others in your household or work group are ready to change their bad habits, too! The more changes you can make in the patterns of your daily life to support your quit and your new habits, the more successful you will be.

Your Quit-Commitment Contract

There's something about "putting it in writing" that makes any decision feel like a solid commitment. We sign contracts to buy cars and houses, accept jobs and work assignments, get married (What? You didn't know that a marriage license is a legal contract?), and adopt a pet from the animal shelter (even celebrities like Ellen DeGeneres).

So write a quit-commitment contract for yourself right now, while it's fresh in your mind. Your contract should include:

◆ The specific habit you're quitting and your reasons for leaving it in the dust

◆ The quit methods you intend to use

◆ How you plan to reward yourself for the changes you make

◆ The timeframe of your quit

◆ The people who know about your quit

Be Mindful _____

Millions of Americans make New Year's resolutions to change their old habits—and nearly 20 percent of them succeed in sticking with their changes for two years. What's the secret to their success? They reduce or eliminate cues and triggers for the old habit and reward themselves for their new habits. Most important, they believe they have the ability to change.

Date it, sign it, make copies, and put them with your important papers. Keep the original where you can see it every day. You might also want to write reminder cards to yourself, and notes for what you can do if you lapse. Keep a diary or journal to record your daily experiences, including the challenges you confront and what steps you take to meet them.

Successful change requires setting and meeting reasonable goals that matter to you. You know yourself; you know what makes you tick. Even if you don't pay that much attention, you do know. So choose quit methods you know give you a fighting chance.

Passport to Change: The New You

You have a lot of resources and support going for you. Everyone wants to see—and help—you succeed. But you know better than anyone that beneath the excitement and the hope lies the experience of every day living. You've traveled this road before, and you know it's bumpy and deceptive.

So this time you're setting forth with an entire destination packet, just like you're traveling to an exotic location. You're going to create this packet, your change itinerary, just as you'd put together a travel itinerary: step by step. Your plan defines where you want to go and what you want to avoid, so you act and feel like you belong and not so much like you're a tourist.

You might feel like a stranger in the land of your new habit, at first. This is unfamiliar territory, even if you've visited here before. But now you want to live here. That takes a different approach than does simply passing through. You need to learn the local customs—how people behave in this new realm where your old habit does not exist and your new habit thrives.

From Here to There

A journey starts with an intended destination. Where are you going? Looking ahead on your journey of change keeps your focus on your new habit—your destination—instead of looking over your shoulder at the old habit. You waste a lot of energy trying to keep your eye on what you're giving up in the old habit. Instead, see yourself fully engaged in the lifestyle you want to live.

Say, for example, your old habit is overeating, and the new habit you want to replace it with is healthy eating. By focusing on the healthy eating, you set your sights on making healthy food choices and the benefits you gain from them. Will you miss those other foods? Most certainly! But when your desire to change comes from the core of who you are, you can allow such feelings to come … and to go. They aren't who you are anymore.

When you write down your intentions and plans, they become real. You can look at them, read them out loud, and, if you choose, show them to other people. So take a few minutes now to write in your responses for the habit change you're making.

When I look at myself living my new habit, I see _____

_____

_____

I'm making this journey of change because _____

_____

_____

Three ways my new habit can bring joy into my life are:

1. _____

2. _____

3. _____

Keep it positive! Frame your new habit for what it is, not how it differs from the old habit. For example, instead of calling your new habit "not smoking," how about "live smoke-free." Instead of "lose weight," how about thinking "achieve and maintain a healthy body." You get the idea!

Are We There Yet?

Your journey of change is an ongoing experience. You, like everyone else, have only 24 hours in each day, and you really should spend seven or eight of them with your head on your pillow. Of the hours that remain, your waking hours, each holds its own challenges and its own joys. As eager as you are to immerse yourself in your new habit, you still must take one day at a time.

But you are the driver on this journey, and you make the decisions that get you through the day. Some days you may feel desperate for a shortcut, anything to get you through with the least amount of anguish and frustration. Other days, you may wish you could stop time itself so you soak in the joy of your accomplishments.

Three things I can and will do today to take me closer to my destination habit are:

1. _____
2. _____
3. _____

Create a new list each day. It's okay to do the same things for several days, even a week when the going gets tough and these are the things that make everything worthwhile for you. But stretch yourself to find more ways to make this new habit so interesting that you'll wake up one morning and struggle to remember the old habit. It will happen, you'll see.

The Measure of Your Travels

Have you ever driven across the United States? It's a grand adventure to see the country in such a way. It's also a great lesson in relativity: how 500 miles can zip by when there's lots to see along the highway, and how 500 miles can drag out when there's nothing but highway to see.

Some days will be more productive than others. You can't predict; you've got to go with the flow, just like driving across the country. But you can establish measures for yourself that show you your progress, even when it's been one step forward and two steps back all day.

Three measures of my success today are:

1. _____
2. _____
3. _____

As with the ways you can move toward your new habit, create a new list each day or every couple days for the measures of your success. As you move more solidly toward your destination habit, your success markers will change.

About Those Voices in Your Head

Everyone responds better to reward than punishment, even lab rats. Yet when we disappoint ourselves, the first thing we do is beat ourselves up! We talk trash about ourselves, and we believe it. We see ourselves as—and feel—worthless. Lab rats, when repeatedly punished, stop trying to seek reward. There is little wonder that old habit calls to us so enticingly!

So don't listen—not to the siren song of the old habit, not to your own trash talk. You're doing fine. Take a look at your success measures. Better yet, take a look in the mirror. That face staring back at you is the face of determination, and it deserves your respect and your confidence. Tell it so!

When You're Telling Yourself ...	Stop, and Instead Say ...
I'm such a loser!	Each day I have opportunities to learn something new.
I just can't do this.	I can find a way if I look beyond the surface.
Whatever I do, it's not good enough.	I do my best.
My life is such a mess!	I'm a work-in-progress, and some days are better than others.
My bad habit doesn't hurt anyone.	My bad habit hurts me, and that's one person too many.

Self-talk is a powerful tool. It can tear you apart if you let it take a negative tone, or it can build you up if you give it positive energy. You are your own best cheerleader, and sometimes you've got to cheer even when you don't feel like it. There's some good, somewhere, in every situation.

Reward Yourself

Every day, reward your successes. Do it every hour if it helps you stay focused. You can't spoil yourself. Even if the best you're able to muster is to stand still, that's progress enough to be worthy of recognition.

Choose rewards that support the changes you're making and that have personal meaning for you. Rewards and treats can be tangible or intangible, big or small, public or private. You choose. After all, this is your journey.

Five ways I can reward myself in my new habit today are:

1. _____

2. _____

3. _____

4. _____

5. _____

Your brain loves rewards and will do anything to get them. Keep it focused on the rewards that support your quit from the old habit and your journey to the new habit—to the new you.

Calm Yourself

Understandably, you're feeling a lot of stress about the changes you're making. We don't need to tell you that. But we do want to tell you the stress you feel is real—you're not making it up. However, you can do things to calm your mind so you can then calm your body. And when you can do this, you can put your old habit in its proper perspective.

Meditation is one of the most effective methods for relieving stress and helping you feel centered in yourself. In a certain way, it's the flipside of addictive behaviors, a positive and healthy melding of mind and body. Meditation is widely used in many medical settings as part of an overall, integrated healing approach.

There are many forms of meditation, and likely meditation classes are offered in your local community. (We talk more about Vipassana meditation in particular in Chapter 7.) But you don't have to go to class to benefit from this ancient method. The key principle for most forms of meditation is the same: focus the mind.

def•i•ni•tion

Meditation is a practice of focusing the mind as a method for increasing nonjudgmental awareness. Many forms of meditation have been in use for thousands of years. Though spirituality may be, and often is, a component of meditation, meditation is not in itself a religious practice.

You might choose to focus on your breath (a common meditation technique), a specific aspect of your old habit that is causing you anxiety, or an inner vision such as a peaceful garden. You might find it helpful to visualize the old habit's pathways in your brain receding and the new habit's pathways growing strong. A few minutes of meditation can bring surprising calm to your entire being, and you can do it just about anywhere.

Take a few minutes right now to identify three points of focus for meditation, and a circumstance for each where a brief meditation could ease your stress.

1. _____
2. _____
3. _____

Engage Yourself

The more you're out in the world, the less energy you have to direct at any discomforts you feel from your old habit or the changes you're making in your life. Being with other people is a key dimension of many habits, the old ones as well as the new ones. Go to the library, the museum, the park—places where you can be around other people without increasing exposure to cues and triggers for your old habit.

Get moving! Physical activity gets your mind involved in what's going on outside itself. Make daily exercise a part of the new you; nothing improves your health more effectively. When was the last time you had fun like when you were a kid? Fly a kite; ride a bike; take off your shoes and socks and walk barefoot in the grass or on the beach; skip along the sidewalk; toss a Frisbee. Find—or rediscover—what you enjoy, and do more of it.

What interests you? What did you used to do for fun and activity that's no longer part of your life? Write five things you can do today, if only for 10 minutes at a time, to get out in the world in a physical way that you enjoy.

1. _____
2. _____
3. _____
4. _____
5. _____

Easing the Transition: Help from Medications

Habits such as smoking, drinking, and drug use physically affect your body in ways that may cause you to experience withdrawal symptoms. Nicotine, alcohol, and other drugs affect your brain and your body in complex ways. When your struggles to break free from your old habit are particularly intense—as they may be during the first two weeks to two months after you separate yourself from your old habit—you might gain some benefit from medications.

Steer Clear _____

Some medications require a physician's prescription and oversight. Others are available over-the-counter for anyone to purchase. Discuss the possible side effects, including interactions with other medications, with a pharmacist or doctor before taking any medications—prescription, over-the-counter, or herbal—for symptoms related to quitting your old habit. All medications have potential risks.

Medication alone will not end your old habit. At best, it can ease some of your discomforts and help you get your feet firmly on the track of your new path. Studies show about the same rate of success with and without medication for quitting most addictive behaviors. You still must do the work making the change requires.

Nicotine Replacement

The most common addiction aid is nicotine replacement. You can buy some of these products—which come in the form of chewing gum, skin patches, and lozenges that dissolve in your mouth—at drug stores and supermarkets without a doctor's prescription. Other forms—oral tablets, nasal sprays, and inhalers—have higher concentrations of nicotine and need a prescription from your doctor.

Talk About It _____

A new, non-nicotine medication to help with smoking cessation is varenicline, available by prescription in the United States under the trade name Chantix. Taken by mouth in tablet form, varenicline works by blocking the effect of nicotine in the brain so you get little pleasure from smoking. The medication also reduces cravings and other physical symptoms that may occur in the early stages of quitting.

Nicotine replacement works by delivering a small dose of nicotine into your blood circulation. The nicotine makes its way to your brain, where it binds with nicotine receptors. Your brain sometimes isn't all that smart because this binding convinces it that you've had a few puffs on a cigarette. (But you don't feel quite the same way about it because you know better.) It's not enough nicotine to give you the full jolt you'd get from a smoke, but it is enough to calm those agitated brain neurons and bring the craving intensity down a few notches.

Follow the package directions for whichever product you choose; it is possible to overdose on nicotine, which isn't pretty or fun. It's especially risky to smoke while using a nicotine replacement product because doing so rapidly raises the level of nicotine.

Antidepressants

The antidepressant bupropion (available as the brand-name products Zyban and Wellbutrin in the United States) has a not-so-secret second life as an aid for ending addictive habits such as smoking, alcohol abuse, and some kinds of substance abuse (notably methamphetamine and opiates other than heroin). Because depression often accompanies many addictive behaviors, doctors may prescribe bupropion as the antidepressant for people who have compulsive habits such as gambling and overeating.

Other antidepressants that appear to help with quitting an addictive behavior are the SSRIs—selective serotonin reuptake inhibitors such as Prozac. This class of drugs boosts the level of serotonin, a mood-elevating neurotransmitter that naturally occurs in the brain. Researchers believe higher serotonin levels help to stabilize the brain's quest for dopamine-releasing pleasure sensations.

Anti-Alcohol

Disulfiram, best known as Antabuse, is a medication that prevents the liver from metabolizing alcohol. If you drink while taking disulfiram, higher levels of a toxic waste byproduct (acetaldehyde) accumulate in your blood, causing many very unpleasant symptoms. Doctors may prescribe disulfiram for people who've been unsuccessful over a long period in their efforts to stop drinking.

Naltrexone is a medication that works by blocking the sense of euphoria that comes with drinking. It also reduces cravings for alcohol and can help you get back on track when you have a lapse.

Methadone Maintenance Treatment (MMT)

Methadone is a synthetic drug that binds with opiate receptors in the brain the same way opiates do (such as heroin and dilaudid), but without the euphoria, intoxication, and sedation. Used in this way, methadone relieves cravings. Physician addiction specialists may prescribe MMT for people who have opiate addictions.

Diet Aids

Numerous over-the-counter products claim to suppress appetite and control hunger. Many of these contain caffeine, which acts as both a stimulant (making you feel less like eating) and a diuretic (pulling fluid from your body so it appears that you're losing weight). Some products may contain decongestant drugs also found in cold medications; these drugs are also stimulants. Herbal products often contain bitter orange, an extract that increases heart rate and raises blood pressure. Doctors may also prescribe medications that suppress appetite or block the absorption of dietary fat.

Live in the Moment

You've made a bold and courageous move, to quit your bad habit and redirect your life for positive experiences. Your old habit has cost you plenty. Now have the opportunity to make changes that benefit you and carry you in the direction you want to go. Even in this early stage of change when your main focus is on quitting the old habit, keep the new you in your sights. You're much closer to him or her than you might think.

The Least You Need to Know

- As important as it is for you to focus on where you want to go in your efforts to change, you first must leave your old habit behind.

- The "best" quit methods are the ones that work for *you*.

- There are many resources to help you through the tough spots of your quit.

- Putting your commitment to change in writing, as a contract with yourself, helps you focus your intentions and your actions.

What About Tomorrow?

In This Chapter

- ◆ Getting to know the new (and real) you
- ◆ Life in the eye of the storm
- ◆ What do you mean, I can't have it now?
- ◆ Strategies for change
- ◆ In good company

Now that you're past the first few weeks of quitting your habit, the tides turn. You've settled into a new daily pattern of behavior that emphasizes different, healthier habits. For the most part, you're doing well. You want this change, and it suits you.

The part you've mastered before—quitting a habit—is behind you. Ahead lay the sometimes smooth, sometimes choppy waters of living in this new way. This is where you've floundered in the past, and where you're eager to succeed this time. You know, however, that your old habit's not going to cut you loose without a few final rallies for your attention.

So let's take a look at the currents and rocks beneath the surface you might expect to encounter over the next two years—and beyond. Though unfamiliar to you, these are well-charted waters. All you've got to do is navigate them!

Life, Unaltered

Maybe this is the first time in your life, or at least for as long as you can remember, that you've been without your old habit. It might be the first time your friends and family are experiencing the "real" you. Feels pretty good, doesn't it? And yeah, you feel a bit exposed, too, like stepping out onto the beach in a new swimsuit—in February.

However long it's been since you've known this part of yourself, it's always been there, somewhere within you. So let it out! People around you may see this "new" you as someone exotic and different, but you know better. This is the real you, and you've got a lot to offer. Unaltered.

Still Life

Bad habits often thrive because they create their own contrived excitement—the thrills that come with indulging them. There's never a dull moment when the old habit's at the helm. You're always sailing the swells, flying and falling.

But that, of course, is much of the problem. When you pack your life with perpetual excitement, you lose track of just how "on" you are all the time. So you keep looking for more—and more, and still more. You can never get enough.

Even when your old habit is one that, on the surface, is more sedate—say, overeating—it still carries its own form of excitement. Maybe you have to sneak to indulge—holding late-night raids on the fridge, stashing snacks in the car, hiding wrappers and remains—or pretend the old habit isn't really a problem. Your brain loves the rush of these actions, even when you think they're providing comfort rather than thrills.

> **Talk About It**
>
> In the 2007 season of the successful reality TV show *The Biggest Loser*, the four finalists had lost close to 50 percent of their body over the course of the show—well over 100 pounds each. During the season finale, each had the opportunity to talk about what the experience meant to him or her. One contestant worried most about the potential for relapsing into old habits after she was back in her daily environment, observing that according to statistics 90 percent of them would do just that.

Life in calmer waters might seem, well, boring. It's not, really—real life is its own rush. You just have to get your "land legs" under you to enjoy it. And real life has something you've likely not experienced much with your bad habit wearing the captain's hat: peace and quiet. Quiet feels weird and unnatural when you've been used to riding the eyewall of the storm.

Now that you're in the calm, you might fidget, move things around, or look for things to do. If you're doing all those chores that have piled up while you've been focused on other things, by all means keep at it! But if all you're doing is looking for ways to busy yourself, stop. You're only seeking new ways to indulge those old urges for excitement, and you don't want to go there. More important, you need the quiet. Your body, thoughts, and feelings need predictable down-time so you can relax and unwind.

Quiet is normal, even though it may not feel that way to you just yet. It's how people who don't have your meddlesome old habit live. Quiet is good. Once you get used to having quiet in your life, you'll wonder how you ever made it through the day without it. Though you might not believe it now, soon enough you'll even look for opportunities to cultivate stillness in your life.

(Re)Claiming Your Life

It's so great to finally break free from your old habit! But when you look around, does your life look like it belongs to someone else? Some bad habits have significant consequences, particularly if you've been arrested, convicted, or jailed as a result. You may have to deal with financial repercussions, especially from compulsive shopping or gambling. And you might face health issues or relationship challenges no matter what your old habit was.

Picking up the pieces may seem daunting. As with other facets of your journey of change, though, it's a process of putting one foot in front of the other. All change takes place one step—sometimes one impossibly small step—at a time. This is an ideal opportunity to take stock of things and to build the life you want to live. Will it be easy? In a word, no. But it'll get easier. Will it be worth the effort? You bet! And you'll be pleasantly surprised to see the ways in which other people are willing—and even eager—to help you succeed.

The Joy of Living

Life is not all about the quiet, of course. You want to have fun, and you should! Chances are your old habit was the source of much of what you'd come to think of as fun. Truth is, it wasn't—it was just what you did. It came to replace genuine fun.

Dig back: what's your favorite childhood memory of something fun, something you did for no other reason but the sheer joy of doing it? Maybe it was playing baseball or riding your bike, walking your dog, swimming, or building with Legos. You're all grown up now, of course, and life is more complicated. But as an adult, you have pretty much free rein when it comes to choosing what you'd like to do. So what keeps you from doing what you'd really like to do?

> **Talk About It**
>
> For fast-acting relief, try slowing down.
> —Lily Tomlin, American comedienne

Try this: each morning when you're in the shower, think of one activity you'd like to do that's fun. Just choose something small, like walking barefoot in the grass, sitting in the library to read a chapter in a book, or skipping instead of walking.

See and feel yourself doing this activity. Then think about what's on your agenda for the day. How can you fit in your fun activity? Schedule it in, like any other appointment or responsibility. Then keep it—and enjoy!

You may need to start out very small, to work your enjoyable activities into your daily life. When what you want to do seems bigger than your available time, consider how you can break it into smaller pieces. How can you rearrange your daily demands? Where do you have natural breaks in your schedule?

These meetings with yourself are just as important as anything else you could do to support the changes you're making in your life. We tend to set aside things we'd like to do that have no purpose other than to make us happy because we have so much else we *should* do. But the things we do for ourselves are *shoulds*, too, and we need to learn to make time for them.

Take a few minutes right now to examine your day today. Write your activities in the appropriate column, "shoulds" or "wants." Things you "should" do are often things you do for other people or to meet obligations. Things you "want" to do are usually things you do for yourself. For example, finishing a customer's order or running your clothes to the drycleaner over your lunch break is a "should"; using your lunch break to eat lunch (what a concept!) or take a walk is a "want."

Shoulds   **Wants**

_____   _____

_____   _____

_____   _____

_____   _____

_____   _____

Now, how's the balance look to you? Lopsided, of course, is not balance. Most of us find the "shoulds" side of everyday life to be quite heavy. Balance may come from relieving some of the "shoulds" as well as adding more "wants." You'll be pleasantly surprised to see how much difference even small changes can make, and how easy it can be to spot any stealth appearances of your old habit by tracking what you're doing by design … and desire.

Negotiating with the PIG

When we want something, we want it now, not in 10 minutes, not in 2 hours, not in 3 weeks. *Now.* Alan and other addictive behavior specialists call this the *Problem of Immediate Gratification*, or *PIG*. Addictive behaviors are all about the PIG: they please our pleasure pathways. The PIG is all those cravings and urges the old habit called on to draw us in. The PIG has an insatiable appetite. The PIG awaits your return, greedy and selfish. Turn this PIG into bacon!

def•i•ni•tion

The **Problem of Immediate Gratification (PIG)** refers to the behaviors we've developed to instantly satisfy the appetite of our cravings and urges.

Negotiating with the PIG is the process of learning new behaviors that allow you to feel comfortable with delayed (also called deferred) gratification—waiting to experience fulfillment and pleasure. Not impatiently, like a child dancing around on the sidewalk in front of the ice cream store but calmly and matter-of-factly—which can be its own form of satisfaction, contentment in a steady state.

Talk to your PIG! Tell it, "I'd rather have a hug than a drug." Tell it, "I know you can make me feel good right now. But I'd rather wait, and feel good for a long time." Tell it, "I'd rather swim the length of the pool underwater than have a cigarette." What are your PIG's top three demands? Write them here. Then, write what you'd rather have or do. Be creative, and keep it real for your life and circumstances.

What My PIG Demands

1. _____

2. _____

3. _____

What I Want Instead

1. _____

2. _____

3. _____

Practice having or doing what you want. When your PIG makes a demand, say the demand out loud, and then speak your counter-offer. When you've mastered these three demands, move on to the next three. Your greedy PIG will keep you on your toes, but you're smarter than your PIG!

Dueling Brain Cells

Pigs are considered among the smartest of farm animals. A Penn State researcher even taught pigs to use joysticks to manipulate images on a computer monitor, for rewards of M&Ms and Skittles! The PIG of your habit is right up there on par with its namesake when it comes to manipulation. It knows just what to do to get what your brain's pleasure centers want.

Your cravings and urges call on the pleasure pathway and other structures in your brain (see Chapter 2). Your efforts to balance the rush of immediate gratification and the steady satisfaction of delayed gratification pit one part of your brain against another.

Your prefrontal cortex—the PFC—is responsible for complex thought and reasoning, language, and intellect. It loves long-term planning, which gives it the opportunity to strut its stuff. You'd think, with this structure being the largest part of your brain, it would easily win out in any battle of balance.

But two primitive structures, the amygdala and the hypothalamus, are pretty good at tag-teaming for the end-run around reason. Your amygdalae (you have a pair of them) direct your basic responses to emotions, particularly your desires; your hypothalamus is the gateway that grants passage for nerve and chemical signals to travel from your brain to your body. The PIG lives in these structures.

When you must choose between now and later, these structures all jump into the ring. It's conditioning versus cognition. The PIG is sneaky, but in the end, the PFC is smarter. With enough time to think, reason rules. You just need to know there is a battle and plan your strategies to give reason the advantage.

Learning to Wait

Our culture fattens the PIG. Everything happens in an instant. Are you hungry? By the time you put your credit card back in your wallet, your meal's waiting at the second window. Are you bored? Hundreds of channels await the click of your remote. Are you lonely? Text your Fave 5s and beyond, if they don't respond in a heartbeat.

Tomorrow is all about "not now." The ability to wait comes more easily for some people, but for others, it's a constant struggle. Though you can take tomorrow as it comes, most of us do at least a little planning if only by setting the alarm clock. The PFC loves tomorrow.

Make the PIG Work for You

Habits live in a push-pull world of feels good/feels bad. We strive to indulge that which is enjoyable (*positive reinforcement*) while at the same time avoid that which is unpleasant (*negative reinforcement*). Sometimes one or the other becomes more important, so we shift our efforts accordingly. We slip into behaviors that allow us to feel good without giving much thought to why we might feel bad.

def•i•ni•tion

Positive reinforcement is a consequence that feels good enough to encourage repetition of the behavior. Negative reinforcement is alleviation of unpleasant feelings.

When you can identify the push and the pull of your old habit—how it makes you feel good and how it makes you avoid or escape feeling bad—you can develop ways to reward yourself for continued progress in your new habit. Often the threat of returning to the old habit is enough in the way of negative reinforcement; we don't need to create further avoidance actions. (We'll talk more about the abstinence violation effect in later chapters.)

But we do often need to create more positive reinforcement. We're not always so good at rewarding ourselves. It's natural to feel a bit touchy about this when giving up an old habit that used to be the source of reward. Remember, though, that now we're talking about *positive* reinforcement. That old habit was anything but positive, no matter how it made you feel.

It's really great when other people recognize our good efforts and work, and compliment or praise us. We also need to compliment and praise ourselves. Affirmations are one way to do this. Another approach is to give yourself points for actions and behaviors that carry you forward on your path of change, with a major reward for accumulating a certain number of points. Your reward could be a weekend getaway to someplace you've always wanted to go, an afternoon playing golf, or an evening without answering the telephone. What matters most is that the reward is important to *you* and supports your path of change.

Will and Way

We hear and talk a lot about willpower, often in an all-or-nothing way; either we have it or we don't. When we're struggling with change, we take the cliché "where there's a will, there's a way" as evidence (or condemnation) that we're doing something wrong: if only we were strong enough, we could beat this old habit into the ground. Nothing could be further from the truth!

The "will" part is your desire, your motivation. It's what you want to do. The "power" part covers the strategies available to you to make your "will" happen. As you learn new coping skills, you gain improved ability to shape the events of your life.

These two parts nurture each other. The more you learn, the greater your motivation. You begin to see results from your methods, and you dare to desire greater change, so you seek further knowledge. It's an endlessly upward spiral.

Steer Clear

Here's one test you should never take: *I'll just try it to see.* Though it might sound like a good way to see how far you've come—just one drink, only one cigarette, a single cookie, 20 minutes at the blackjack table—testing your resolve by confronting temptation is a slippery slope more likely to lead to a lapse than to prove your progress. Better to test yourself by finding new ways to experience your path of change.

Change Strategies That Work

Do an Internet search for "changing habits," and you'll get tens of thousands of hits. Some websites offer valuable insights and suggestions (see Appendix B). Others are really out there, suggesting approaches we don't even want to repeat. How do you know what to do when it comes to quitting a troublesome habit?

def•i•ni•tion

Evidence-based approaches are methods and techniques tested through conventional scientific research and demonstrated to be effective for specific purposes.

When working with people who are changing their addictive behaviors, Alan and other psychologists focus on approaches, which they call *evidence-based approaches*, that they know work. And they know these approaches work because scientific studies demonstrate their effectiveness.

Evidence-based approaches are the essence of every-day life, whether or not we recognize them, from the routes we take to get to work to the ways we prepare meals. We do things in certain ways because we know those ways work. We run into difficulty when we don't know for sure how something works. Then we often try just about anything, just to see. If it works, great—we'll do it next time, too. If it doesn't work, we try something else.

This have-at-it approach works fine with jigsaw puzzles and cooking experiments. But when it comes to our well-being, it's good to know what really works.

Mindfulness

Habits, by their nature, are fairly mindless. That is, we engage in habitual behaviors without thinking about what we're doing or why we're doing it. We're on autopilot. What are you doing right now? Of course, you're reading this paragraph. But what else are you doing? Are you tapping your foot, twirling your hair, pulling at your moustache, eating? None of these things is bad! It's just that if you're doing them, you're likely unaware of them.

Mindfulness is the state of being aware, on a moment-to-moment basis, of being in the here and now, without passing judgment. It's rather like taking a feeling or experience and holding it in the palm of your hand so you can examine and explore it from every possible angle. Then, when you choose a behavior, you can do so with consideration for its benefits and consequences. Check in with mindfulness techniques by taking a look at *The Complete Idiot's Guide to Mindfulness* (see Appendix B).

Be Mindful

Alan teaches a mindfulness technique he developed that he calls "urge surfing." When a craving or urge strikes, envision it as a wave and envision your breath as the board you ride to "surf" the urge. Focus on your breath as the surfboard. Concentrate to keep your breath on top of the craving. Hold this imagery until the wave finally breaks and the urge fades. It's the basic nature of cravings to be short-lived; urge surfing allows the craving to exist and dissipate in a controlled, mindful way.

Habits get the better of us when we lose objectivity. When we can observe our behaviors as though we step out of ourselves, we can better see them for what they are and how they affect our lives. Our thoughts and actions are then the result of conscious choice. Of course, we still can choose the less desirable behaviors, but we're much less likely to do so when we know we're making the choice.

Meditation

There are many forms of meditation, some associated with spiritual practices and some that are not. We present meditation simply as a technique. You might choose a form of meditation that is consistent with your faith or incorporates your practices into your personal belief system.

In its core form, meditation focuses your thoughts. Like clearing the clutter from your desk, this process of focusing establishes a sense of calm and order to your thoughts. Meditation is particularly effective for settling the mental and emotional chaos that you feel when worry and fear fill your mind.

Talk About It

Alan and his colleagues conducted a research study to evaluate how well a Buddhism-based form of meditation, Vipassana (a Buddhist word that means insight), might help jail inmates with alcohol dependence or substance abuse problems maintain sobriety. While incarcerated, inmates learned Vipassana meditation techniques and then met with researchers three and six months after their release. Those who used Vipassana had significantly greater success than those who participated in conventional treatment or who did not receive any treatment at all.

An effective and simple meditation technique is to focus on the breath. You always have your breath with you, so there's no need for any special equipment! This meditation can be brief, helping with cravings and temptations. You also can extend it, helping to relieve stress and anxiety.

Breath Meditation

1. Focus your conscious attention on your breath. Don't make any effort to alter the pattern of your breathing; just observe your breath going into and leaving your body.

2. Engage your physical senses in your observations. Listen to the sound of your breath. Feel your breath as it enters your nose, expands your chest, and enters your lungs. Envision your breath bringing life-giving oxygen into your body.

3. Let the focus on your breath become the content of your thoughts. Whatever other thoughts appear, gently return your attention to your breath.

4. Feel this awareness relax your body; everything is about your breath.

5. When you are calm and centered, gradually return your attention to the environment around you.

You can expand this simple meditation to a mindful exploration of the source for your worry, fear, anxiety, or stress. If you feel yourself slipping back into these emotions, return to your focus on breath. With practice, you'll be able to engage this meditation in nearly any circumstance, often without others around you even noticing.

12-Step Programs

The first break-through in recovery methods was Alcoholics Anonymous (AA), a faith-based program featuring twelve steps of participation. In the decades since its inception, AA has helped millions of people with alcohol dependence and abuse to maintain sobriety. Today countless programs for a wide variety of addictive behaviors build from the 12-step platform.

These programs have in common three fundamental principles: anonymity, belief in a higher power, and absolute abstinence. Most also require participation in weekly meetings to share experiences and support. For many people, 12-step programs are very effective—and that's great. It's important to recognize, however, that the basic design for such programs came into being during a time when we knew little about the processes of addictive behaviors.

As we've gained knowledge and understanding in the decades since the advent of AA, however, we've come to recognize that while abstinence is a desirable goal for most addictive behaviors, it is not likely to be absolute. Relapse is part of the change process, and it's important to acknowledge and accommodate this.

Temptation Lane

Risk has many faces. The face you worry about the most, of course, is that of your old habit. And it seems like every time you turn around, there it is, lurking in the shadows. It's okay; you'll get used to seeing it, and eventually you'll be able to look past it.

Confronting—and embracing—risk in a positive context is a challenge of a different sort. This is the risk of change, the risk of success. "Oh, c'mon," you might be thinking, "why would success be a risk?" But it

> **Talk About It**
>
> I still see things that are not here. I just choose not to acknowledge them. Like a diet of the mind, I just choose not to indulge certain appetites ….
>
> —Russell Crowe as the brilliant but psychotic mathematician John Nash in the 2001 movie, *A Beautiful Mind*

takes a lot of effort to change, and you put yourself out there in ways that others can see and judge. Remember, though, that most of those others are pulling for you to succeed. They find encouragement in your efforts and may themselves be inspired to make positive changes in their lives.

The Company You Keep

You need the company of others, and you need those others to be people who share the new habits you're cultivating. You need people who truly support you in the changes you're making. Moving forward with your life may mean moving on to new friends.

Who are your friends, and what do you have in common with them? This is a good time to make a list. Keep it simple: names and common interests. What do you do together? Where do you go? It might surprise you to discover that the bonds you have are the interests of your old habit. This is not you!

Now, make another list. What *are* your interests? What do you like to do? Where do you like to go? This is you.

Of Like Minds ... and Habits

Many habits, good and not so good, encircle themselves with a select group of other people who share the habit. If you love to play tennis or hike, odds are so do many of your friends. You may belong to clubs or organizations that support these activities and spend much of your leisure time enjoying both the activity and the friends.

Be Mindful

Writing in a journal can help you express your thoughts and emotions so you can explore them without judgment. A journal also lets you look back on your journey of change to see the progress you've made and can help you identify specific challenges and relapse threats. You can also use a journal to self-monitor your cravings and urges.

On the flipside, many of your friendships may have unbreakable links to the habit you've ditched. Are you suddenly alone after work and on your days off because you no longer smoke, drink, do drugs, or gamble? Are you left behind on recreational shopping excursions and fast-food lunches? Are you dateless?

It's hard not to feel left out and unloved when the people you once spent all your time with don't invite you anymore. And it's even harder when you have to turn down their invitations. Even through the haze of your habit, you shared your life with these people.

But going back to the old group means going back to an environment where the old habit thrives, and that's not the direction you want to travel.

Special Occasions and Celebrations

Birthdays, holidays, and special events are often like magnifying glasses that intensely focus the beam of temptation. People gather who might have little else in common, bringing their habits to the party. Along with your gift, make sure you bring your relapse prevention plan. Your approach for staying the course depends on the old habit you've left behind and the new habits you're cultivating.

Before you leave for the party, sit down with a pen and paper. On the left side of the paper, write the risks you're likely to encounter at this event. On the right side of the paper, list three methods for countering each risk. Remember, too, that leaving early is always an option. Carry this list with you, and take a look at it when temptation challenges you.

That Which Feeds Your Soul

It's easy to find yourself caught up in the details of changing your habits and your lifestyle. After all, such details are the crux of your change efforts. But it's easy to feel bogged down in this focus. You're more than your habits, and it's important to nurture your spirit.

Plan some time for yourself each day, and use this time for yourself. You might meditate or pray, walk in the woods or along the beach, or sit on your porch or a park bench and watch the sunset. Consider this your time to recharge and renew. Tomorrow is another day—you want to be able to greet it with enthusiasm and joy.

The Least You Need to Know

- ◆ Habits often create an artificial excitement that makes life without them seem boring.
- ◆ Mindfulness counters the need for immediate gratification.
- ◆ Willpower is a combination of motivation and strategy.
- ◆ A simple breath meditation can ease cravings and relieve stress.
- ◆ Keeping yourself mindfully focused in the here and now helps you resist social pressures.

Part 3

Wanting and Needing

Do you really need a smoke, a drink, a big bowl of chocolate ice cream? Or do you simply want it so intensely that it feels like a need? Needs, we must have to make it through our daily lives. Wants, we like. Our habits make both easier but don't always get us what we need.

Part 3's chapters explore our desires and our efforts to meet and control them. Chapter 8 presents methods to improve awareness and focus intent. Chapter 9 looks at shifting emphasis from what we can't have or do to what we truly want to do and be. Chapter 10 presents ways to harness bad impulses for good purposes. Chapter 11 cuts through the fog of despair and depression that surrounds us when we relapse to look at the circumstances in our lives that challenge our efforts to change.

Chapter 8

In-Dependent

In This Chapter

- ◆ Your mind has amazing power!
- ◆ Needs, wants, and habits
- ◆ Changing perspectives on addictive behaviors
- ◆ A "back to the breath" mindful meditation

Remember when you first left home? Not the time you stuffed your bedtime bunny and a package of graham crackers into your Power Rangers backpack and marched resolutely into the far reaches of the backyard. Rather, the time you packed everything that was yours to claim and moved it to your own place—a college dorm room, an apartment, or maybe even a house.

Whether you wanted to actually go back home or not, there were times when you missed it more than anything. In that part of your memory where fun things float to the surface and chores sink beyond the level of rapid recall, you long for the comfort of having someone else fix your meals, do your laundry, and turn off the bedroom light when you fall asleep with a book.

As much as you couldn't wait to be independent, maybe it wasn't really what you expected. And what's with those electric bills, anyway? Being a dependent doesn't look so bad from a distance, especially when you forget what it was like to live under house rules.

Old habits are a lot like leaving home. They were comfortable when you lived there. They took care of you, although not in ways that were in your best interests. Like home, you sometimes miss them. But do you really want to go back? Not any more than you really want to return to your childhood home!

The Power of Your Expectations

At the University of Washington's Addictive Behaviors Research Center, there's a room that's not quite your conventional classroom. It has no whiteboard, no desks, and no books. Instead, this room features a bar with tap pulls and liquor bottles, neon beer signs, a scattering of tables and chairs, and dimmed lighting.

Though this looks much like a tavern where you'd meet friends for drinks, it's no Do Drop Inn. This is the BAR-LAB, a convenient acronym for Behavioral Alcohol Research Laboratory. Here, the "mixologists" are researchers. What they're serving up as beer may or may not actually be an alcoholic beverage, although those partaking—student volunteers—believe it is. And when you sidle up to the bar for your next real/fake beer, smile … you're on candid camera! That long mirror behind the bar is actually a one-way window.

> **Talk About It**
>
> What we see depends mainly on what we look for.
> —Sir John Lubbock, English parliamentarian

During one research session, about an hour's worth of drinking, there's a happy and somewhat boisterous crowd in the BAR-LAB. People talk and laugh as they toss down a few pitchers. Inhibitions drop away; one table gets particularly raucous. Several drinkers at another table stumble when they get up from their chairs. To the casual observer, the scene is that of a typical Saturday night on the town.

When researchers question the revelers at the end of the session, many describe that they're feeling quite a buzz. They talk about feeling themselves loosen up and become more social with each drink. There's some embarrassed laughter, red cheeks, and slurry speech. But one or two admit, with an edge of confusion, they're not feeling as buzzed as they should for the amount of drinking they've done.

Then the bomb drops: researchers reveal to the volunteer subjects that no alcohol was in the drinks. None. Nada. Well, only the miniscule amount, a fraction of a percent, that unavoidably slips through in the brewing process. But for all practical purposes, this happy crowd might as well have been chugging apple juice. Sudden, pin-drop silence greets this revelation.

Some are embarrassed, some are disbelieving, some are puzzled, but all are surprised. Then someone laughs, and one by one these suddenly sober volunteers talk about how they felt when they thought they were drinking real beer. Alan calls this the beer goggles effect. The point of this kind of BAR-LAB session is to investigate the extent to which expectations influence behavior.

In technical terms, such research demonstrates that a clear and powerful *placebo effect* exists when it comes to indulgences of pleasure. And though these studies focus specifically on alcohol, an abundance of research supports the same kinds of results with other substances.

The value of such research is that it gives question to what, exactly, causes the feelings you experience when you indulge your addictive behaviors. Is it the behavior or is it your expectation of how you will feel? When you have a few beers, play a few hands of blackjack, eat two bags of chocolate chip cookies, or cruise the web during your lunch break, do your feelings come from what you're actually doing or from what you expect to feel in doing it?

> **def•i•ni•tion**
>
> The **placebo effect** is a much studied phenomenon in which people experience the same result from an inactive substance or procedure as from an active or "real" one. Placebo testing is an important part of clinical research.

The answer is most likely a blend of both, even with substances known to create physical changes in your brain and your body. The good news for you, in this ambiguity, is that you can harness your expectations in ways that support your efforts to change.

What We Need, What We Want

The night before her first two-day bicycle tour, a fully supported ride with an overnight stop at a motel, Deb laid out everything she needed to take along: three pairs of bike shorts, three jerseys, four pairs of socks, regular shorts and a T-shirt for after the first night's ride, regular shoes, jammies, slipper-socks, a fleece vest, a rain jacket, long-fingered gloves, short-fingered gloves, eight energy bars, a dozen energy gels, back-country first aid kit, sunscreen, aloe, shampoo, conditioner, antiperspirant, bar of soap, toothbrush, toothpaste, floss, comb, towel, and a packet of tissue.

A friend came by to offer a few parting words of encouragement but instead burst into laughter. "You're gonna need one of those little trailers!" she said. An experienced overseas traveler, the friend took over. Ten minutes later, a 1-gallon Ziploc freezer bag held a day's change of clothing, shorts and T-shirt, toothbrush and toothpaste, rain jacket, and a pair of flip-flops. The sealed bag fit, with no cramming or maneuvering, into the bike's front pack.

It's easy—and common—to confuse what we want for what we need. When it comes right down to it, our needs are pretty basic. Mostly, it's our wants that get out of control, masquerading as needs. We often don't have so many choices when it comes to responding to our needs.

Habits feed wants. But with our wants, we have a lot of options. More important, we have plenty of time to consider the pros and cons, so we can choose with intent. It's all too easy to feel rushed and anxious, even with the smallest of decisions, and default to autopilot: we do what we've always done, without thinking about why. The situation makes us feel as though we really don't have a choice about what to do or how to respond.

Every action, and even each thought, is a choice. The feeling that you *have* to behave in a certain way is like waving a red cape in front of a bull: charge! But turn this on its head to make choices with mindful awareness of their possibilities (positive and negative), and you calm the anxiety and agitation. The poor bull doesn't have what it takes to think about that red fabric fluttering in the wind. If he did, he'd certainly snort and saunter off to graze in a sunny field somewhere. But you do have what it takes to stop, think about the choices, and make mindful decisions. After all, you're the one in control. Right?

Addiction, Old-School Style

Though views on addictive behaviors have shifted substantially in recent years, many old perceptions linger. Because these may still be on your mind, we want to address them here.

Until the last decade or so, nearly everyone—researchers, clinicians, people with addictive habits, and the people in their lives—held a rather narrow view of addictive behaviors. This view was mostly anchored to substance abuse and the physical and psychological effects of alcohol and drugs.

The Moral Weakness Myth

From the beginning of recorded history, there's been drinking, drug use, gambling, and indulgences of excess. Without the ability to understand the functions of the brain and the processes of habit, people considered these indulgences vices—moral weaknesses.

Efforts to remedy these vices ranged from ostracizing to preaching. Some societies took an even harsher approach, imprisoning or otherwise punishing "offenders." Of course, such an attitude and environment fostered secrecy and shame, unfortunate holdovers that linger still today.

The Disease Model

Around the end of U.S. Prohibition in the early 1930s, the concept of alcoholism as a disease began to emerge. Quick to follow was the concept of addiction as a disease. Within this model of understanding came disease-oriented terms like treatment, recovery, and relapse. Other terms, such as addiction, dependence, tolerance, and abuse, gained specific meaning.

In this narrow definition, addiction referred to seeking behaviors, one's efforts to obtain whatever it was he craved. Dependence was the way in which he changed, physically or psychologically, because of his habit. Tolerance was the escalation of fulfillment—there was never enough, no matter what it was. And abuse was the continued process of indulging one's habit despite the harm it caused.

Within this model also came a premise of absolutes. Like with pneumonia or a heart attack, one was either sick or well. There was no middle ground, no gray area, no "living with" context. Quickly the model expanded to include narcotic and other substance abuse—the dominant addictive behaviors of the time.

Steer Clear

Many people, especially young people, tend to view tolerance as evidence that they can "take a lot" and still function. Alan cautions that tolerance is, instead, an indication that one's addictive behaviors are out of control. Tolerance tells an individual that he's grown accustomed to a particular effect, such that it takes more to gain the experience the habit provides.

The benefit of this perspective was that it shifted away from the model of moral weakness. It also gave scientists legitimate reason to study addictive behaviors and established treatment approaches within the framework of medical care. And it gave added credibility to the raft of health problems that arise from addictive behaviors. Treating the addictive behavior as the underlying cause of a health problem (for example, smoking and lung or heart disease, or overeating and diabetes) gave doctors new avenues for dealing with the whole picture. By the 1980s, the disease model ballooned to include just about every circumstance of addictive behavior.

The drawback of this perspective was that it gave rise to the perception that there was little, if anything, a person could do about his or her addictive behaviors except seek treatment and hope to stay in recovery.

Co-Occurring Disorders

From recent research comes the recognition that addictive behaviors seldom live alone. That is, habits often develop in the effort to self-treat underlying conditions that may or may not have an official diagnosis. Clinicians call this *dual diagnosis.* Some studies suggest as much as 80 percent of people who have an addictive habit also have an underlying psychiatric diagnosis, depression being the most common.

def•i•ni•tion

Dual diagnosis is the presence of at least one underlying psychiatric condition in addition to an addictive habit. Often, a person may have multiple underlying psychiatric conditions as well as multiple addictive habits.

Popular country-western songs of the 1950s and 1960s were often called "crying in your beer" songs, an observation that a lot of drinking was intended to drown one's sorrows. Today we call this drinking to self-medicate depression. Other addictive behaviors may serve the same intent, from overeating to gambling to excessive web surfing. These are often habits of escape.

Removing the habit tends to lift the veil on the underlying condition, so that many people then seek medical treatment for their symptoms. It's important that your doctor knows about the habits you're changing, and that your therapist, if you're seeing one, knows about any medical diagnosis your doctor gives you. This lets each integrate with the other for treatment and care.

Habit, Interrupted

Habits gain rapid traction because you don't notice what they're up to until they're in full gear. By that time, bringing them to a halt takes considerably more effort. This is where mindfulness comes in. Being mindful—being aware of the present moment without criticism or judgment—helps you recognize patterns of response before they gain much ground.

Beyond Cravings and Triggers

You already know that certain settings, events, and even people set in motion the behaviors of your old habit. If you let this cascade gain momentum, you're in the lap of a lapse. Let it gain control and you're on the path of relapse. How is it that this can *still* happen?

Cravings and triggers are not as straightforward as they seem, particularly as you get further down the pathway of your now not-so-new lifestyle. Sure, in the beginning any association with the old behaviors triggered intense cravings. But you've gotten past that. Now when desire surfaces, it's not always so easy to identify its cues.

Remember, the path to building habits is a long and winding trail through experience and memory. One thing leads to another … to another … to another. It's like unraveling a ball of string. There are many points of contact, each of which can take the ball in a different direction. The key to making sense of the connections is to follow them, one at a time, to where they begin.

In Chapter 7 we talked about urge surfing and also gave a breath meditation—both mindful techniques to help quiet cravings. Here's more focused mindful meditation.

Mindful Meditation for a Craving: Back to the Breath

When a craving surfaces, let it emerge. A craving that senses you're trying to squelch it becomes even more intense; the smaller space you give it, the more pressure it generates. This breath meditation helps you allow cravings and other stresses to exist without driving you out of your mind.

1. Stop what you're doing and sit or lie in a calm and quiet location.

2. Focus on the sensation of your breath at the edges of your nostrils. Draw all of your attention here as you breathe normally.

3. Mindfully experience how each breath feels, increasing awareness of the breath as it moves in and out at the edges of the nostrils.

4. Meanwhile, let your thoughts pass like a parade. Keep your conscious effort on drawing your awareness to the experience of the breath.

5. Continue the focus on the breath until the parade of thoughts through your mind slows enough for you to examine your thoughts without being controlled by them. Here, you begin the serious work of separating your conscious mind from your craving.

6. Keep your focus on the breath at the edges of your nostrils, concentrating until you feel more relaxed, calm, and centered within yourself.

This meditative breathing serves a twofold purpose. First, you stop what you were doing—or what were about to do, like reach for a cigarette or a Twinkie. Second, the meditative breathing brings your mind to a more relaxed focus that allows your thoughts, including cravings, to simply exist without action or judgment.

The Endless Road

"Are we there yet?" The battle cry of the impatient leaps ahead to the trip's destination. How can you help but feel frustrated, and even angry, when the answer's always, "not yet" or "almost"? When you focus on the end of the road, the road seems endless. When it comes to countering cravings, this is a good thing!

Cravings and urges are a lot like little kids on a long trip. They require constant attention and entertainment. Try ignoring them; they quibble and bicker. Pretend they're not there; they pinch each other and yell. Eventually your brain feels like it's going to explode. It's the helplessness of that ageless threat, "You don't want me to stop this car!" Of course they do! That's the whole point—to get you to stop what you're doing and pay attention to them.

> **Steer Clear** _____
>
> OMG! Little has changed our lives as rapidly and extensively as cell phones and text messaging. Do you use your commute as a traveling conference room? Can you send text messages with your phone in your pocket? Shift focus! This is one habit worth separating from, whatever else you're doing. Though it gives you the illusion of accomplishing more with less, it's really only more of a distraction. Focus your mind on the driving—or whatever else you're doing—and leave the texting for a time when you can give it your undivided attention.

When your focus shifts to the journey itself, the endless road becomes an experience to savor and enjoy. Suddenly there's no pressure to be in any particular place at any particular time. Whew—what a relief! You can sit back and just get there when you get there. There's time and space enough for everything.

Instead of trying to shush those clamoring cravings, you can listen to what they're really telling you and respond to the underlying needs rather than their outward expressions. As you might plan frequent rest stops and fun activities for kids in the car, take time to plan ways to deflect triggers and pacify urges that support your new habits and lifestyle. Turn off the cruise control, and enjoy the journey!

The Least You Need to Know

- Your expectations can significantly influence your experiences and behaviors.

- Habits generally accommodate our wants, not our needs.

- Underlying conditions such as depression often coexist with addictive behaviors and may require medical treatment.

- Mindful meditation methods can lessen the intensity and frequency of cravings and urges.

Always the Last One

In This Chapter

- ◆ The last is such fun, let's do it again!
- ◆ What's *your* psyche? Perspectives from Freud, Jung, and Skinner
- ◆ Breaking the links to potential relapse
- ◆ Learn to cherish your firsts

What's *your* favorite "last"? Your last summer vacation from school? Your last day of being in your twenties? The last time you drove your first car? The last time you lugged a diaper bag on an afternoon outing? The last time you paid less than a dollar or two a gallon for gasoline? Ah, those were the days!

We seem to celebrate our lasts even more than our firsts. A unique antici-pation and excitement grows as the last one approaches, and fond memories of it linger for a long time after. We feel a sense of pleasure about many of our lasts, even though at the time they weren't, maybe, quite so much fun.

The Seduction of the Last One

Author Italo Svevo wrote a classic novel in the form of a diary that explored the seduction of the last one through what was, at the time, the new lens of *psychoanalysis.* Svevo titled his novel *The Confessions of Zeno* (*La coscienza di Zeno,* in its original Italian version).

def•i•ni•tion

Psychoanalysis is a method for treating emotional and psychological symptoms by uncovering and interpreting unconscious feelings and thoughts. Austrian physician and psychologist Sigmund Freud is widely acknowledged as the "father" of psychoanalysis.

The main character Zeno Cosini starts smoking cigarettes as a preteen, a common trend in his generation and culture. When serious illness strikes him at age 20, Zeno's been smoking for half his life. When the doctor tells him smoking is making his condition worse, Zeno vows his next cigarette will be his last.

But that cigarette is—you guessed it—only the first of a lifetime of last cigarettes. Zeno eventually establishes a complex system for quitting based on important dates, but even that is not enough to make the quit stick. The fictional Zeno is a poster child for relapse— always quitting, and obsessively focused on the *ultima sigaretta.*

Determined to understand his persistent inability to move past the last cigarette, Zeno seeks help from a Freud-trained psychoanalyst who tells him to begin a journal (hence the format of the novel). Through Zeno's self-explorations, the reader comes to recognize (as does Zeno himself, by the end of his life and the end of the book) that Zeno's addiction is not to the cigarettes but instead to the experience of the last cigarette.

Every cigarette is but another step in that direction, a tiny thrill building to the big rush. So when that last cigarette finally arrives, Zeno's inner tension is so high he can barely contain himself. The seduction of this "high" proves more intense for Zeno than the desire to smoke.

Psyche Diving

Modern researchers explore the mind through high-tech methods like magnetic resonance imaging (MRI) and positron emission tomography (PET) scanning. These imaging methods allow scientists to peek inside the brain to "see" how it functions under various circumstances. One direction of this exploration is the biochemistry of habit and addictive behavior, which Chapter 2 discusses. This is a study of *how* our habits form—how our repetitive behaviors pave themselves into our brains.

But *why* do we engage in these behaviors in the first place? No one knows, entirely. Until the sixteenth century, physicians and philosophers debated the existence and function of the mind. Some believed the mind was a layer of the brain; others believed the heart held this structure of emotion and intellect. This idea seems rather silly to us today, but these early scientists didn't have much to work with. However, over the past hundred years or so, researchers have done a pretty good job digging below the surface of our thoughts and emotions to arrive at some general insights and understandings.

Lie Down Here on My Couch, and Talk to Me ...

Of all the ground-breakers in modern psychology, probably none is as famous—or infamous—as Sigmund Freud (1856–1939). Though Freud's reputation is in the field of psychology, he trained first as a physician and neurologist. He was also a prolific and provocative (okay, controversial) author.

In the early twentieth century, when novelist Svevo (whose real name was Aron Schmitz) was writing *La coscienza di Zeno*, Freud was working on a new approach to the study and understanding of human behavior: psychoanalysis. Freud had some addictive behaviors of his own, notably cocaine use and cigar smoking. In trying to understand himself and his behaviors, Freud began to think about the concept of an unconscious mind—layers of thoughts and emotions that exist beyond awareness.

Talk About It _____

From error to error, one discovers the entire truth.

—Sigmund Freud, Austrian physician and psychoanalyst

Though Freud was not the first to consider the mind as complex and multi-layered, he was the first to take the approach to a practical application. And that approach—psychoanalysis—is the first structured method to delve below the surface of memory and conscious awareness. The fictional Zeno, like his creator Svevo (also a heavy smoker), sought help to understand and change his addictive behaviors from a Freud-trained psychoanalyst—all very cutting-edge in its time.

Freudisms

So what do you know about the venerable Dr. Freud? Before we take a closer look at Freud's influences on our understanding of habitual behavior, let's have a little fun at the good doctor's expense and at the same time see what you know—and what you think you know that really isn't so (to paraphrase humorist writer Artemus Ward)—about the father of psychoanalysis. Test yourself on these Freudisms, the snippets of Freud's ideas and theories that have made their way into popular culture.

1. A Freudian slip is …

   a. An undergarment your great-grandmother wore to poof out her wedding dress.

   b. An Americanized version of a German phrase for stumbling when you step off a curb.

   c. Saying something that isn't what you intended to say but is what you really mean.

2. The Oedipus complex is …

   a. The largest hotel/casino/resort in Las Vegas.

   b. A stage of childhood development.

   c. A chain of movie theaters.

3. Free association is …

   a. Saying whatever comes into your mind.

   b. Membership clubs that charge no fees.

   c. Connecting your dreams with events in your life.

4. Repression is …

   a. A serious, long-lasting downturn in the economy.

   b. Burying fears and worries so you don't think about them.

   c. Feeling deeply sorry about something you've done.

5. *The Ego and the Id* is …

   a. An ancient Greek poem.

   b. A little-known song by The Beatles released on the B-side of "I Am the Walrus."

   c. A book describing the components of the consciousness.

How much do you know about the frontrunner of modern psychology? Here are the answers:

1. The answer is (c), saying something that isn't what you intended but is what you really mean. Classic examples include calling a significant other by a previous lover's name and altering words ("You look really petty tonight.")

2. The answer is (b), a stage of childhood development. Freud believed it was a normal part of growing up to feel competitive with one parent for the attention of the other. His early musings on this concept put it in the context of his personal feelings of competing with his father for the attention of his mother.

> **Talk About It**
>
> In ancient Greek mythology, Oedipus Rex was a king of Thebes foretold to leave his kingdom as a child and return as a man to kill his father and marry his mother, not knowing who they were. The ancient Greek playwright Sophocles immortalized the tale in a series of three plays. Though the trilogy explored the full gamut of family relationships, the marriage of Oedipus to his mother is what underlies the discord (some say dysfunction).

3. The answer is (a). Free association became the cornerstone of psychoanalysis.

4. The answer is (b), burying your fears and worries deep in your unconscious mind. Repression, Freud believed, was the key to understanding one's behaviors.

5. The answer is (c). Freud described three components of the mind, or psyche, in his landmark book, *The Ego and the Id* (published in 1923). The id, the primitive self, dealt with basic drives—survival, pleasure, sex. The superego was the moral self, keeping the id in check. The ego was the balance between the id and the superego, the aware self.

Freud's concepts of the mind stemmed from his perspective that the thoughts and worries that consumed adults arose from unresolved childhood issues—primarily relationships with parents and siblings. Identifying those issues, Freud believed, would allow resolution.

The Talking Cure

Though for us today this theory seems a no-brainer, in Freud's time the common perception was that the mind was simply a means for imposing one's will over one's life. This perception was, in large part, the foundation for the prevailing belief that addictive behaviors were matters of will: by directing the force of one's mind, one could control his actions and behaviors.

def•i•ni•tion

Free association is the process of talking or writing about whatever comes to mind, without interpretation or judgment.

Such a simple concept of an obviously complex matter made no sense to Freud, and eventually his elaboration on the multi-layered mind shattered this perspective. Freud came to believe that through talking in *free association* to a neutral listener, a person could release the contents of his or her inner mind. Then talking about what emerged could provide insight and understanding about those thoughts and behaviors.

Freud saw addiction as a problem of ego attachment and the illusion of control. Freud had his own issues with nicotine and cocaine and used his methods on himself, which led him to recognize his own connections between his emotions and his behaviors. He further believed strong connections existed between the mind (thoughts and emotions) and the body (especially in the manifestation of symptoms and illness). However, at the time, he understood little about addictive behaviors (especially those associated with drugs like cocaine and nicotine).

The recognition of multiple layers or levels to the consciousness marked a fundamental shift in understanding emotional and mental processes and the start of a new specialty, psychology. Freud's theories and methods were the pivot point of this shift, though not everyone accepted them.

The middle of the twentieth century brought a flurry of offshoots and even contrarian movements, all aiming to reveal the sanctum of the inner mind. Psychoanalysis morphed into the more generalized *psychotherapy*, with a growing emphasis on the role of the psychologist or therapist being to provide people with methods to help themselves.

def•i•ni•tion

Psychotherapy is a treatment approach in which a psychologist helps a person gain insight and understanding into thoughts and behaviors that create dysfunction in his life. The goal is to make changes that improve the person's ability to function and participate in the activities of daily life.

Dream Weaver

Though Freud's first breakthrough work was *The Interpretation of Dreams*, which he published in 1900, Freud's breakaway colleague Carl Jung (1875–1961) was the one who established the concept of the dream as a bridge between the conscious and the unconscious. Jung was drawn to the mystic even as a child and incorporated spirituality into his theories and methods. He observed common imagery in dreams, which he came to view as universally symbolic.

Like Freud, Jung trained as a physician. The study of the mind was far enough along by the time Jung entered the arena, however, that he was able to specialize in the new field of psychiatry. Also like Freud, Jung was fascinated with the workings of the unconscious mind and how they influenced behavior.

Early in his career Jung wrote a book, *Studies in Word Association*, which he sent to Freud. Freud was impressed with the similarities to his own theories and arranged to meet Jung. They became close friends, and their friendship lasted a half-dozen years before it fragmented over their differences of opinion.

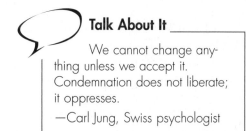

Talk About It

We cannot change anything unless we accept it. Condemnation does not liberate; it oppresses.

—Carl Jung, Swiss psychologist

Jung even had a hand in the founding of Alcoholics Anonymous (AA). As the story goes, Jung had a friend who'd lost count of the number of times he took his last drink. When the friend asked Jung for advice, he told him to seek a spiritual connection and relinquish himself to this higher power. The friend shared Jung's comments with Bill Wilson, who took them to heart in developing the concept of AA as a faith-based method for maintaining sobriety.

Of Myth and Man

In an episode of the long-running NBC sitcom *Frasier*, Frasier Crane's psychologist brother Niles (played by actor David Hyde Pierce) fills in on Frasier's radio show. Niles opens with the announcement, "While Frasier is a Freudian, I am a Jungian so there'll be no blaming mother today!"

What do you know of Jung's theories and interpretations of behavior? This short, fun quiz will put you to the test!

1. The collective unconscious is ...

    a. A cult.

    b. A rock group from the 1960s.

    c. The combined experiences of humanity as a whole.

2. A complex is ...

    a. Condos, offices, and shops in connected buildings.

    b. A pattern of suppressed thoughts that expresses itself through unexpected or inappropriate behaviors.

    c. The tendency of dreams to follow themes.

3. An archetype is ...

    a. A symbol.

    b. A style of building.

    c. A twelfth-century style of book-making.

4. Synchronicity is ...

    a. Uncanny coincidence.

    b. Unrelated events that occur simultaneously.

    c. Having a sense of something happening before it happens.

5. Active imagination is ...

    a. Daydreaming.

    b. A polite term to describe a precocious child.

    c. Letting all the characters in your dreams or thoughts act themselves out while you watch.

Are you a Jungian at heart? Here are the answers:

1. The answer is (c), the combined experiences of humanity as a whole. Jung viewed the collective unconscious as a reservoir we all tap into for expressing concepts beyond our individual ability to understand.

2. The answer is (b). Jung perceived that our unexpected or inappropriate behaviors arose from the mind's efforts to balance expressed and suppressed thoughts and emotions. Such balance was so essential that the mind would find whatever ways it could to achieve it.

3. The answer is (c). An archetype is a symbol that has universal meaning across cultures. For example, the sun represents light, life, the outward self, and the father-figure. The moon represents shadow, dormancy, the inner self, and the mother-figure.

4. The answer is (a), an apparently uncanny coincidence. Jung believed such occurrences arose from their connections in the collective unconscious. They weren't so much uncanny as that we were unaware of their connections.

5. The answer is (c). Jung believed that allowing the imagery of your mind to play out while you observed them in nonjudgmental fashion would let you reach interpretations and insights that would bring you to new understanding.

Jung believed symbolism to be the essence of how the mind functions. Symbols—archetypes—appear consistently in thoughts and dreams because they have universal meaning. Paying attention to them, Jung believed, was key to interpreting the "language" of the unconscious mind. These symbols, or archetypes, were not burying themselves and waiting for you to uncover them but were always present in thoughts and dreams. Jung viewed them as shadow elements of the personality.

Archetype, Myth, and Understanding

Jung developed the concept of a collective unconscious to explain the common connections of these archetypes across time and culture, theorizing that these symbolisms are somehow "accessible" to all human minds through spiritual bonds. Archetypes are common in art and literature and are the basis of mythology—the stories we tell to explain what we observe but don't understand.

Within the context of archetypes, Jung also developed the premise that thoughts, emotions, and actions exist in paired opposites—flipsides. As social beings, we constantly make choices that exclude one of the opposites. This is fine, Jung believed, as long as we acknowledge that the opposite exists. In a sense, such an approach is quite mindful.

Archetypes are not only about ancient myths but are also part of our most sophisticated and modern technology—the computer. You choose archetypes to represent yourself every time you select an *avatar*, tag line, screen name, or quotation that appears in your e-mail signature. What do your avatars reveal about you?

def•i•ni•tion

An **avatar** is an icon that represents a user in a virtual community. It can be a character (as in computer role-playing games), a symbol, or words (as in screen names). The term comes from the ancient Sanskrit word *avatara*, meaning incarnation.

Carl Jung himself became an element in an archetype. He appeared on the famed cover of the 1967 Beatles album *Sgt. Pepper's Lonely Hearts Club Band*. In case you don't recognize him, he's in the top row, seventh from the left, between eccentric comedian W. C. Fields and master of the macabre Edgar Allan Poe. Hmmmm ….

The Secrets of Your Dreams

Many theories exist about the meanings of dreams, ranging from the idea that your brain "dumps" all the data it's accumulated through the day to premonitions and mystic encounters. Your dreams are often the only stage where your fears and worries can safely play out. No one else can see or experience them, and you can choose to ignore them when you awaken.

A dream journal is one way to take a look at what runs through your mind when it's free from the filters you put in place when you're awake. This journaling can be as simple as keeping a notepad and pen beside your bed, so that immediately upon waking, you can jot down key characters, story lines, and such. The longer you're awake, the more those filters will interfere so you want to make your notes before you make your coffee.

After two weeks or so of keeping track, what themes do you see? Have your dreams changed since you started noting them? Do you see things about yourself that you haven't noticed before? Can you draw connections between events in your dreams and people or events in your waking life? Do you dream about your old habit, or about relapsing? A good dream dictionary can help broaden your understanding of archetypes and their possible meanings. Appendix B includes some books we recommend for this purpose, including *The Complete Idiot's Guide Dream Dictionary* by Eve Adamson and Gayle Williamson.

Shaping Behavior

Born the same year Jung published the book that brought him to Freud's attention, B. F. (Burrhus Frederic) Skinner (1904–1990) studied both Freud and Jung as a post-graduate psychology student. But Skinner was more interested in developing methods to change behavior than in understanding the motivations behind behaviors.

Skinner wanted to be a writer, not a psychologist, and first went to college to study literature. The publishing industry was not as enthralled with him as he was with it, however, and after spending a few years in New York City writing newspaper articles, he decided to follow a different career path. He settled on psychology as a natural course for his curiosity about people.

Skinner was nonetheless a prodigious writer, publishing dozens of papers and books. Ironically, one of the best known of his works was his 1948 novel *Walden II*, a fictional account of a utopian commune where his behavioral theories play out.

If It Feels Good, You'll Do It

Though Skinner is not as familiar to the average person as Freud and Jung are, Skinner's contributions to the understanding of behavior are just as significant. So are you ready to see what you know about this ground-breaking behaviorist's theories? Choose the answer for these questions:

1. Operant conditioning is …

   a. An early form of cooling the air in a room.

   b. A method to encourage the repetition of specific acts.

   c. The sterile environment in which surgery takes place.

2. The Skinner box is …

   a. A device that gives you a great tan so you're ready for your vacation to the Bahamas.

   b. A type of slot machine.

   c. A controlled environment for the study of behavior.

3. An aversion stimulus is …

    a. A secret interrogation technique.

    b. An experience unpleasant enough so as to avoid repeating.

    c. A type of kit-built airplane.

4. Schedules of reinforcement are …

    a. Learned patterns of consequences.

    b. Military troop rotations.

    c. On-the-job performance appraisals.

5. Mentalist constructs are …

    a. Movie sets in science fiction films.

    b. What kids build with Legos.

    c. Ideas and values.

Let's see how you did. Here are the answers:

1. The answer is (b). Operant conditioning uses rewards (and sometimes, though less effectively, punishments) to encourage the repetition of specific acts that lead to desired behaviors. The underlying premise is that rewarding each small step in the direction of the desired behavior eventually results in change. For example, a lab rat receives a treat for happening to stand in a particular corner of its cage, so it begins coming to the corner to receive a treat. The rat then receives a treat for standing on its hind legs in the corner, so it begins doing that to get the treat. And so on, until the rat performs an entire sequence of actions.

2. The answer is (c). A Skinner box, designed, as you might suspect, by B. F. Skinner, provides a controlled environment to make sure nothing will interfere with the stimulus and response. Though if your choice was (b), a type of slot machine, you wouldn't be far off.

3. The answer is (b). Aversion means to avoid. The medication disulfiram (Antabuse) is a form of aversion therapy to treat alcohol abuse.

4. The answer is (a). Schedules of reinforcement are patterns of consequences that we learn. For example, that lab rat in the Skinner box learns that every time it

presses the lever it gets a treat. But if the lever releases a treat with only every three presses, the rat learns to quickly press three times.

5. The answer is (c). Skinner viewed subjective factors—intangibles—as mentalist constructs because they exist only in the mind. He believed change arose from manipulations of observable factors—tangibles—notably environment and behavior.

Skinner's theories and methods became the springboard for cognitive behavioral therapy, a method of developing an awareness of our thoughts and actions so we behave with conscious intent rather than through automated behaviors—habits.

One Change Leads to Another

While he was a struggling writer in New York, Skinner spent a lot of time observing the behaviors of pigeons on the ledge outside his window and on the roofs of buildings. He noticed that the birds seemed to learn in small steps which they eventually combined into more or less complex behaviors. He could get them to move in certain ways, such as turning around in a circle, by giving them bits of food each time they took a step. When he returned to school, Skinner applied his observations to behavioral experiments with lab rats and other creatures—sometimes even human volunteers!

Talk About It

In his early study of operant conditioning using pigeons, behavioral psychologist B. F. Skinner observed that pigeons became more persistent in their behavior when the reinforcement was unpredictable. A pigeon that was turning its head at the time it received a reward of food would persist in turning its head and looking for food to appear. Skinner observed this was the most difficult behavior to alter. He also later speculated that such false cause-and-effect correlations formed the basis of superstitious ritual, such as is common in addictive behaviors like gambling.

Skinner demonstrated that change most often, and most successfully, took place as a series of very small steps in the desired direction. Reaching the full behavior was a process that required patience, practice, and time. Skinner's work also laid the foundation for later models of understanding, such as the Stages of Change (see Chapter 2).

The Quest for Understanding

Most of us want to know *why* we do the things we do and benefit from gaining insight into the needs that drive us. As the saying goes, those who fail to learn the lessons of history are destined to repeat them. So we want to understand what compels us to do things we know aren't in our best interests—or at least to make conscious connections between our behaviors and their consequences in day-to-day, tangible ways.

Sometimes we find comfort in discovering there are reasons—and let's be clear here, we're talking about explanations, not excuses—for how we feel, and knowing the reason takes the wind out of its sails. The habit loses its power. We lose interest. Behavior changes. The connections between the "why" and the "what" of our habits are often at the core of heading off relapse.

Promises Made, Promises Broken

What happens as soon as someone tells you, "Don't …"? You do! Or at least you want to. It's human nature. You can't resist one last look, one last taste, one last thrill. After all, it's only one—and it's the last. Promise. But without something else to capture your attention, this is not a promise you can keep.

Maybe you, like Zeno, chose a special date (or many special dates) on which to make your final indulgence of the old habit: the last day of a month, the day before your birthday, New Year's Eve, a holiday or anniversary that has personal meaning for you. You chose such a date because it's a natural marker. Something else worthwhile took place on that date; maybe the power of that success will rub off on your efforts.

But the seduction of this is that the date then becomes special for what you are giving up, not what you are going to gain. The challenge is to keep your eye on the benefits of your changes and to establish markers that celebrate the new you. The fictional Zeno truly meant to quit, every time he smoked his last cigarette. But with no other focus for his desires, the next cigarette became all he could think about.

Those old habits are sneaky in this way, lurking just below the radar of your consciousness, silent but ever-present. Then when you least expect it, they leap out and snare you, unaware. Or do they? Research tells us that for as much as relapse may appear to be a sudden event, we get plenty of warning that it's coming. We ourselves may even unknowingly set the stage.

Why We Struggle So with Firsts

Certainly we relish, or at least remember, our firsts—first lost tooth, first bicycle ride, first walk to school alone, first date, first kiss. First can be a great joy. We all like to finish first, to be the winner. But going first is not always easy. Being the first one means there is nothing to follow. You're on your own, whether it's your first experience with something totally new (think Wright brothers) or with something everyone eventually experiences. What feelings accompany your memories of your first dance, your first job, your first move away from home?

Most first memories come with a lot of emotional baggage. The first one, no matter what it is, is fertile ground for the sense of failure. What if we don't do it right? What if everybody notices that we don't do it right and laughs at us? Or worse, doesn't laugh? What if we have to do it again and again, until we finally do get it right?

Well, you are going to do most of your firsts again. They won't be firsts anymore, of course, but they'll be the same kinds of experiences. You'll have more first dances and get smoother with each one. You'll have more first days on the job and get calmer and more confident with each one. You'll have more moves, and each will become easier. This you know and probably take comfort in knowing.

Firsts and Failure

Odds are, you do very little in your personal life today that doesn't involve microchip technology, from texting on your cell phone to checking e-mail on your Blackberry to doing research on your computer. But do you know who produced the first commercially available personal computer? No, it was not Chuck Peddle (Commodore), though props to you if this was your guess. Nor was it the pair of Steves, Wozniak and Jobs (Apple). And it wasn't high school buddies Bill Gates and Paul Allen (Microsoft), either.

It was John Blankenbaker, a physicist who created the Kenbak-1 and began selling it in 1971. The price—$750—was a bit steep for a time when eggs were 25 cents a dozen, gas was 36 cents a gallon, and a CB radio went for $150. But color television and push-button dialing were about all the technology most people desired; Blankenbaker sold only 40 or so computers before closing up shop.

Is this first a success, or is it a failure? You could see it either way. And often we do see first successes as failures because whatever follows is more successful. Sometimes being first isn't best, in the long haul—sometimes it's better to be at least second and often third, sixth, or even twentieth. Each cycle of failure and success produces a better result.

It works the same way with changing your habits. You learn from your experiences, good and not so good. Something different comes from each round. And each cycle becomes more of a success, over the long term, even when it looks like a failure.

Making Peace with Your Firsts ... and Your Lasts

If you think back to your very first experience with your old habit, it's likely not an entirely fond memory if you're straight-up with yourself. Maybe you were scared you'd get caught. Maybe you got sick. Maybe you got hurt or hurt someone else. Maybe you spent a lot of money that you really didn't have to spend in such of a way. Through time, of course, these memories soften and fade until what you remember has little to do with what actually happened.

You're always going to remember your firsts and your lasts in different ways. The key to successful change is to let them be what they are, to experience them for what they are, without judging or comparing. We often look at a first as an experience we'll do better the next time. Okay, so be it; but let it be a *good* thing, not a remedial matter. Think about this: which would you like to have as a favorite moment to cherish long after it ends, a last cigarette or the first underwater swim the full length of the pool?

The Least You Need to Know

- Sometimes the lure of the last is so strong we strive to repeat it again and again.

- When we can understand why we do the things we do, we can make informed choices about whether to do them and what to do instead.

- No first is perfect, but then, neither is any last.

- We should be proud of our firsts, even when they leave plenty of room for improvement—that gives us space to grow.

Chapter 10

Good Enough

In This Chapter

- ◆ Coming to terms with your best
- ◆ The principle of good enough
- ◆ What do you expect?
- ◆ Thrills! Excitement! Adventure!

Your path to change is dynamic and ever-changing, which is not to say you never quite get there. On the contrary, your goals themselves morph and evolve as you move toward them. But after a while, you begin to feel like it's been long enough. You've been throwing your best at this change thing—shouldn't you be done by now?

But this isn't like acing a history exam, making class valedictorian, or winning it all in a tennis tournament. No matter how much effort you put out, you can change only so much. And it's hard to know when you're giving enough of yourself to make this change thing happen.

As the World Turns

When you were a kid, your world held endless possibilities. In grade school you believed you could be an astronaut, an artist, a doctor, a pitcher, a quarterback, a rock star—and all at once, even, if you wanted. You had your own little field of dreams going, and you knew you could play any position you chose.

> **Talk About It** _____
>
> You are never too old to set another goal or to dream a new dream.
>
> —C. S. Lewis, British author

By eighth grade, you realized you had to narrow your options. You began to get the idea that you couldn't quite do everything, if for no other reason than there just wasn't enough of you to go around. And you were starting to see (sometimes with a little help from your friends) that there were things you didn't do very well.

Maybe you got dizzy spinning in circles—not so good for wannabe astronauts. Maybe the sight of blood made you queasy or the family dog howled whenever you sang in the shower. Maybe the teacher had to assign you to a volleyball team in PE because no one picked you to join.

It didn't matter that you could solve complicated algebra problems in your head, craft a paper mache replica of Michelangelo's *David*, or explain Walt Whitman to your friends. What good was any of that, when you weren't good enough to do what you really *wanted* to do?

Now that you're an adult, you know everyone has strengths and weaknesses. You don't believe, anymore, that you could be the best at whatever you want to do. Instead, you're probably doing what you do best, and you're really good at it. You're not so concerned about the things other people do better than you, because you know that's how we work together. Maybe you even play on a recreational volleyball team now—and you're the team's high scorer.

What's Good Enough?

From the outside, addictive habits look like behaviors a person should be able to control. You probably feel this way about them yourself, at times. You got yourself into this situation because of choices you made; you should be able to get out. Even now that you know better, the idea of it still plagues you. You want, with all your heart, to be good enough to rise above your old habit and simply make it go away. (Chapter 7 talks about willpower.)

Your supporters—friends and family—are cheering you on. They applaud every forward step you take. As great as this feels, sometimes you wonder whether you should or could be doing even more. You know, in your heart of hearts, that you're already giving it all you can. But still, you worry. What *is* good enough?

Like much that has to do with the process of changing behavior, good enough is a dynamic concept. American cognitive psychologist and computer science researcher Herbert Simon (1916–2001) received the 1978 Alfred Nobel Memorial Prize in Economic Sciences for developing a problem-solving model based on the *principle of good enough* (*POGE*). POGE has become a standard in computer application and systems development. Now you know what's up with downloading all those service packs!

In a broader context, the POGE looks for the point beyond which there's a diminishing return on the investment of effort. It's a companion to the *80/20 rule*. To put forth good enough effort is to meet your needs most of the time.

def•i•ni•tion

The **principle of good enough (POGE)** defines a decision-making approach that gets a new computer application into use with minimum frills. POGE assumes work to modify, expand, and correct the application will continue after it's in use and that the application will continue to evolve. The **80/20 rule** holds that in general, 80 percent of results come from 20 percent of effort. The amount of additional effort necessary to achieve 100 percent of results is generally so excessive that it's not worthwhile. The 80/20 rule is also called the Pareto principle, after the Italian economist Vilfredo Pareto (1848–1925) who first made the observation that 80 percent of income in Italy went to 20 percent of the population.

Being good enough is not something that comes easily for many of us. We learned, way back in kindergarten, to strive to be the best at everything we try. This isn't a bad lesson, but it can set us up to feel as though we've failed if we're not *the* best.

What It Means to Give Your Best

What does your best look like? We're not talking *the* best, but *your* best. It's hard for us, sometimes, to know. Or more accurately, it's hard for us to explain what it looks like when we're giving our best because it comes from within us.

In competitive sports, athletes compete against each other and often the clock for places. Those who are *the* best take the top positions. Their efforts and achievements may make them regional, state, national, or even world champions in their events.

Who doesn't love being in one of those spots! But even more important to athletes at all levels is the achievement of personal best (PB): the highest achieving result an individual has obtained to date in his event, no matter the level of competition or the results of other competitors.

A PB might be a fastest time, a longest distance, a highest climb, an achievement of skill—whatever goal someone has been striving toward that he achieves. Sometimes the result means a win, but often wins are not PBs for the athletes that achieve them. A PB is a moving target. Each time he marks a PB, he creates a goal for the next time.

When it comes to your journey of change, your PBs might be goals of "withouts" that you achieve related to your old habit: a day away from the game consol, three days without a cigarette, a week without a drink, a month away from the poker table. As you get further along your path of change, you'll find that your PBs shift to incorporate goals related to your new lifestyle: a week of walking 45 minutes every day, a month of riding your bicycle to work, three months of volunteering at the food bank on Wednesdays. Eventually, nearly all your personal bests will be goals within your new lifestyle.

The Specter of Failure

The premise that we can succeed through our efforts has a flipside: we can fail through our lack of effort. When things don't go as we want them to, we tend to view the situation as failure. But is it, really? Everyone loves the idea of success. It sounds so positive! But when you don't succeed, does that mean you've failed? No one likes the idea of failure; it sounds so negative.

The problem with the success/failure *dichotomy* when it comes to making changes is that it doesn't much allow for the context of progress. Everything is black or white; there's no gray area. In real life, this is seldom the case. When you take a step along your path of change and take it with conscious choice and full awareness, you're making progress. It doesn't matter how big the step, or even if the step goes sideways rather than straight ahead. And every now and again you're going to take a step back; that's just how it is.

def•i•ni•tion

A **dichotomy** is when two things are mutually exclusive; they exist in an either/or context.

Do you fail because you step off track? No! Your sidesteps—and even backsteps—are messages of learning for you. Think of these as prolapses: falls forward, not backward. Consider what happened. What were the cues that triggered the irresistible craving?

How did you feel right before? Right after? What skills can help you miss the misstep next time? Take the time and effort to analyze the experience, and you're sure to come up with fresh insights into your emotions and thoughts as they relate to your habits. How can this possibly be failure?

Aren't We There Yet?

Twenty-one, thirty, ninety, three-sixty-five. What is this, an auction? Everyone, it seems, has a different idea about how long it takes to end an old habit or start a new habit. It would be great to put a timeframe around change, like the growth charts pediatricians use to monitor childhood development. Then we'd have some sense for where we are in the scheme of things. We'd know how far we've come and how far we've yet to go. But there is no clear calendar of progress when it comes to unlearning one set of behaviors and learning another. It takes as long as it takes.

Your circumstances are unique to you, no matter how much alike someone else's they may seem to be. Even if you stand beside someone who's just like you, for as shared as your experiences feel, they're very different. Sure, you might have the same cues and cravings. But how you respond comes from within you. You might get it right away, that you can't drive past the golden arches on your way home from work every evening because the temptation to pull into the drive-thru is too great. So you drive a route that takes you 5 miles out of your way to miss it. The other person might give up driving to work altogether and instead ride the bus.

Overcoming Your Insecurities

One reason those old habits are so tough to shake is that they make us feel good, not only in general but also about ourselves. We all have insecurities—worries that we're not good enough, fears that we can't live up to the expectations other people have about us or that we have about ourselves.

What expectations are you battling? They might be positive or negative. When you pull them out into the light of day for closer examination, you may be surprised to discover they're not what you thought. You may be struggling to meet expectations from childhood, which, of course, is now

Be Mindful

Visualization can be a useful tool for evaluating expectations. Can you see yourself fulfilling the expectation? How does it look different from your life right now? What do you see yourself doing that would let this vision become reality?

long gone. Your significant other may have certain expectations of you. Your boss has a different set. How are you to meet them all and still be you?

Take a few minutes to think about the expectations that you hold yourself to right now. Make a list of them. Beside the expectation, write down where you think you got the expectation. Finally, write what it would take for you to meet the expectation. We'll give you space for five; use a separate piece of paper if you have more.

Expectation	Source	What It Would Take to Meet
_____	_____	_____
_____	_____	_____
_____	_____	_____
_____	_____	_____
_____	_____	_____

Now take a closer look at your list. Which of these expectations could make a meaningful difference in your life *today?* Why? Put a star beside them. How many have no meaning for your life as you want to live it? Draw a line through them; they're now history. For the expectations with stars beside them, what keeps you from doing what it would take to meet them? Most likely, you need only to get out of your own way. Expectations, too, are moving targets. As you fulfill one expectation, replace it with another.

The Eye of the Storm

Stress is a key consequence of worries about whether you're living up to expectations and doing all you can to reshape your life. Sometimes it's good to take a "stillness" break or a breathing break and remove yourself from the chaos that surrounds you. Let things swirl while you rest safely in the center of the whirlwind. Calm yourself before you venture back into all the activity.

Thrill Me!

As human beings, we love excitement. What emotional and psychological factors drive our desire to seek thrills, even when the result is potentially harmful or even fatal? Some scientists believe thrill-seeking behaviors like bungee-jumping and free-fall amusement park rides are more hormonal than emotional, the modern-day outlets for our primal "fight or flight" response. Other researchers believe we just learn to crave the adrenaline rush that intense fear generates.

Talk About It

Maybe you'd like to take an adventure vacation to feed your need for excitement. The fastest growing segment of the travel industry right now is among companies and locations that offer exotic expeditions. From heli-skiing mountain peaks to scuba diving tropical coral reefs, we're finding new ways to get our thrills.

Some addictive habits are outright thrill-seeking, like gambling. Casinos make the most of this with controlled lighting (you never know whether it's night or day), flashing lights, strobe lights, ringing bells, and other gimmicks designed to keep the excitement level at fever pitch. Even electronic slot machines make the kinds of noises we associate with them, despite there being no need for them to make any noise at all. The thrill of other addictive habits may lie in doing something illegal, like using illicit drugs or shoplifting.

Take It to the Limit

Addictive behavior experts know the craving for excitement underlies many addictive habits. There is even a line of thinking that advocates the habit itself is less the addictive factor than is the desire for excitement. Research using magnetic resonance imaging (MRI) scanning shows the same areas of the brain become intensely active when thinking about risky behaviors like bungee jumping or when thinking about a cigarette (people who smoke) or drugs (substance abuse).

We've seen a surge in popularity of thrill-seeking adventure events and vacations over the past decade or so. It's as though we've tired of ordinary intensity and have to bump it up a few notches. Once it was challenge enough to run a full marathon. Now extreme marathons keep competitors on the course for 24 hours or longer.

Maybe you'd like to take an adventure expedition to feed cheetahs in Namibia or cruise to Antarctica. Maybe you'd like to ride a mountain stage of the Tour de France, drive an Indy race car, or join a cattle drive on horseback in Argentina. All are possible.

Are such activities safer outlets for drives within us that would otherwise seek addictive habits? Or is it simply that our world community is smaller and travel is easier and more affordable? Probably a bit of both.

> **Steer Clear**
>
> Many adventure vacations are arranged and conducted by businesses that special-ize in such recreation. Because the activities are inherently risky, it's important to thoroughly check the company's qualifications, staff training and expertise, and insurance coverage before signing on the dotted line.

Channel Your Need for Thrills

In the 2006 movie *A Good Year* (featuring Russell Crowe, Albert Finney, and Marion Cotillard), main character Maximillian, as a child, tells his Uncle Henry, "I want to be a professional poker player when I'm older, or a comedian." Max instead grows up to become an aggressive investment banker who takes very little in his life seriously. His "take no prisoners" tactics combined with his unshakeable belief that he's right nearly costs Max his high-powered job.

Many occupations build on the love of excitement. Firefighters, police officers, and soldiers can find themselves putting their lives on the line at any moment. Pilots talk about the rush they feel every time they pull back on the throttle and feel that 30-ton jet strain against gravity to rise into flight. Even insurance underwriters must be drawn to the thrill of the gamble—what is risk assessment if not pure speculation?

These occupations are necessary and respected in our society. But not everyone can do them; it does take someone who has the love of excitement. Similarly, not everyone who engages in potentially addictive behaviors develops an addictive habit. Statistics vary widely on the correlation between occupation and addictive habit, so we don't yet have a very clear picture of this relationship.

One Addictive Habit for Another?

Some experts question whether indulging our love for excitement, through recreation or occupation, is itself an addictive habit. If we're chasing intense adventures because we're after the thrill, are we simply swapping one addictive habit for another to feed the PIG?

We probably won't know the entire answer to such a question until we learn more about brain function and the roles of the stress hormones in addictive behaviors. A bigger question might be to examine the need we seem to feel to engage in activi-ties that put us in harm's way or at risk for danger. Is it, as some scientists believe, a means for dealing with an alarm system we've inherited from our primitive ancestors?

Talk About It _____

Money was never a big motivation for me, except as a way to keep score. The real excitement is playing the game.

—Donald Trump, American entrepreneur

The Least You Need to Know

♦ "Good enough" is not a compromise but rather an opportunity for you to evolve as your changes progress.

♦ When you're always looking for your personal best, you're doing the best you can.

♦ A surprising number of the expectations that shape your sense of how well you're doing are no longer valid for the new lifestyle you're creating.

♦ High-risk adventures and occupations may stimulate the same parts of the brain as do addictive habits.

Chapter 11

Why Try Again?

In This Chapter

- ◆ You've come a long way!
- ◆ Be kind to yourself
- ◆ Relapse risks
- ◆ Things to remember when you're blue

In professional baseball, there's not a player on the field who *ever* wishes he were somewhere else than right there on that field. It's a dream come true, to step onto the field and look up into the stands where thousands of fans watch and cheer. For all those kids who turn out for Little League, only a talented and fortunate few make it to the big leagues. Just taking the field is a tremendous accomplishment.

Each player steps up to the plate and gives the pitch his best swing. He pushes aside all worries and anxieties to focus on only one thing: the ball coming at him. In his mind's eye, all he sees is bat and ball connecting. Sometimes it happens; sometimes it doesn't. When it doesn't, his turn's over. Three strikes, he's out.

But he's not done! He's only out for this inning. It's someone else's turn to step up to bat. It's temporary. His turn is over until he comes up in the rotation again. He gave it his best shot, and he'll give it his best shot on his next at-bat. It's the nature of the game.

Life, of course, is more complex than a baseball game. But the basic concept holds true. You always keep your eye on the ball. Sometimes you swing and you hit, sometimes you swing and you miss. It's a great feeling to hit, but it's okay to miss. What matters is that you step up to the plate and take the swing.

What Was I Thinking?!

Do you feel, sometimes, that you'd be just as well off had you simply stayed with your old habit, for better or for worse, instead of taking on the challenge of changing? Most of us wonder this at some point in the change process.

We get bogged down in the everyday-ness of maintaining our efforts. We maybe even start to feel depressed that so much of our energy goes to always being on the alert for choices and decisions that get away from us before we know it. Those old habits are always there in the shadows, ready to step out whenever the slightest opportunity presents itself. It seems that if we never make the effort to change, at least there's nothing lost. Well, there's nothing gained, either!

The Learning Curve

Remember when you first started a new job? You had a certain level of experience and ability, enough to land you the position. But you by no means knew then what you know now. It seemed like 10 minutes couldn't go by without your asking someone how to do something. During your first few weeks on the job, you probably asked yourself every day, "What have I gotten myself into?"

> ### Talk About It
>
> When you make a mistake, don't look back at it long. Take the reason of the thing into your mind and then look forward. The past cannot be changed. The future is yet in your power.
>
> —Hugh Lawson White, American politician

But then you began to learn your way around. You made contacts in different departments and made connections with people whose jobs dovetailed with yours in some way. You learned new skills and different ways to do things. You became adept at identifying problems and finding solutions. Now coworkers come to you with questions and for advice.

Did you make mistakes along the way? Sure you did. You're human! Did those mistakes keep you from sticking with the job? Nope. Mistakes are part of the learning curve, and everyone expects them to happen. Of course it's better when someone else makes the mistakes and you can learn from them, but it seems the way of life that you've got to make your fair share of mistakes all on your own. Did you feel like quitting? Probably so, at times. But you stayed. You stuck it out. And now you're very good at what you do.

Your process of change unfolds in the same way. You can no more close your eyes, turn around three times, and instantly be someone different in your habits than you can be the go-to expert on your first day in a new job. You'll make mistakes, which often take the form of lapses, along the way. But you'll get better, and your mistakes will be fewer. And sometimes your mistakes will take the form of prolapses—falls forward that move you closer to your goals for change, because you gain understanding and experience in managing challenges.

You've Got the Skill Set

In mountain biking, when a person can handle trail obstacles with some degree of competence, he's got the skill set. He's not the best, but he's not the worst—and most important, he's not a risk to himself or other cyclists. It's very likely he'll always ride somewhere in the center of this continuum between best and worst—even as his abilities improve.

On your path of change, you now have the skill set. You're in stage 5 of the Stages of Change: maintenance. You still encounter unexpected twists, turns, and bumps in the trail, even though you now know the trail pretty well. But you can recognize the early warning signs that you're at risk for slipping and take action to regain your traction before you slide out of control. And just like the skills one uses riding a bike, on the job, or with any other activity that's part of daily life, the more you use your skills, the better with them you become. You learn to keep your balance.

One Step Forward ...

When Wayne's weight hit 350 pounds and he couldn't walk up the stairs to his bedroom without stopping halfway to catch his breath, he knew he wanted to make changes in his life. He was only 32 years old, yet he moved like he was decades older. Wayne turned to the Employee Assistance Program at his job, which helped him locate a fitness expert and a dietitian. They helped him develop a plan of exercise and healthy eating that would bring his weight down and improve his overall health.

Wayne stuck to his plan for two years and lost 150 pounds. He looked and felt great. His girlfriend also lost weight once she began to join his workouts, and he made many new friends of the people he met through the activities that became part of his everyday life. He shopped for fresh fruits and vegetables at the market on his way home from work every evening and fixed his own healthy meals so he had leftovers to take for lunch the next day.

He parked at a commuter lot 3 miles from his work and walked the rest of the way every day, no matter the weather. He played basketball Tuesdays and Thursdays after work and swam laps on Mondays and Wednesdays at lunch. He filled his weekends with activity—outdoors whenever possible and at the pool, bowling center, and gym when the weather was uninviting.

Then stress started to pile up. Wayne's company was sold to a competitor, and the new ownership consolidated operations. Half of Wayne's department was laid off and the other half was transferred to a location 20 miles out of town. Wayne's girlfriend got a new job in a city 200 miles away, and they could see each other only every other weekend.

Wayne switched his lunchtime routine to workouts in the onsite gym and bumped them to every day. He had to drive to the site and park in the employee lot, but going for a space in the far corner gave him about two blocks' worth of walking to and from the building. The toughest accommodation was shopping for meals; his favorite market was now a destination rather than a stop on the way home. Wayne's eating habits became the first casualty of the changes in his lifestyle.

With fewer people to handle the workload, lunch shrank to 20 minutes, and Wayne started to eat at his desk so he could continue working on the computer. More people were laid off, and Wayne began coming in early and leaving late to get everything done. Within six months he'd gained 30 pounds. Despondent, he broke off his relationship with his girlfriend. Why would she want to be with someone like him? He should've just stayed the way he was, he thought. Then there wouldn't have been anyone to let down, no downslide for other people to watch.

Steer Clear

Stress is the most predictable reason we slide back into old habits. When pressure piles up on us, we lose the ability to think clearly and rationally. We default to whatever's easiest because we feel we just don't have the time to do anything else. Though for most of us stress comes from all directions in our lives, the factor that carries the highest for old habit relapse is difficulty in our relationships with other people. Arguments and fights with spouses, partners, kids, coworkers, and bosses are big red flags.

... One Step Back

Wayne wallowed in his funk for a few more months, putting on another 30 pounds. He had to dig to the back of his closet to find clothes that fit, clothes he hadn't worn for nearly two years. But he felt oddly uncomfortable; his old ways didn't suit him anymore.

Wayne was surprised to discover he really didn't like the old version of himself. He didn't even know who that person was, staring back at him from the mirror in the morning when he shaved. What surprised Wayne the most, though, was the support his friends, coworkers, and family continued to give him. For as down as Wayne was on himself, no one else wanted to see his tremendous gains slip away. And, he realized, neither did he.

That Wasn't So Bad

The first step back was a lot easier than he expected. All he had to do was take it. He wasn't where he'd been, but he wasn't starting over, either. He simply picked up where he was and started working his way to where he wanted to be. The anxiety anticipation creates—worries about how others will react and even about how we ourselves will feel—is nearly always far more intense than taking that first step.

That Pesky Abstinence-Violation Effect

Sometimes the slide back to an old habit happens so fast we don't recognize what's going on until we've got both feet firmly planted in old behaviors. Then we get depressed, frustrated, and angry. We figure, what the hey, might as well stay. At least it's familiar, and it's what everyone expected anyway, right?

Wrong! But it's what we tell ourselves, and it's a leading factor of relapse. Alan was among the first addiction researchers to recognize and document this pattern as the abstinence-violation effect (AVE), which we first talked about in Chapter 2. The AVE is a sense of failure about a back-stepping behavior that is way out of proportion to what we've actually done. It encompasses feelings of guilt and self-blame.

Some people, like Wayne, step on and off the path for quite a while before the reality of what they've done sinks in. For other people, the step off is more like a leap. Maybe you indulge your craving for a cigarette, a drink, a chocolate chip cookie. Maybe you sit on the sofa channel-surfing instead of going to the gym for your six o'clock aerobics class. Maybe you stop at the mall on the way home from work and buy that set of Callaway Big Berthas, even though you don't really need a third set of golf clubs.

Steer Clear

Are you feeling a little down, a bit blue? Then it's not a good time to head out to the mall! A recent study confirms that sad shoppers are likely to spend up to four times more than shoppers who are emotionally neutral. Miserable shoppers also tend to be unaware of how they're feeling as well as of how much they're spending.

You've taken a single detour back to your old habit. It's only one misstep, but guilt and shame overwhelm you. You don't know what came over you. You feel you've let everyone down, including yourself. You might as well jump; it's faster than falling.

And it sure enough is. Before you know it, you're right back in the hug of that old habit, which is happier than a bear in salmon season to have you back. Of course, it's a hug that's already smothering you. But you haven't noticed that yet; you're too busy trying to juggle your feelings of guilt and your sense of relief.

Hold everything! You don't have to travel this AVE. Once you recognize the warning signs, you can choose a different route. A lapse is, well, only a lapse.

The Relapse Set-Up

Through his years of researching addictive behaviors and working with people to change theirs, Alan came to recognize that when certain circumstances converged, the risk for lapse—a single return to the old habit—was particularly high. He also came to recognize that when we know what these circumstances look like in our lives, we can act to redirect our responses and prevent, or at least contain, the lapse.

These circumstances fall into two general camps, and between them account for more than 80 percent of relapse experiences. *Intrapersonal risks* exist within us. These are our anxieties, fears, worries, and desires. Negative emotional states are the main intrapersonal triggers. These feelings and emotions surface when we're bored, angry, tired, scared, depressed, frustrated, or otherwise unhappy. We want to make these feelings go away. Other intrapersonal triggers are testing willpower, exposure to environmental cues, and negative physical states.

The old habit is all too willing—eager, even—to step up and do this for us. But it's a game of smoke and mirrors. Eventually, as we know all too well deep in the core of our being, the old habit is even more of a problem. Rather than relieving our stress, it compounds it. And on top of everything else, we feel bad that we slipped to another "last one."

Interpersonal risks exist in our interactions with other people. Though we may feel anxious, angry, frustrated, or otherwise unhappy, these emotions arise from encounters, often arguments and disagreements with other people. Our spouse or partner, boss, coworkers, kids, siblings, neighbors, and even the anonymous guy in the blue car who cut us off on the freeway can all be sources of conflict in our daily life.

def•i•ni•tion

> **Intrapersonal risks** are emotions and feelings that arise from within us. They are risks for lapse and relapse because they tempt us to return to our old habit to make ourselves feel better. **Interpersonal risks** are emotions and feelings that arise from our relationships with other people, particularly conflicts.

Who needs it? Certainly not you! Who cares? Certainly not anyone else! You could disappear into orbit around the moon, and no one would even notice, so why not go back to the old habit? At least it doesn't argue with you. But, of course, it's your old habit that doesn't care about you. And that alone is reason enough to think twice about going back to it.

Because these two factors—intrapersonal risks and interpersonal risks—are so complex, we discuss them here, in this chapter, in an overview way and also give them their own chapters later in the book. Chapter 16 explores inner struggles, and Chapter 17 examines the influences and challenges of relationships with others.

Dealing with Your Feelings

Often, feelings of sadness, uneasiness, and loneliness are vague and unattached to specific events. This makes it more challenging to find ways to turn your mood around. When you find yourself in a funk, focus on what you're feeling. Let your mood, however dark, simply exist without judgment or feeling that you have to change it.

You might be the kind of person who does this best through writing, like in a diary or journal. Or maybe you think better when you're engaged in a physical activity, like running or swimming. Maybe yoga or meditation helps you sort through your

Steer Clear

Intense feelings of sadness that continue for longer than two weeks and cause you to lose interest in activities you used to enjoy, change your sleep patterns, or cause you to eat significantly more or less than usual may be indications of depression. Depression can be a serious condition that requires treatment from a doctor or other health-care provider.

thoughts and emotions so you can recognize, accept, and let go. Remember, you're not trying to change anything yet; that comes later and will likely require much less effort than you anticipate.

There are two points to this process. One is to clarify how you truly feel. Sometimes you might believe you're feeling sad, when really you're angry or frustrated to be in this situation (whatever the situation is). Or you might think you're angry, but really you're hurt. The other point of this process is to reveal what specific circumstances, usually people or events, trigger these feelings so you can develop methods that let you respond differently.

Dealing With Pressure from Others

Everything we know about fitting in or feeling left out, we learned in kindergarten or maybe even earlier, in daycare. We've gotten more sophisticated in our practices, to be sure, but those core lessons carry throughout life. From our first exposures to group situations, we learn to care what others think about us and to behave in ways that let us feel included rather than left out. These lessons carry through our entire lives and can be especially compelling in patterns of behavior.

Even when we want to feel different, we strive to be the same. Look around any high school or college campus to see just how hard we work at this! No matter how old we are or what we do in life, we still like to be included. As human beings, we are social creatures. We respond to social pressures.

Countering the Pushy Approach

"Aw, c'mon! Just come sit with us. You don't have to do anything else, just hang out and have fun!" You know this type—loud, insistent, persistent. This is the guy or gal who throws an arm around you and leads you to the slaughter, laughing all the way. Once, you went willingly. But now you make other choices.

This makes other people uncomfortable. *They* feel left out. (Imagine that! Didn't think of it that way, did you?) They want to draw you into the fold—especially back into the fold, if that's the way it used to be. When you're in there with them, they don't have to think about whether they should be making other choices. And when the pushy one is someone important, like the boss or your partner, the stakes skyrocket.

It's a challenge to deal with pushy people no matter who they are. Here are some approaches that might work for you, singly or in combination, depending on the situation:

◆ Be direct and say no, with no explanation, no waffling, no feigning of polite consideration. Just "no." Sometimes confronting someone head-on is what he or she least expects and lets loose of the effort to corral you right away.

◆ Become a broken record. No matter what the other person says, continue to say, "No, thanks." If the person persists, add an explanation: "I'm following a very structured diet for health reasons and I eat only the foods I prepare."

◆ Be honest and say that you don't do whatever it is anymore. If you choose this approach, decide before you use it whether you want to provide further explanation.

◆ Take aside the pushiest person and explain why you're not interested in joining the group. Sometimes taking a person into your confidence provides a connection between the two of you that gives the other person a sense of compassion or at least a begrudging agreement to leave you alone.

> **Talk About It**
>
> People often say that motivation doesn't last. Well, neither does bathing—that's why we recommend it daily.
>
> —Zig Ziglar, American author and motivational speaker

◆ Make up an excuse that is so wildly far-fetched no one can respond. "I have to take my cat for obedience classes." Then walk away. People will either laugh or stare at you, but they're not likely to keep pushing.

◆ Excuse yourself to go to the restroom or run an errand and leave. This is the option of last resort in most situations, and it may catch up with you the following day.

Choose the methods that are most natural for you. Politeness and humor are always great complements for any method you choose.

Sidestepping into Temptation

When Peg came around one morning selling raffle tickets to raise money for the food bank, Steve didn't give a second thought to buying 10. The money was going to a worthy cause, and he could end up with a free lunch, a week's paid parking in the underground garage, or even a weekend getaway. Not a bad investment no matter how you slice it.

When Peg came around a few months later with the office football pool, Steve didn't think twice about putting $10 in the pot and picking his numbers. Ten bucks for the chance to win $200 was not a bad bet. And really, it wasn't a bet at all. What's $10— a couple lattes? Half the money from the pool went to buy coffee and supplies for the break room, anyway.

When Peg stopped by Steve's desk to say a group from the office was planning to spend the coming long weekend in Las Vegas and asked him if he wanted to join them, Steve looked at her in amazement. "Peg, you know I don't gamble anymore!" he said.

The challenge with many of the habits we want to change is that they live in the realm of normal, everyday life. The lines are not always clear when we step across them.

Fighting the Blues

First, we want to emphasize that it's fine and normal (and some would say, even necessary) to feel blue every now and again. We all do. But when our mood causes us to feel so unhappy that our thoughts wander to old habits, it's time to step in and realign our emotional responses.

Maybe your old habit helped you block these kinds of emotions. Habits involving drinking and other drugs block your feelings directly, like anesthesia. Other habits hinder emotions indirectly, providing a group of people for you to hang with and activities to keep you busy. Smoking (smoke breaks), playing the slots, and shopping marathons are high on the list of such habits.

It's natural, too, for you to miss the sense of connection your old habit might've provided—even when other things in your life now give you the same satisfaction. It's like the longing you might feel at the start of summer for when that was the beginning of three months of no school. But this is only your brain on nostalgia. Remember how eager you became, toward the end of summer vacation, for school to start again?

Be Mindful _____

Is it hard for you to go home after work, because you used to go elsewhere when your old habit was in charge? Find positive outlets for this restlessness. Go to the gym; stop at the library to read magazines that relate to your job or your interests; volunteer to serve dinner at a homeless shelter or to be a Big Brother/Big Sister. There are many positive ways to use your energy!

Your real life is in the here and now. Once you figure out what kinds of experiences cause you to feel certain ways, you can change either the experiences, or when that's not possible, change your responses to them.

The only rule is, do something that gives you a sense of satisfaction. If you engage in activities that don't really mean much to you, you'll soon come to resent them, and they'll become what they are: meaningless substitutes. Be willing to try different things. For most people, activities that involve being with others are the most satisfying.

Fork in the Road

One allure of the forbidden indulgence is that it's forbidden. You can't have it, so you want it. But in reality, you're the one who's decided you can't have it. You're the one who put your old habit on the list of things you can't have or do. And you're the one who has the power, every time this old habit calls to you, to decide how to answer.

Each time you come to a fork in the road—a decision point—you make choices about which direction to take. The more aware you are of your range of decisions and their consequences, the more effectively you can choose those that keep you on your path. Alan encourages clients to use a *decision matrix* to identify and evaluate choices.

Though this sounds sort of complex, it's really a simple approach you may already use without knowing that's what you're doing. Here's how it works: at the top of a piece of paper, write the decision you're facing and the possible choices you could make. Next list the specific short-term consequences and long-term consequences, positive and negative, for each choice.

def•i•ni•tion _____

A **decision matrix** is a model for evaluating the consequences, positive and negative, of a choice.

When you're finished, consider each option and its consequences. Which options appeal most to you? Which consequences are most acceptable? You may decide certain risks are worth the potential benefits. When this is the case, you can minimize the risks by creating a plan, or even a script, for behaviors you can choose that will still keep you on your path.

For example, you've worked hard to lose weight through lifestyle changes and you know overeating is your greatest risk, but a client wants to meet in a restaurant, so suggest one that you know offers healthy menu choices. Or if the client chooses the restaurant, call ahead or look up the restaurant's menu online to identify items that will keep you on your path of healthy eating.

Keep Looking Ahead

Relapse thrives on looking back. Sometimes when we look back on the old habit, it doesn't look so bad—especially when we're under a lot of stress or feeling down. Sometimes that old habit looks pretty good, but this is our brain's selective memory at work, trying to seduce us.

But there's never a need to rush into a decision. You always have enough time to make the right choices; it takes no longer than making the wrong ones. When your focus is on the path in front of you, the path behind has a lot less influence.

The Least You Need to Know

- The more you practice your new skills and habits, the better at them you become.

- It's easier than you think to get back on your path.

- Risk for relapse comes from within (intrapersonal risk) and from outside influences (interpersonal risk).

- Being prepared for high-risk situations helps avert relapse.

Part 4

You Can't Do It Alone

It takes a community to change a habit—a community of supportive and encouraging family, friends, coworkers, and other people who are making similar changes. We need others to watch out for us, to help us back to our feet when we stumble, and to recognize our progress.

The chapters in Part 4 look at what it takes to build such a community and how to separate who's helping from who's hindering. Chapter 12 discusses how we can nurture our relationships with those who truly support our changes so we can distance ourselves from those who don't. Chapter 13 explores how those closest to us—our loved ones—help and hinder our efforts. Chapter 14 looks at the special risks for relapse that kids face. And Chapter 15 goes beyond our inner circle to identify support within the larger community.

MY COMPULSIVE SHOPPING HAS GOTTEN SO OUT OF CONTROL, I'VE DECIDED TO JOIN A SUPPORT GROUP TO HELP ME QUIT.

LET'S GO TO THE MALL SO I CAN BUY A NEW OUTFIT FOR MY FIRST MEETING!

Chapter 12

Together We Rise

In This Chapter

- ◆ Asking for help is not always an easy thing to do
- ◆ Everybody has a word (or two) of advice
- ◆ Your personal helpline
- ◆ Helping yourself

It's hard, sometimes, to know when we need help. And it's even harder for many of us to ask for help. Somehow we've gotten the idea that asking for help is a sign of weakness, proof we really can't make these changes on our own. Well, guess what? We can't! Not because we're weak—but *because we're human.*

We all need support and encouragement from others. Some comes from the people in our lives who are important to us—friends and family who want to see us do well because they love us. Some comes from people who maybe aren't part of our inner circles, but because of shared experiences, they *get* us.

Success in making life changes depends, of course, on what we do for ourselves. But just as much, it relies on the support systems we build that help us change.

I Need Somebody to Help Me!

We need people who can effectively support our efforts to change. Some people, especially in our personal lives, may not do well in this role. (We talk specifically about personal relationships in Chapter 13.) We need people who'll tell us when they see us making decisions that put us at risk. We need people who'll hug us when we're down, cheer us on when the going gets tough; celebrate our successes; give us a hand when we slip; and tell us, straight up and without judgment, what's what.

Your support team is the collective of people that keeps your best interests front and center, even when you don't (or don't want to). Like any other team, you want to pick those who are best for the game. It's more fun when these team members are your friends, but sometimes your friends aren't quite the best at helping you face difficult choices, especially when they're part of the behaviors you're trying to leave behind (more on this in Chapter 13). And friends often lack the knowledge and skills to give you the support you need. They love you and will take your calls in the middle of the night, but they're not addictive behavior specialists.

Dear Abby ... I'm Not Good at Asking for Help

It's one thing to drive a hundred miles out of your way because you're too stubborn to stop and ask directions or to turn on the GPS in your rental car. You might even turn the experience into an adventure, seeing places you otherwise wouldn't—make lemonade out of lemons and all that.

But when it comes to your life, do you really want to wander around? So many people, so many resources, are just waiting to help! All you have to do is ask. But many people struggle with this. We like to feel independent and strong, and having to ask for help sometimes makes us feel insecure and weak.

We talked in earlier chapters about the intertwining of undesirable habits and secrets. When a big part of our old habit was keeping it hidden from others, we also developed the habit of keeping things to ourselves. We didn't want others to notice our habit, so it wasn't a topic of conversation. Asking now for help along our path of change makes it so.

In a certain sense, to ask for help is to open the book on any lingering secrets. Most of us don't want our lives to be completely exposed to others and rightfully so. Privacy protects our vulnerabilities and gives us opportunity to explore deep feelings without fear.

Psychologists, doctors, therapists, and other health-care providers are ethically, and in most circumstances legally, bound to maintain confidentiality. And they know a bigger picture than the one we see from our perspective. They are great resources to turn to for help.

Be Mindful _____

Asking for help is not the same as looking for someone to tell you what to do. The most effective help does the opposite; it presents you with perspectives and options for you to consider. You make the decisions, not someone else. Advice is just that—advice. You've got to determine what will work for you.

Filtering Advice

One thing about advice is that everyone has some to share. Whether the advice others give to us is really helpful … well, that can be another matter. We have to balance what we know about ourselves and our circumstances with what others observe about us that maybe we can't see.

Other people tend to offer suggestions and advice based on their own experiences. It's good to listen to what they have to say, because it might be information you otherwise wouldn't stumble into. In such situations, think about why the particular solution or strategy worked for the person telling you about it and how your situation is both similar and different.

You don't have to take all of what someone else suggests. You might take the parts and pieces that fit you and your circumstances. Through this process of filtering and adaptation, you build your own structure of insights and skills.

I've (Still) Gotta Be Me!

Christopher Moltisanti, the fictional mobster on HBO's critically acclaimed drama *The Sopranos*, had a lot going for him. He was charming, attractive, rich, and loyal. He was his boss's confidante.

But Christopher also had a problem habit—well, several problem habits. After a season-long downward spiral, he finally made it to stage four of the Stages of Change: action. He got himself into AA and NA, cleaned up his life, got married, bought a house in the 'burbs—the whole nine yards.

Then he slammed into the wall of his biggest problem: his, um, career. To be a good gangster, he had to play by gangster rules, and those rules included the habits he was trying to shake. It's tough to break from the bottle when your business meetings take place at the Bada Bing Club.

Your circumstances aren't so extreme (we hope!), but the point remains the same: you've got to figure out how to be who you are and still be who you want to be.

Cleaning House

No one wants, or expects, you to give up the essential you. But your old habit might've taken you so far from who that is that you don't quite know, right now, who you really are. It's not so much that you *have* to make a clean break and fresh start but that now you've got the opportunity to do so. This is an ideal time to take stock of your life; keep what works and toss out what doesn't.

> **Talk About It** _____
>
> Wonder where the time goes? The U.S. Census Bureau reports that the average American spends the equivalent of five months a year engaged in "virtual" activities—watching television, listening to iPods and other personal electronic devices, and surfing the web.

Daily life tends to wind along on its path without a whole lot of conscious thought or direction from us. The alarm goes off; we shower and dress, grab a cup of coffee and something to eat, and off to work we go. Schedules and deadlines dictate the workday, and then it's home for the evening ritual of dinner and family.

To stand back and look at your life as it truly exists is like having a guest over who opens the door on an overstuffed closet. You knew the closet was bad, but you didn't really know how bad. For a moment, everything stays stacked and crammed. As you stare at all that stuff, you can't imagine how it all fits or what keeps it from falling out. And the instant you spot and pull out that T-shirt you've been looking for (like opening the door had been your idea), the closet's contents come crashing down on you.

However crazy things might've gotten to be in your life, this is your chance to restore structure and regain control. Don't just shove things back and slam the door! Take a close look at what's in there—the people and activities that fill up your life. Evaluate what's worth keeping, and let the rest go. Once you clear away the stuff that's accumulated over the years, you can see the you that's under there.

Reclaim Yourself

Are you having trouble seeing beyond the chaos and confusion? Choose a day to follow yourself around, so to speak, to report on your life. Literally. You'll need to plan this because it'll take some extra time.

First, write yourself a note that summarizes who you think you are and how the ways you spend your time support that. Then as you go through your day, take notes. Who places demands on your time and energy, and what are those demands? What do you do to meet them? Who benefits from your meeting those demands? How much do the expectations of others override your own interests and intentions? Does meeting the expectations of others put you at risk for slipping back to old ways?

Be Mindful

Just for one day, unplug yourself. Let e-mail collect at your ISP. Turn off your cell phone. No more texting. Leave your iPod at home. Turn off reality TV—you've got your own real life to live. If you have errands, walk or bike to the store, post office, or library. You can't make such of a break in your life? Then start small. Take 20 minutes every four hours to do something for yourself. Work your way up to a morning or afternoon away from your regular responsibilities and then a full day. Who knows, before long you might actually have weekends off!

At the end of the day, compare notes. How does the reality of your life match up with who you believe yourself to be? It's sometimes startling to recognize how far removed from the real you your life has gotten. Don't let this overwhelm you; you're a good person with a lot going for you, and you're on the right track with the changes you're making in your life.

On a clean sheet of paper, write down three things you can do tomorrow that will move you closer toward being who you want to be. At the end of the day, make yourself a few notes about each. Then write down three things for the following day. You can use the same three things—it's your life! Each day, keep track of what you do compared to what you want to do. When you master one change, drop it from your list and add something new.

Someone to Pull You Back

Melodie was smoke free for six months, the longest she'd been able to sustain a quit. No more wafts of hidden smoke smell filled her apartment. She could walk past the smokers clustered on the sidewalk outside her office building without feeling like she wanted to snatch a cigarette right out of someone's mouth. Though she couldn't yet swim the full length of the pool underwater, she was now swimming for a full hour, three evenings a week. It was so great to take a deep breath!

One night after coming home from a swim, Melodie put her bags on the counter and burst into tears. For no apparent reason, she craved a cigarette like her life depended on it. Waves of panic left her shaking. She started ripping through the drawers in the kitchen, frantic to find a forgotten cigarette somewhere, anywhere. Then she caught her reflection in the window and froze.

"I'm healthy, strong, and vibrant because I do not smoke!" Melodie spoke the words of her distress mantra, a message to herself she crafted when she wrote her change contract (see Chapter 6). Then she picked up the phone and dialed Paul, the first person in her safety line. Paul talked her through the urge until she was calm and centered within herself again.

Instead of ending with a cigarette and a lapse, Melodie's sudden trip to the edge stayed just that. Paul's guided urge surfing (remember this from Chapter 7?) helped Melodie ride out her craving until, like a wave at the beach, the craving peaked and then faded. She let the craving simply run itself out until it disappeared just as mysteriously as it had arrived.

Be Mindful

The U.S. Department of Health and Human Services (DHHS) offers toll free access to instant support for people who've quit smoking but feel the urge to light up again. The hotline 1-800-QUITNOW puts callers in immediate contact with cessation counselors who can provide encouragement and referral to local resources. Many local health departments also have crisis hotlines to talk people through the tough spots of quitting.

Virtual Support

The Internet puts at our fingertips a seemingly endless bank of resources. Just about anything we want to know is somewhere out in cyberspace, and all we have to do is tap into it. If we have a question, there's an answer! Whether it's the correct answer, or the right answer for us, is another matter, but more on that later.

Industry experts tell us that 70 percent of American households have Internet access. We use the Internet to find restaurants and shopping, get directions and maps, communicate for business and personal reasons, play games, acquire music and videos, look up our names to see what's out there about us, and even do our banking. The Internet is part of daily life for most of us, both at home and at work. If we want to know something, we Google it. It's hard to imagine life without the Internet. Like most marvels of technology, however, this is both good and bad.

Digital Dialogue: Where Nobody Knows Your Name

Internet communities thrive. People log on and type in their comments, questions, and concerns. Others respond. It's a great way to hear the experiences and suggestions other people have about issues similar to ours and to share ours with others. Time and distance don't matter; we can chat online at two in the morning with someone who's halfway around the world.

Chat rooms and forums are Internet-based communication structures. A chat room functions in real time, somewhat like a telephone conference call, with participants sending messages back and forth when they're online. A forum is more like a bulletin board or e-mail, where one leaves a message and others respond whenever they read it. Chat rooms and forums may be moderated or not. When there's a moderator, there's more structure to the dialogue. The moderator can remove inappropriate content and otherwise keep user comments in line with the chat room's or forum's intent and topics. Some people like the immediacy of real-time communication typical of chat rooms, which feels more like conversation. Others prefer the e-mail feel of online forums where they can leave a message that others respond to over time.

A popular aspect of online communication is the sense of anonymity it offers. Although most chat rooms and forums require users to register and establish online identities, we don't have to reveal who we are. Others know us by our screen name or our avatar. There's less a sense of judgment attached to what we say, and what others say to us when no one knows our real name.

As with everything on the Internet, caveat emptor (buyer, or in this case, user, beware). We don't really know anything about the people who are giving advice. It's best to think of Internet interactions in the same context as conversations we strike up at social gatherings.

What's true for one person is by no means a universal truth. There's often value in hearing how others handle certain situations, and taking from that what might fit for us. But we have to evaluate what others say within the context of our own life and circumstances and decide what will work for us and what won't.

Electronic Library: Informational Websites

Knowledge is empowering. The more you learn about the new lifestyle you want to live, as well as about the old habit you're leaving behind, the better able you are to make the changes you want to make. The Internet makes it easy to find out just about anything you might want to know.

Many websites present reliable information. Some websites, unfortunately, distort information, present misinformation, and even intentionally provide erroneous information. The website's owner might believe the information is true, but there is little objective substantiation—you're getting opinion passed off as fact. It's up to you to determine.

Steer Clear

If your old habit had to do with the computer or the Internet—from games and gambling to compulsive web-surfing—then using the Internet as a resource is likely not the best choice for you.

When it comes to getting the straight facts, stick to the "big name" websites. These are the sites of professional, educational, government agency, and health organizations. Many of these websites feature peer-reviewed or otherwise authenticated articles. We used to suggest staying with the dot-org websites, but this no longer carries assurances that the site's noncommercial. Appendix B lists some trustworthy websites where you can find reliable, objective information.

As with anything, beware that which sounds too good to be true. It nearly always is—which translates into bad news for you. At best you waste your time; at worst you can find yourself following a yellow brick road to relapse. Miracle cures seldom are, and lavish promises are usually empty.

D.I.Y.

Regardless of other support systems in place for you, in the end you're the one responsible for the changes you're making. So a certain amount of the work you're doing, you must do yourself.

Quite a few methods can help you keep yourself on track. Most are ways to defuse episodes of anxiety or stress so you can regain your bearings. You also can use them as regular practices to keep your stress level manageable and as measures to head off a lapse.

Meditation

Meditation is a practice that aims to connect mind, body, and spirit to produce relaxation and calm. It's not necessarily religious or spiritual, though many people do incorporate meditation with their belief systems. The origins of meditation are thousands of years old. Many of meditation's key practices are common across various forms of meditation.

There are many types of meditation. Some use chanting and mantras—repeated words or phrases that may have universal or personal meaning. *Yoga*, *qi gong*, and *tai chi* are forms of meditation that blend movement with mental focus. Prayer, probably the most common form of meditation, exists in many belief systems as a method of communication with a higher power.

def•i•ni•tion

> **Yoga**, which comes from an ancient Sanskrit word that means to yoke, is a mind-body practice that combines poses (body positions) and meditation. **Qi gong** is a traditional Chinese medicine (TCM) method that combines movement and meditation. **Tai chi** is a martial art that uses slow, graceful movements to focus and integrate the energy of the body and of the mind. You can do all three practices individually, though it's best to learn in classes or from teachers because proper technique is essential.

Because meditation, in its simpler forms, requires only that you be able to go within yourself for 5 or 10 minutes, it's a method you can take anywhere and do any time. You can practice basic meditation techniques at work, in the car, on your lunch break—even in the bathroom if that's the only place you can get a few minutes of solitude!

Affirmations

The great thing about saying encouraging things to yourself is that the more you hear them, the more you believe them. Before you know it, the words come to life— they become *your* life. Affirmations are positive statements you repeat to yourself and can be either general ("I'm a strong, loving person") or specific ("I speak to my boss with confidence and authority").

Write affirmations on note cards or Post-It notes, and put them in places where you'll see them—on the bathroom mirror, the front of the fridge, the dashboard of your car, around your computer monitor, or on your desk or the walls of your workspace.

Appendix C provides a "starter set" of daily affirmations you can use and also space to write your own daily affirmations. Pick up a copy of *The Complete Idiot's Guide to Creative Visualization* (Shari Just, Ph.D., and Carolyn Flynn, Alpha Books, 2005).

Visualization

If you can see it in your mind's eye, it can become your reality. Visualization is popular among athletes (from pros to weekend warriors), performers like musicians and actors, and even politicians. Visualization is kind of like focused daydreaming: you create in your mind a picture of your doing whatever it is that you want to do. The picture, as you continue to focus on it and replay it, then becomes a self-fulfilling prophecy.

When you've struggled a long time with an addictive behavior, many of your self-fulfilling prophecies—the ways you see yourself in your mind's eye—are negative. You see yourself engaging in the old habit, even as your life is moving in a different direction. The pull of what's in your head is powerful, sometimes more powerful than what's really happening in your life. This can increase your risk for relapsing to the old habit. So make a conscious effort to see yourself as the person you want to be, rather than the person you don't want to be.

Take a Breathing Space: SOBER

Often the most effective action you can take is to stop what you're doing. Alan calls this "taking a breathing space" and uses the acronym SOBER to remember the steps of this simple but effective exercise:

S = Stop

O = Observe

B = Breath (focus on)

E = Expand awareness

R = Respond mindfully

Journaling

Writing your thoughts is a great way to sort and filter all of what's running through your mind. Teachers have long known a connection exists between the hand and the brain, which is why they want students to take notes instead of giving handouts. Writing forces your thoughts to line up and come out of your brain in an orderly fashion.

Don't worry about your writing skills! The point is the process of writing more than what you write. Although it's sometimes instructive to go back and read what was on your mind, the main function of writing your thoughts is to get things out so you can examine, and then release, them.

Steer Clear

If you write in a journal or diary, think about where you keep it and who might see it. Putting your thoughts and feelings on paper is great for you but has the potential to create problems if others read what you never intended to share.

Remember our discussion of Freud's psychoanalysis methods in Chapter 9? Freud's premise was that speaking aloud the thoughts that came to you, without attempting to formulate them or make sense of them as you're talking, is a way to get at what lies deep in your unconscious mind. Getting these thoughts out in the open where you can examine them then leads you to insight and understanding.

Stream of consciousness writing transfers this approach to journaling. You write your thoughts as they occur to you, in all their jumbled glory, with no worries about sentence structure, grammar, commas, or periods. No one else will see this writing (unless you choose to share it); no one will judge or grade you.

def•i•ni•tion

Stream of consciousness writing is a method of writing your thoughts as they come to you, without concern for grammar, structure, or punctuation.

At first, this kind of writing may feel awkward. After all, we're trained from about the second grade on to shape what we put on paper so that it follows the rules of writing. But keep in mind that some of the world's greatest writers have used stream of consciousness as an art form in fiction—James Joyce, Marcel Proust, and Gertrude Stein, to name three.

As with free association (the cornerstone of Freud's talk therapy), stream of consciousness writing often reveals concepts and beliefs we hold about ourselves that we've buried pretty deep and otherwise might not express. The words on the page bring such thoughts into our awareness so we can then explore them in a mindful way. Sometimes reading aloud what we've written—speaking our thoughts out loud, essentially—helps us more easily identify worries and concerns.

Reach Out

For the most part, other people are more than willing to help you stay on track and meet the goals of your efforts to change. (In Chapter 13 we talk about the other part—when other people are not so helpful.) Friends and family will sign on to be your helpline when times get tough, giving you someone to call even when it's the middle of the night. Just ask!

Then when you find yourself facing temptation or feel yourself at the edge of lapsing, call or contact one or more of these people. Fifteen minutes on the phone can save you a day, a week, or longer of beating yourself up because an urge got the better of you. And you can enlist your helpline in preventive acts, too. Have someone go with you if you must attend an event that will challenge your resolve. You might even designate one person on your call list to screen activities in advance for you so there'll be no surprises—that's a good thing.

You may never need to call on your helpline. But knowing that other people are there for you, ready to step in when you need them, is sometimes itself safety net enough.

The Least You Need to Know

♦ Not all advice is good advice, no matter how well-intended or sincere.

♦ You're a unique individual; what works for someone else may or may not work for you.

♦ Internet resources can provide useful information as well as connections with people who share your concerns and experiences.

♦ Even if you never use it, having a helpline gives you a sense of confidence and security.

Chapter 13

For the Ones We Love

In This Chapter

- ◆ The danger of mixing old relationships with new habits
- ◆ Is your relationship nurturing or poisoning you?
- ◆ Sometimes you have to let go
- ◆ It's your skin—be happy in it!

It may be hard for you to recognize, consumed as you are with the changes you are making, but these changes are affecting everyone else in your life. Others, too, must change—sometimes only their perceptions of you, but sometimes their entire ways of interacting with you. Such change is not easy and may not come as willingly as you expect.

These others in your life might work with you to keep you on your path. Or they may do their darndest—and not always be aware of it—to entice you to stray. They may tolerate your struggles and slips or issue ultimatums that make your journey more difficult. When the new you returns to the old environment, how much of your life must you redefine? What can you keep, and what must you let go?

New Habits, Old Relationships

What role did your old habit play in your relationships? Was it the hinge pin that held everything together? If so, those relationships may now have little foundation. Shared habits are often what draw us to other people. They give us ways to engage and something to do. If we pull the old habit out of the picture, what's left? Sometimes, not much except an increased potential for relapse.

To what extent do your relationships center on your old habits? This short self-quiz can help you identify the threads that hold you together. Choose the answer that best fits. You can do the quiz for as many of your relationships as you like—romantic, work, friendships, even immediate and extended family.

1. When we're with each other, we talk about …

   a. The weather.

   b. The day's sports scores.

   c. Family and kids.

   d. Not much of anything.

2. We first got together because …

   a. Of our jobs or school.

   b. We live near each other.

   c. Our kids are friends.

   d. To smoke, drink, eat, shop, gamble—any or all.

3. When I think about this person, I feel …

   a. Excited.

   b. Anxious.

   c. Depressed.

   d. Dread.

4. Since I've changed my habits, we …

    a. See each other more often.

    b. See each other less often.

    c. See each other about the same.

    d. Go out of our way to avoid each other.

5. Other people …

    a. Try to keep us apart.

    b. Try to get us together.

    c. Feel welcome to join us.

    d. Talk about us when we're not there.

If you answered "d" to all five statements, then it's time for you to evaluate the connections you have with other people in your life. It might well turn out that the relationship is healthy and positive for both of you. But it could be that sticking with the relationship is risky when it comes to staying on track with your new habits.

Lovers and Others

Your loved ones are often your biggest fans. They cheer you on to make changes in your life. They stand by you. They've been there to catch you when you've stumbled. And now that you're back, they're overjoyed. But your change is their change. As you know better than anyone, change is not easy.

When your old habit ran the show, you were not the one in control. Maybe you thought you were, but you weren't. Mostly, your habit called the shots. Depending on the nature of your habit, your friends and family may've had to step in to rescue you—and often enough that they began to feel like your guardians.

Now that you've banished the old habit, you're eager to step back into your life and retake the wheel. But those who've been taking care of you might find it difficult to become passengers again. They've been on their share of wild rides with you and maybe aren't so confident that this time is any different. They'd rather do the steering, so when you slip off track the pieces don't have much chance to scatter.

It's not exactly a vote of confidence, is it? But it's what their experiences have taught them. Now you've got to teach them otherwise.

Toxic Love

A toxic relationship exists when one person (and sometimes both people) will do just about anything to remain in the relationship and get the other person to do so, too. This kind of relationship isn't much good or fun for anyone—not those who are in it and not those who observe it. People outside the relationship usually can see the problems and may even try talking to you about their concerns. When you're inside the relationship, you're often blind to its troubles, or you chalk them up to "everybody has issues."

> **Steer Clear** _____
>
> Mostly when we think of toxic love, we think of intimate partnerships—spouses and lovers. But hurtful and dysfunctional behaviors can exist in any kind of close relationship—siblings, parent and child, and friends. The risk is highest in relationships where you feel, for whatever reasons, you can't leave.

Like anything else toxic, a toxic relationship is not good for you. Its negatives far outweigh the positives, which you probably know in your heart of hearts, even if you can't acknowledge it; yet the two of you stay together. Does this sound like anything you've been reading about lately … hmmmm, maybe like a habit? If you think so, you're exactly right. Though the patterns of behavior that exist in a toxic relationship are damaging, it's still easier to follow them than to create new patterns.

Such a relationship might be what sets you off on the path of an addictive habit. The habit becomes your way of coping, your way to escape the unpleasantness. Or the relationship might arise from shared addictive habits. In either case, the relationship puts you at great risk for slipping back into your old habits.

How Healthy Are Your Relationships?

Is a relationship working for you or against you? See what you think after choosing the best answer for each of these questions. Go through this short quiz for each relationship that's part of your daily life.

1. When it comes to the changes I've made, the other person …

    a. Says encouraging things to me every day that support my new path.

    b. Tells me I'll never really change.

    c. Makes fun of me.

    d. Puts me in situations to test me.

2. When I go with the other person to an event or activity that challenges the changes I've made, the other person …

    a. Pats me on the shoulder and tells me, "You can handle it!"

    b. Recognizes the challenges before I do and suggests we leave.

    c. Tells me I've become boring and rigid and need to lighten up.

    d. Tells everyone there that I've given up the old habit.

3. When I feel myself on the brink of a lapse …

    a. I hide my feelings from the other person because I don't want him/her to be disappointed or angry.

    b. The other person can tell even when I don't say anything and taunts me or makes fun of me.

    c. The other person is the first one I go to because he/she always says the right things to help me regain my sense of direction.

    d. I try to suck it up and blast through it.

4. When I slip back into the behaviors of my old habit, the other person …

    a. Yells at me and tells me I'm a loser.

    b. Never finds out about it, if I can help it.

    c. Hugs me and says, "It's one slip, no big deal. Let's get you back on track!"

    d. Asks what he/she can do to help me from slipping again.

5. When we're making decisions about what to do when we're together, we …

    a. Wing it; plans bog us down.

    b. Just do what the other person wants to do.

    c. Call other friends to see what they're doing.

    d. Intentionally choose activities and events with low risk for exposing me to my old habit.

6. When I've had a particularly stressful day, the other person ...

    a. Gives me some quiet or alone time to calm down and gather my thoughts.

    b. Tells me what I did wrong and what I should've done instead.

    c. Doesn't notice.

    d. Starts telling me about his/her bad day, which was much worse than mine.

7. I have a relationship with the other person because ...

    a. We have a lot in common and enjoy being with each other; we're better together than solo.

    b. I have to—we're family.

    c. I'm such a wreck, no one else would want me.

    d. I feel better about myself and my life when I'm with him/her, no matter what kind of day I'm having.

Finished? Okay, then let's take a look at the possibilities your responses suggest.

1. An answer of (a), the other person is encouraging and supportive on a daily basis, is a sign of a healthy relationship. The other three responses suggest the other person doesn't believe in you and may say or do hurtful things that leave you not believing in yourself.

Steer Clear _____

Some relationships are toxic because of physical or emotional abuse. In the United States, the National Domestic Violence Hotline provides assistance and information 24/7. The number is 1-800-799-SAFE (7233) or TTY 1-800-787-3224 for the hearing-impaired. The call is toll free from anywhere in the United States.

2. Answer (b) suggests the other person in this relationship is looking out for your best interests. Answers (a) and (d) imply the other person has faith in your ability to resist temptation but doesn't really understand the struggle that might be taking place within you. Of course, you can't avoid every situation that could trigger an urge to indulge the old habit; (a) can be a positive, healthy response when you have a strong repertoire of coping skills. Answer (c) is a red flag that shows the other person does not support you or the changes you're making in your life.

3. It's unhealthy in a relationship for you to fear the other person's response such that you're afraid for him or her to know you're human, which is what making mistakes is all about, right? You might be able to power through on your own, answer (d), which speaks volumes about your integrity and determination though. But this response also suggests you're afraid to tell the other person. And no one should make fun of you or taunt you, answer (b), in your time of need or, really, at any time.

4. Answers (c) and (d) both imply a supportive relationship; (c) takes a position of shared responsibility with the other person in the lead, while (d) puts the onus on you. Again, fear of the other person finding out, which is what's behind efforts to hide the slip in answer (b), is unhealthy in the relationship. Yelling and belittling you, answer (a), are toxic behaviors.

5. Answer (d) shows you both understand the risks you face every day and share a commitment to helping you maintain the changes you're making. Making a few calls to friends, answer (c), is a good place to start as long as you make decisions with intent. Winging it, answer (a), is not the most supportive of solutions. And just doing what the other person wants to do, answer (b), says this is a one-sided relationship—and it's not on your side.

6. Just because you've had a stressful day doesn't mean you've done anything wrong! But your stress should not go unnoticed, either. And when your day's been a black cloud, the last thing that's going to help you feel better is hearing the other person's day was even worse. (How could that even be possible?) So answer (a) hits the mark square on for a supportive, healthy relationship.

7. Answers (a) and (d) are close, and either suggests the two of you are good for each other. Answer (c) says this relationship is no good for you.

If you end up with three or more answers that are unhealthy behaviors, it's time to evaluate the relationship with an eye toward change. In its current form, the relationship's not doing you any good. It's not very good for the other person, either, although when the balance of power tips that way it's even harder to see how harmful it is.

You may find that some of the relationships you currently have in your life are healthy and others are toxic, though often the same themes run through all your relationships. And of course, relationships are complex. No seven-question quiz can tell you whether one is right or wrong for you. But you should come away from this quiz with a little broader view.

Giving It Up for Someone You Love

Sometimes your dilemma isn't so much how others are affecting your ability to stay true to the new you but rather how you're affecting someone else. You believe you're doing all the right things, but suddenly you recognize that your efforts are bringing about all the wrong results. Instead of getting better, things are getting worse.

Maybe you're too empathetic because you've changed your own habits. You've been there, done that, and you know it's not easy. You're trying to be supportive but instead, to your dismay, you end up supporting the other person's undesirable habits.

def•i•ni•tion

Enabling behaviors are things you do for someone else that allow the person's undesirable habit to continue. It is a pop psych term. **Codependency** is an entrenched pattern of enabling behaviors in partnerships and family relationships in which one person has an intense emotional need to control and care for another.

Sometimes when you think you're helping, you're really not. Words we often hear in this context are *enabling* and *codependency*. These are not terms health professionals generally use but are rather pop psych concepts that have become part of the lingo associated with addictive habits. Codependency, as a clinical term, refers specifically to a predictable, dysfunctional dynamic within the families of people who abuse alcohol.

It's popular to look at these concepts—enabling and codependency—as the reasons why a person continues an addictive habit. Though the behaviors of others can (and often do) subsidize someone else's addictive habits, responsibility for the habit lies solely with the person who has the habit. The concepts of enabling and codependency do get at the bigger picture of addictive habits, however, because they broaden the focus to look at how environment and relationships influence the habits we develop.

The Elephant in the Room

When you're in a relationship with someone who has an addictive habit, what's your role? Are you the one always picking up the pieces, making excuses, covering up? Though the short-term result may seem positive, it's really not. It doesn't take long for the cumulative effect to be painfully unhelpful for both of you or the entire family.

As hard as it is at first, you've got to back away and let your loved one stand alone with his habit. This is especially tough when the consequences will affect you and other family members. When you stop calling in sick for your partner who's passed out on the sofa, for example, you might feel you're putting your family's financial security in jeopardy.

But what security is there, anyway? You've got to know you're not the only one who knows! Right? A bad habit, whether it's yours or someone else's, is often the worst-kept secret. Other people know something's not right, even if they don't know what it is. If you're acting as though everything's just fine when really it's pretty awful, you're not helping anyone—not your loved one nor yourself.

Changing How You Relate

The way you relate to a loved one is your own pattern of behavior—a habit. And it's your own path of change when you decide to do it differently. It might take you a while to get used to thinking this way because your old way of relating revolved around your loved one's addictive habit. Your new approach puts the focus on that habit in a very different way.

It's tough, we know. It hurts to feel like you're turning your back on your loved one. But you can't change someone else; heaven knows, you've tried. Sometimes all you can do is step away so the other person can—and has to—stand alone. She might fall. But that might be what it takes for her to finally recognize the hold of the addictive habit and the need to change.

> **Be Mindful**
>
> If you love someone who has a problem with a bad habit, do you love that person enough to take yourself out of the picture if that's what's needed for the person to change? This is sometimes the most difficult decision to make and also the most selfless.

Mending Fences

Your old habit may have pushed your relationships to the brink or even over the edge. Maybe you lost your job or your partner moved out. Now that the new you is back in the picture, you must decide what to do about these matters. When someone's broken off with you because of your old habits, is this a relationship you want to salvage?

This is a complex issue. You need to consider how the relationship ended and what's changed since then. Did the other person call it quits because you did not want to change or because of fallout from your behaviors (like facing financial problems, being arrested, losing your job)? Did you change because you want this person back in your life? What do you see happening if you reconnect?

In what ways did the relationship support, or at least tolerate, your old habits? Because it did, in some fashion, even if it ended because of them. How many times have you been in the position of trying to regain the relationship? If your partner left you before and then came back, what kept the relationship from growing in ways that supported you in your changed habits? What happened that let you slip back to your old ways?

Sometimes the best way to move forward with your life is to accept what the relationship brought to you when it was good and now move on. We know this sounds harsh. But if things weren't working before, they're not going to miraculously start working now, and no amount of *magical thinking* will change that. You must have a reasonable and realistic expectation that the relationship, too, can change. Otherwise, going back to it has "Warning: Relapse Ahead!" signs posted all over it.

def•i•ni•tion

> **Magical thinking** is a perception that events, thoughts, or actions share connections when there is no true relationship. For example, you run into a former lover in the grocery store, then at the coffee shop, and then at the movie theater. Magical thinking interprets these encounters as beyond chance even though you live in the same neighborhood. You saw each other before you were in a relationship; why wouldn't you see each other now? Yet magical thinking lets you believe these encounters are signs you should get back together.

Your Line in the Sand

We all struggle with boundaries, especially when it comes to the people we love. It's human nature to want to be helpful and to do things for other people. But sometimes it's hard to define "enough," especially when we really want something. A boundary is a way of saying, "this is my personal space, and within it I make the rules."

People who've had addictive habits take over their lives have a particularly difficult time saying one of the smallest, yet one of the most powerful, words in the English language: no. When out of control feels normal to you, "no" has little meaning—whether you hear it or say it. But now you're free from your addictive habit, and you need to redefine yourself so you and others know what to expect.

You've got to have faith in yourself to feel comfortable saying no. You must be confident that you're right and that your rightness matters. If you're not used to saying no, it can be scary. You might fear the other person will laugh at you, yell at you, ridicule you, or—worse—leave you. Well, if someone who's important in your life makes fun of you or ignores your needs, maybe you're the one who should leave!

Although boundaries are all about limits, setting them restores your freedom to be yourself. Limits on how you spend your time, your money, and your efforts help you structure how much of yourself you give to others. Though at first you might feel selfish, in reality setting boundaries is an act of generosity through which you give to yourself first. When was the last time you did that?

Be Mindful

It's tough, when you're in the throes of reestablishing yourself, to remember why you're doing all this work. Other people may seem confused, which confuses you. Such times of pressure are ideal for pulling out yet another of your coping skills: affirmations. Have a half-dozen or so positive statements you can tell yourself when life seems overwhelming. And when you feel stressed, stop what you're doing; pull out an affirmation; and say it aloud three times, five times, seven times—however many times it takes for you to believe the words.

Be Comfortable Being Yourself

We're all social beings. We like to be with other people, to have others care about us and to care about them. Social interaction is a fundamental human need and a basic function.

We've stressed the need to surround yourself with people who support your efforts to change, the friends and family you can turn to when you need someone to remind you of why you're making these changes, someone to help you stay on track.

In part, you need such a support network because it's so essential for you to separate yourself from your old network, the one that supported your undesirable habits and would like to draw you back to your old ways.

But it's equally essential for you to become comfortable with who you are, as an individual, and with being by yourself. Learning to feel calm within yourself helps you develop patience. We talked in earlier chapters about the challenges of instant gratification—getting what we want right now instead of waiting. When you're comfortable in your own skin, you're comfortable with waiting—delayed gratification.

And you can be alone without being lonely. You just have to recognize that it's okay to be alone and to relax within yourself so you can enjoy your own company. You're an interesting, engaging, enjoyable person all on your own. You don't need others to prove it!

The Least You Need to Know

♦ Relationships are also habits, and like other habits, they can either serve you well or cause you great grief.

♦ The changes you make in yourself affect all your relationships with others.

♦ Toxic relationships keep you from reaching your potential and fulfilling your goals.

♦ Leaving someone because the relationship is harmful is one of the most difficult things you can do, but it's also, in some cases, one of the most generous gifts you can give to yourself and to the other person.

Chapter 14

Kids

In This Chapter

- ◆ Habits through the stages of childhood
- ◆ What to ignore, when to take notice
- ◆ Dealing with problem habits
- ◆ Heap on the praise

Bad habits in kids create concern and stress for everyone. Sometimes parents are the first to recognize the situation, and sometimes they're the last to know. Some habits, like thumb sucking, seem as inevitable as teething and are likely to run their course without all that much intervention from worried parents. Kids leave them behind in the same way they ride away from training wheels, and that's that.

Other habits are more troublesome and need for parents and other adults to step in. Some habits might speak to underlying health issues. You know how hard it is for you as an adult to recognize a habit isn't doing you any good. Kids often don't see the potential consequences of their habits, especially when "everybody's doing it!"

Factors that make kids vulnerable to developing undesirable habits also put kids at special risk for relapse. Parents, teachers, and other adults can help kids make decisions that establish positive, healthy habits. Kids aren't always eager to accept such help, of course. So let's take a look at some ways to redirect behaviors that leave both child and parent feeling good.

The Age of Innocence

Everyone loves babies! They're so cuddly and cute—how can anyone not melt when that toothless, drooly smile beams their way? But how can that sweet little bundle of joy lie in her crib and bang her head against the headboard? It gives *you* a headache, doesn't it hurt her? Surprisingly, no, it doesn't. Head banging and body rocking are two habits that send parents of infants into panic. But for the most part, as pediatricians try to calm us, these are harmless methods baby uses to calm herself. Yep, even babies have habits.

These habits, not in any particular order, most worry parents of kids from infancy to about five years of age:

- Body rocking/head banging
- Nose picking
- Bedtime battles
- Thumb sucking
- Hair pulling/twisting
- Teeth grinding (*bruxism*)
- Breath holding
- Throwing tantrums
- Tattling
- Picky eating

def•i•ni•tion

Bruxism is the medical term for teeth grinding. In children bruxism often appears during teething and then goes away. In adults bruxism may be a stress response. A doctor or dentist should evaluate teeth grinding that persists beyond late childhood.

Like we adults, kids develop habits to help themselves feel better. Unborn babies suck their thumbs even in the womb. Many kids play with their hair, especially when they're falling asleep. Some kids rub their blankets or favorite toys. Like thumb sucking, such self-comfort habits may continue through late childhood, particularly when the child feels stressed or tired.

Habits also mark our child's path of development. Behaviors of the body—thumb sucking, hair twirling, playing with toes—expand as the child's awareness of himself and his surroundings broadens. Young kids don't see anything wrong with picking their noses or scratching where it itches because they don't yet have a sense of what's socially appropriate.

> **Steer Clear** _____
>
> Hair twisting and pulling that becomes uncontrolled may be trichotillomania, an obsessive-compulsive disorder. Trichotillomania commonly begins in adolescence, though can affect people—kids and adults alike—of any age. A key symptom of this disorder is the pulling out of clumps of hair, often resulting in patches of baldness. Some people pull their eyebrows or eyelashes or hair on other parts of the body.

As our child's communication skills improve, habits that primarily serve as attention-getters, like tattling and throwing tantrums, begin to fade. Of course, other habits are waiting in the shadows, eager to step in. But we get ahead of ourselves.

Temper, Temper!

Watching a two-year-old thrash around on the floor and hold his breath until his face turns blue is enough to make most adults want to pull their own hair. But most of the time, these behaviors are not going to harm the child. Pediatricians recommend that when a child throws a tantrum, a parent should stay alert to protect him from inadvertent injury or hurting others. Otherwise, she should let the tantrum wear itself out while appearing to the child to be no more interested than if he were coloring or playing with toys.

The occasional tantrum is inevitable and is a marker that your child's brain is growing. But throwing frequent tantrums is a habit you (and your child) can do without. To block this habit's progression, try to figure out the common factors that are at play when your young child has a meltdown. Is she tired, bored, frustrated, angry, not getting attention from you, or not getting what she wants? Though it might seem that a single event sets her off, more likely it's an "all of the above" situation that pushes her over the edge.

Shaping Early Behaviors

Because most early childhood habits disappear on their own, the most successful approach is simply to ignore them and instead reward the behaviors you want to see. Praise the picky eater for eating his fish rather than chiding him for pushing his peas aside. Offer easy choices—green beans or carrots? Bath before or after teeth brushing?

Young kids like routine and feel secure knowing when things are going to happen. This is to your advantage for developing good habits around routine activities, like brushing teeth, taking a bath, and going to bed.

The Wonder Years

As kids get older, their worlds expand. School exposes them to a broad spectrum of new behaviors and attitudes as they meet new people. Television, movies, and the Internet literally bring the world into your home. Social challenges and skills move to front and center as kids work to figure out how and where they fit in the scheme of things.

School-age kids are learning how to interact with one another. While the habits of early childhood fade as your child grows and develops, the habits of middle childhood test behaviors that will eventually become the social patterns of your child's life. These are the times that try parental patience. Yet this is a great window of opportunity, if you can pull aside the curtain and see the possibilities.

Talk About It

Though hard numbers are tough to come by, surveys suggest that kids watch between 20 and 35 hours of television a week. That's more hours than many states permit teenagers to work! Younger kids don't always know that what they see on TV isn't real, even when they're watching cartoons.

Here are the most common habits among kids from about age 5 years to 10 years, again in no particular order:

- Watching too much TV
- Not doing their chores
- Biting nails and cuticles
- Back-talking
- Squabbling with siblings
- Lying
- Bullying
- Whining and nagging
- Dawdling
- Developing tics (No, not the bugs!)

As eagerly as we await and celebrate those first sounds we can interpret as words, there comes that moment when we look at the beloved offspring spouting off in front of us and long for those days of meaningless baby babble! Back talking, whining, and nagging replace tantrums and tattling as ways to guarantee attention.

With more structures in place to direct their lives, kids struggle to balance their need to control their daily activities with the demands of schedules and calendars. While there's never enough time to do chores, there's always plenty of time to watch favorite TV shows. Bedtime battles shift from night to morning as kids push the limits for getting themselves ready for school.

That's what this period of childhood is all about—limits. You set them, your kids push them. As frustrating as this is, it's a key part of your child's emotional and social development.

Habits to Relieve Stress

Some kids continue to suck their thumbs and twirl their hair, especially when they're trying to fall asleep or are sitting quietly watching television or reading. These habits soothed them when they were younger, and sometimes they resort to them now. Nail and cuticle biting is an extension of such habits.

At this stage of development, these habits can result in consequences that require attention. Thumb-sucking, for example, can pressure incoming adult teeth enough to change their alignment. Biting the nails or cuticles risks infection. A matter-of-fact approach that emphasizes an alternative behavior will help redirect your child's behavior without embarrassing him. Maybe he can take comfort in holding a favorite stuffed animal.

Some kids develop motor or vocal tics—repetitive actions, like blinking, twitching, and throat clearing—as a stress response. The child often seems unaware of the tic or has trouble controlling it. Though alarming to parents, habitual tics are common and tend to go away as a child acquires other skills for handling stressful situations. Tics that continue into adolescence or that include outbursts of sounds or words may be symptoms of Tourette syndrome,

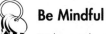

Be Mindful

Kids can learn meditation and other methods to deal with stressful situations. Basic techniques like focusing on the breath can help your child calm himself. Visualization is another effective way to defuse a difficult moment. Chapter 12 describes these methods.

a neurological condition that researchers believe results from disturbances in how brain cells communicate.

Problem Habits

Bullying is a habit that affects more than just the child doing the bullying. It results in emotional, if not physical, trauma to those who become its targets. And the habit's not good for the bully, either, because it reinforces unacceptable behaviors.

As with other undesirable habits, the faster you intervene the more likely you can turn bullying around. Some kids may not realize that what they're doing is hurtful to others, as they may be imitating behaviors they see on TV. Other kids may engage in bullying because it helps them feel confident or superior. Sometimes kids turn to intimidating others in response to pressures or losses they feel.

It's a shock to find out your child's a bully, but don't panic. You and your child can turn this habit around by giving her other methods to deal with her feelings and situations where she feels challenged to be in control. The reasons for these behaviors may be obvious to you, or you may need to dig around to understand her behavior. Ask teachers and caregivers what they observe.

Then talk with your child about how she feels and what might be bothering her. Explain to her that she hurts others with her words and actions. Brainstorm other ways to deal with situations. Let her tell you some of her ideas and see where that leads.

> **Steer Clear**
>
> Childhood bullying is more common, and more serious, than many adults recognize. But adults may also deal with bullies in the workplace—coworkers and bosses who yell, threaten, and otherwise intimidate others. Many experts believe adult bullying has its roots in childhood bullying. It's important to identify bullying behavior in youngsters and to help them develop the skills to interact with others in nonaggressive ways. These habits can last a lifetime.

Sometimes it's helpful to play-act a scenario with you in the role of your child and she in the role of a kid being picked on. Be gentle; remember your mission is to help her understand how her behavior affects others. Praise positive interactions with siblings, and ask teachers to catch your child doing acts of kindness.

Duh!

There comes that morning in every parent's life when he awakens to discover he's become the stupidest person on Earth. How this happens, no one really knows. But it's as inevitable as teething and first dates. His child's become a tween.

Tweens and teens—kids in the stage of development where they're transitioning from childhood to adulthood—take undesirable habits to new heights. *You* know, of course, that your kid is trying to find the right balance between being his own self and fitting in with everyone else. *He* doesn't quite see it this way.

These are the habits that most frustrate and concern parents of kids age twelve and up; you can put them in whatever order you like:

◆ Back talking/rudeness

◆ Not doing homework

◆ Living in virtual reality

◆ Using alcohol and drugs

◆ Messiness

◆ Defying curfew

◆ Sneaking

◆ Eating junk food

◆ Being sedentary

◆ Smoking

Tweens and teens do a lot of hanging out. They may drape themselves all over your family room furniture or sprawl around the benches in the park. To look at them, you might wonder whether they can even stand upright, they're always leaning, sitting, or lounging on something. You worry as much about what they don't eat as what they do eat—what they do as much as what they don't do. Their health habits are beginning to matter, and you know it even if they don't.

This is also the stage where your son is watching you more closely than ever. Even as he craves to be like his friends, he takes his cues from you. Sometimes the best you can do is be the example you'd like him to follow—make healthy eating and exercise choices, drink responsibly if you drink, and follow through with what you say.

Some habits of this stage will fall by the wayside as your teen matures. But many of the habits he develops now are foundations for the future. Homework may become irrelevant, for example, but study habits remain important for learning new job skills. It's no easy task, but the more you as a parent can draw connections for him between his habits now and benefits both present and future, the more he learns to look at choices and consequences.

Be Mindful _____

Does your child get enough sleep? By the time they're teens, most kids sleep far less than their bodies need. Studies show that teens still require about nine hours of sleep each night. If you're the parent of a teen, you know this doesn't often happen! Though it's not a bad idea to let your teen sleep in on the weekends to catch up on lost sleep, it's healthier in the long run to encourage enough sleep on a nightly basis.

Applied Logic

Stephanie's daughter Courtney started working part time when she was a junior in high school. Courtney loved being able to buy clothes and other items with her own money and was generous in treating her friends when they went out together. Stephanie encouraged Courtney to put half of each paycheck into a savings account for emergencies, but every week Courtney had some sort of "emergency" that siphoned her savings.

Trying to be helpful, one evening Stephanie sat down and put together a budget for Courtney that would let her enjoy spending money on herself yet still feed her savings. Courtney took the paper, glanced at it, and tossed it on her bedroom floor. Stephanie was hurt but said nothing. A few weeks later, Courtney came to talk to Stephanie, crumpled budget paper in hand. "So if I follow this thing, I can use my savings for stuff that's important to *me*?"

Stephanie said yes, that was the purpose of savings. Courtney handed the budget paper to her mother and said, "I did some figuring, and this is how I can buy a car." It wasn't quite what Stephanie had in mind, but she could see the effort Courtney'd put into her plan, so they talked through Courtney's ideas and each of them suggested changes.

Courtney stuck to the plan, and after six months she was able to buy a car. It wasn't the car she originally wanted; she scaled back in the reality of sticker shock. And it wasn't quite what Stephanie originally had in mind, but Courtney got a decent enough car and still had money in her savings account to put toward her college fund.

Troubling Habits

Though teens may walk, talk, and act like adults, their brains aren't quite there yet. The hippocampus—the part of the brain that regulates impulse control—is still developing, as are other centers of the brain that give teens the ability to make reasoned, rational judgments. This makes them particularly vulnerable to addictive behaviors.

Research suggests that the earlier alcohol, drug, and smoking experimentation begins, the more likely these habits are to persist in adulthood. Even if you feel adolescent experimentation is inevitable, talk with your kids about the risks and consequences. Clear, open communication maintains a connection for each of you.

When a Good Friend Is a Bad Influence

All kids have friends that seem to bring out the worst, rather than the best, in them. Often a child becomes infatuated with such a friend for long enough to drive a parent crazy, then suddenly drops the friend and moves on. We breathe a sigh of relief. But what about when the friendship continues?

What we see the friendship to be, as adults from the outside looking in, is nothing like what the kid sees. As with any relationship we're able to watch, we can see the actions of both (or all) people as well as the consequences, intended and unintended. And as adults, we have the advantage of experience, and we know some situations just don't turn out the way we'd like. We've had these friendships ourselves. But our kids, of course, think we're out of touch, don't know anything, and want only to keep them from having fun. It's always an interesting moment when our child recognizes the opposite is true!

Although you see the negative, real and potential, influences of the friend, your child sees something else. What? Ask your kid! And listen to what she says. Hold back any desire to judge or lecture; nothing stops a dialogue faster. You might find yourself pleasantly surprised to discover that your child does see both the good and the not so good in this friend.

Even when this is not the case, you'll at least get some insight into what makes this friend so attractive to your child. When you have such an understanding, you're better able to guide her into different activities and, with luck, expanded friendships that more positively support her.

> **Steer Clear** _____
>
> When a friendship puts your child's safety and well-being at risk, you have no choice but to step in—and you should feel confident about doing so, no matter what your child's response. Keep calm, yet stay unmistakably focused and specific in defining boundaries around activities with the friend. Your child might already see the risks but be unable himself to break away. Your intervention takes the pressure off and allows him to save face.

Does Your Kid Have a Problem Habit?

Some habits indicate underlying factors or issues that need further exploration—and often help from a professional. As the saying goes, it's not the behavior itself but the amount of time you spend engaged in it that defines whether it's a problem. When a habit interferes with a child's ability to participate in normal daily activities and schoolwork, the habit's a problem.

And some behaviors are more than undesirable habits. These include …

- Obsessive-compulsive actions such as counting steps, washing hands a certain number of times, repeating certain words or phrases, and other ritualistic behaviors.

- Eating habits that result in health conditions like obesity, anorexia nervosa, bulimia, and binge-and-purge practices.

- Persistent bullying, which may suggest underlying emotional or mental health issues.

- Drinking, drugs, and smoking are always health concerns, no matter the child's age, and can become legal issues for both child and parents.

- Persistent, uncontrollable tics, especially sounds, which could indicate Tourette syndrome.

◆ Intentional self-harm, like cutting, which is always a health concern and requires evaluation and assistance from a health professional who specializes in caring for children and teens.

◆ Persistent lying or stealing, which can result in legal issues that have far-reaching consequences and may also suggest emotional issues.

The bottom line, though, is that any behavior in your child that worries you is worth having the pediatrician or other regular health care provider check out. Ninety percent of the time, your worry will turn out to be baseless—and that's a great relief. The other 10 percent of the time, your child may have a concern that needs further assessment and perhaps treatment. The earlier this happens, the more successful the outcome is likely to be.

And don't hesitate to involve your child's health care provider! There's no better way to understand the spectrum of behavior and to get an objective perspective about where your kid fits along that spectrum. If there's more to it than simply behavior, then you'll have someone else on your side who can help you find appropriate care.

When and How to Intervene

Knowing when to stay out of your child's struggles and when to step in is a tricky balance for parents. Sometimes the mistakes kids make are their most powerful lessons. But we don't want the cost of such lessons, emotional or otherwise, to be overwhelming.

When your child's habit puts her safety at risk, you must step in. Habits such as drinking, using drugs, having promiscuous sex, stealing, driving recklessly, Internet gambling, and smoking (and chewing tobacco) all have significant health and possibly legal and other consequences.

Choose a time to talk with your teen when both of you are relatively free from distractions and other obligations. Be specific as you express your observations and concerns. Present your perspective of the risks and consequences he is facing should he choose to continue in the habits. Also allow him to respond without interrupting him, to hear his perspectives.

When he is underage, this dialogue is not a negotiation, though your goal is to work toward a collaborative solution. It's important for you to remember and your child to perceive that your intervention comes from love and concern. In the end, however, you are responsible for your child's well-being and obligated to do what you can to safeguard it. You might be surprised to discover this is all the intervention you need to make.

When to Seek Professional Help

It's always better to err on the side of caution. If your child's habits concern you, ask an appropriate professional for an opinion. This might be a school guidance counselor, trusted teacher, pediatrician or family doctor, or a therapist or psychologist. Consider seeking professional help when:

- ◆ The habit affects your child physically.

- ◆ The habit causes your child emotional distress.

- ◆ The habit prevents your child from participating in normal, everyday activities like school.

- ◆ The habit causes significant tension in your family.

- ◆ The habit has potential legal consequences for your child.

Most communities have abundant resources to help kids with addictive habits and emotional concerns. Your family doctor, child's pediatrician, and school psychologist or counselor are all good starting points.

Keep It Positive

To see more of a good thing, praise it when you do see it, however fleeting the sighting is. Sounds simple enough, but sometimes we focus so much on the habits we want to see change in our kids (just like we do in ourselves) that we don't notice when they *do* change.

Remember behavioral psychologist B. F. Skinner from Chapter 9? His landmark work produced the concept of operant conditioning—shaping change in behavior through reinforcement. Skinner made two crucial observations very early in his research:

1. Rewards are far more effective in shaping behavior than are punishments.

2. Rewarding the smallest hint of behavior leads to cumulative changes.

As we've said from the beginning, change is a process. With kids, the steps might be incredibly small, but they're steps nonetheless. When your child's struggling, stay calm. Focus on the behavior and its consequences. Help him understand that all habits have both benefits and costs. Sometimes kids feel they can't control or even influence their lives very much.

Collaborate with your child to find solutions that meet his needs. Suggest alternative behaviors. Even with older kids, try diversions. Offer choices that pull him into participating in decisions without creating opportunities for argument. Be patient yet persistent.

And when glimmers of new behaviors appear, reward them! With younger kids, you can't be too enthusiastic. With older kids, you'll probably need to show some restraint. But no matter your child's age, go out of your way to look for reasons to praise his efforts and celebrate his successes (even as you maintain boundaries around problem behaviors). Over time, you're influencing and shaping behaviors in your child. These positive thoughts, feelings, and actions become the basis of habits that can serve him well throughout life.

The Least You Need to Know

- Most kids outgrow the undesirable habits of early and middle childhood.
- When children's habits continue beyond the typical age range, they could be indications of other concerns.
- Habits such as bullying, drinking, using drugs, lying, and stealing can have legal consequences.
- Kids respond best to rewards and praise.

Chapter 15

Who Can Help?

In This Chapter

- ◆ Choosing and finding the right help
- ◆ In the public venue
- ◆ Sharing the caring
- ◆ You're never too old to learn!
- ◆ Employee Assistance and weight management programs

You've come a long way on your journey of change. You've emerged from the tunnel where your focus was very narrow on that spot of brightness, that ray of hope, you could barely see through the darkness of your old habit. Now an entire new world is all around you. You know the best way to keep moving forward, and to lower your risk for relapse, is to connect with resources that support and nurture positive change.

Lucky for you, such resources are abundant in nearly every community. Social, medical, community, church, and government organizations offer a broad network of services that can help you stay on track with your changes and your new life. In this chapter, we look at how to find the ones that are a good fit for you.

Your Brave New World

In the beginning, there was Alcoholics Anonymous (AA). Born of equal parts of desperation and determination, AA was a fresh frontier for those seeking to overcome alcohol dependence. In its day—1935, a year that also gave us Social Security, Elvis Presley, and the board game Monopoly—AA was a new approach to a timeless challenge. Though AA remains at the forefront of recovery approaches even today, myriad other programs and services are out there as well. Some are just right for you, and others couldn't be more wrong.

No matter how good a service or program is, it's not doing much good for you if you can't work it into your daily life. You're devoted to the changes you're making, but you've got to be able to make them in ways that fit with who you are and how you live. Most of us have jobs, families, and other responsibilities. We've already taken from them to get this far; now we've got to work back into a reasonable balance.

When you're looking into the services you'll build into your support network, consider a number of factors:

♦ What costs, if any, are associated with the service? What do you get for your money? If there are costs, will your health insurance pay for any of them?

♦ In what specific ways does the program, service, or provider address your particular addictive behaviors?

♦ Is it one-on-one or group support?

♦ What are the credentials of the program or provider, and who actually delivers the services? Are the approaches evidence-based?

♦ What is the underlying philosophy and what are the goals of the program or service? Is the emphasis on moving toward independence in how you manage your changed lifestyle over time?

> **Talk About It**
>
> It is one of the most beautiful compensations in life that no man can sincerely try to help another, without helping himself.
> —Ralph Waldo Emerson, American writer and philosopher

♦ Can you easily get to the location? Are services available during times you can go, or will you need to reschedule other activities?

♦ Will you learn new skills? Will you have the opportunity to share your experiences and concerns?

♦ What happens if you lapse?

Some approaches want to involve other members of your family or household. Others may not want to know anything more than your first name. What matters as much as the approach is how comfortable you are with it. But we're not letting you off the hook by letting you say, "I'm not comfortable with *any* of it!"

Change is *uncomfortable* at times, especially when other people are holding you accountable for what you say and do. But you should feel that the support network you pull together helps you feel good about your progress and look for solutions to your challenges.

What Do You Want?

What kind of support do you feel you need? Because this is sometimes the toughest part of building your support network, these questions should help you clarify what you're looking for. Choose "yes" or "no" to identify how these statements suit you:

1. I feel calmer and more relaxed when I can talk to someone about stressful situations in my life.

   _____ yes   _____ no

2. I get nervous when I have to speak in front of other people, especially people I don't know.

   _____ yes   _____ no

3. I like to hear how other people have solved problems similar to mine, and I can take away useful information from their stories.

   _____ yes   _____ no

4. I like for someone to tell me my options and suggest the one that is likely to work best for me.

   _____ yes   _____ no

5. I like to brainstorm possible options, looking outside the box for ones that are likely to work best for me.

   _____ yes   _____ no

6. I am deeply spiritual or religious and incorporate my faith in my decisions.

_____ yes   _____ no

7. I look for the science behind everything.

_____ yes   _____ no

8. I don't want anyone to know who I am.

_____ yes   _____ no

9. I prefer to sit back and listen to what experts have to say about addictive behaviors, such as the ones I'm leaving behind, to gain knowledge.

_____ yes   _____ no

10. I prefer to engage in discussion with experts and other people who've been on their paths of change longer than I've been on mine, to gain insights.

_____ yes   _____ no

Be Mindful

Your needs for support might be more complex if you're coming out of an intensive treatment program, inpatient or outpatient. Work closely with your primary treatment provider to get the right kinds of support. Court-ordered treatment, too, often has specific and explicit requirements and conditions.

Your answers can help you decide on the settings most likely to help you. If you answered "yes" to items 1, 3, 5, and 10, you might do well in groups with diverse membership. A "yes" answer to statements 2, 4, and 9 suggests you might feel more comfortable in a very small group or by yourself with a therapist. Or if you answered "yes" to item 9, consider a class or presentation. "Yes" answers to items 7 and 10 suggest you may get more from interactive situations where you can ask questions. If you chose "yes" for statement 6 and/or 8, you might find 12-step or faith-based programs a good fit.

As you can see, there's much variation in what might appeal to you. You might find several options in combination are what best meet your needs. Your interests and preferences are likely to change as your journey of change unfolds. You'll put some challenges and questions behind you and confront new ones. Whatever decisions you make now, they're entirely flexible. You can always change your mind.

How Do You Find the Services You Want?

If you've already worked with some sort of program to kick your old habit out the door, you're already linked into a network of continuing support. Many programs—especially inpatient or residential programs for substance abuse—have progressive structures that help you move from supervised guidance to maintaining on your own.

Your regular health-care provider can also recommend qualified services even if your addictive habit was behavioral, like gambling or compulsive shopping, rather than substance-based. Check community bulletin boards, too. Talk to or visit with someone from the service or support group you're considering, to get a better sense of what to expect. Also you can read books (like this one!) to learn more about what's available. There are books about specific addictive behaviors; see Appendix B to get started with your search.

How Do You Know If You've Made the Right Choice?

Some programs and providers let you attend a meeting or meet with a key person to see whether the service is a good fit for you. Group dynamics are important, though difficult to assess, because the moment you enter the group, its dynamic changes. The make-up of the group matters a bit less in a class-like setting where one person presents information to everyone else. And if you're one-on-one, the interaction is pretty straightforward.

Give the program or provider enough time before you make a judgment, especially if you're thinking it's not what you want. It takes time for a group dynamic to shift and resettle when a new person joins. If you're one-on-one with a therapist, go for at least three sessions unless your reaction is so strongly negative that you can't bring yourself to return. (It happens sometimes and isn't necessarily a reflection on the therapist's abilities.)

 **Steer Clear**

Although sometimes it's the influence of friends that get you to go to a support group, it might not be a good idea to join a support group that any of your friends already attend. You might be less inclined to be candid about yourself and your experiences and about your friend.

It's good when you like the other people who're there, but keep in mind you're not in this to be friends. You're all in this together because you share common challenges (breaking free of the old habit) and common goals (establishing a new lifestyle).

You all understand each other's fears and weaknesses and can keep each other honest when you're slipping toward a lapse. A good example of such groups is the competitive team play on the weight loss television show, *The Biggest Loser.*

Specialists in addictive behaviors caution that friendships formed in recovery groups or support groups may contain an element of high-risk. Even though you're on the other side of your old habit now, you share the dark side of that habit with the others. Yeah, you might be the best thing that ever happened to each other, as friends go. And you could be the worst, as relapse risk goes.

It's great, too, when you can talk about anything in your group or with your therapist. But are you talking about the right things? Odds are you have a lot of emotional baggage to unload—most of us do. And that's sometimes painful. The right support for you is the support that pushes you to dig deep within your psyche to get to the root of your distress (more on this distress—frustration and anger—in Chapter 16).

Your Tax Dollars at Work

In the United States, every state has publicly funded health programs that provide low-cost or free services to help people overcome addictive behaviors. You might find these programs listed as alcohol and drug, substance abuse, chemical dependency, smoking (or tobacco) cessation, and behavioral health. Services to help with other kinds of addictive behaviors, like over-spending and over-eating, might fall more generally within mental health programs.

Talk About It

Many states sponsor or in some way require services for compulsive gambling. Some form of gambling is legal in all states except Utah and Hawaii. Most casinos, race tracks, and other locations where legalized gambling takes place post contact information, often a toll-free hotline, for help with out-of-control gambling.

Most states promote and even advertise their programs. You might find business cards and informational flyers in taverns and lounges, community centers, public libraries, and even grocery stores and shopping centers. If you're having trouble finding help in your state, call your state department of health's general information telephone hotline or check out its website.

Close to Home

Counties and cities also have addictive behavior services. Most target substance-based habits (drugs, alcohol, smoking), though may offer other help under the umbrella of general mental health services. Your local phone book is a good resource for finding and connecting with these programs. Public libraries often have community services display kiosks and educational pamphlets.

What's available depends, of course, on where you live. Smaller communities may offer subsidized services through private providers. If you're having trouble finding the services you need, check with your county or state health department. The Internet is one way to connect with resources beyond your local areas, particularly for information.

SAMHSA

The U.S. Department of Health and Human Services (DHHS) Substance Abuse and Mental Health Services Administration (SAMHSA) is a long name to get to some short and simple connections. The SAMHSA website (www.samhsa.gov) features a treatment facility locator (http://findtreatment.samhsa.gov) to get you to appropriate services where you live or work, whatever your preference.

There are currently 138 providers within 20 miles of Seattle's city center, for example, Alan's home turf. Fourteen within 20 miles of Fargo, North Dakota; three within 20 miles of New Braunfels, Texas; two within 20 miles of Montpelier, Vermont; 103 within 20 miles of Boston. You get the idea. The locator identifies primarily alcohol and substance abuse services, though many providers offer a broader range of help.

SAMHSA is also a great resource for information about addictive behaviors, mental health issues, and the spectrum of treatment and recovery approaches. The agency maintains the National Registry of Evidence-Based Programs & Practices, a comprehensive listing of what works and what doesn't in the context of changing addictive behaviors.

Support Groups

Support groups bring together people who have common goals for change and are the most common form of ongoing help. Often, the hinge pin of a support group is the addictive habit you're trying to leave behind. This can be a challenge—and counterproductive—if the group tends to focus more on the pull of old habit than the successes of new behaviors and attitudes. You want to keep looking ahead, not back.

A support group may be structured, with regular meeting times and locations, and even a moderator who keeps conversations on track. The moderator might be a therapist or counselor or a regular member of the group who has long-term success with change. Some groups embrace particular philosophies or approaches, such as those that are faith-based.

Other support groups are self-moderating. Group members keep meetings on track—a positive expression of peer pressure! The group may rotate leadership for each meeting or have some other process in place to establish and maintain order.

Be Mindful

Organizations are moving increasingly toward Internet-based services to provide information as well as support networks. Chat rooms, webcasts, and slideshows are among the interactive approaches available. If you don't have Internet access at home and want to make use of this method, try your local public library. Most public and many college libraries offer free computer use and Internet access.

Most groups have guidelines for the ways members may express themselves—basically, be nice. Treat others as you'd like them to treat you. It's easy for the emotions of the moment to carry you (and others) away from productive dialogue. You're talking about matters you've long buried deep in your unconscious mind, matters that have become the central focus of your life. These five points can help you keep a clear head when it comes to expressing your thoughts in a group setting:

- Take a deep breath in and let it all the way out before you begin to speak. This helps calm your body and your thoughts.

- Let the person speaking finish before you start talking. If you're afraid you'll lose your thought, jot down a brief note.

- Focus your words on experiences and feelings, not people. "I" is almost always a safe way to start; "you" opens the door to misunderstanding as a personal attack.

- If someone interrupts you, stop talking and wait for the person to also stop. Trying to talk over someone can have the unintended effect of escalating voice volumes as well as emotions.

- Speak loudly enough for others in the group to hear you but softly enough that they lean forward to listen.

> **Talk About It**
>
> Confidentiality is an important cornerstone of any support system. What happens in the meeting or counseling session stays in the meeting or counseling session. This lets people feel free to express their thoughts and concerns. Laws and ethical codes govern confidentiality in some settings, and mutual agreement (trust) prevails in others.

A growing number of support groups have online communication networks to let members reach out to one another whenever they feel the need for such a connection. Some support groups meet exclusively online, with scheduled chat room sessions. (We talk about online support in Chapter 12.) An advantage to this kind of support group is that you don't have to go anywhere to participate. A disadvantage is that you miss the camaraderie of knowing others in face-to-face conversation.

Health-care centers, mental health clinics, local health departments, and some churches and community organizations often sponsor support groups. The group may simply meet at the sponsoring facility, or the facility may provide group leaders or facilitators and conduct the group's meetings. The majority of support groups are self-policing; that is, they monitor themselves and address any concerns directly with one another.

Twelve-Step Programs

As stated at the beginning of this chapter, the original and current model 12-step program is Alcoholics Anonymous—AA. Dozens of offspring programs exist today: Narcotics Anonymous (NA), Gamblers Anonymous (GA), and Overeaters Anonymous (OA) are but a few. AA came into existence when Bill Wilson, desperate to break the hold of alcohol dependence, met Bob Smith, a physician who also struggled with drinking. Dr. Bob, as fellow AA-ers knew him, opened his home to group meetings. Over time the "Twelve Steps" emerged as the guiding principles.

Though their particular 12 steps may vary in how the group expresses them, 12-step programs generally have these core elements in common:

- Anonymity—members know each other only by first name.
- Spirituality—there's an underlying belief in a higher power.
- Strength comes through the group's ability to unify around common goals.

◆ Admitting to an addictive behavior and acceptance that the addictive behavior is beyond the individual's ability to control.

◆ Philosophy that addiction is an incurable, progressive disease.

◆ Belief that understanding and putting right past mistakes is the only way to free yourself to start a new life.

◆ Obligation to help others overcome their addictive behaviors. An experienced member of the group takes on the role of sponsor for a new member.

Twelve-step groups are open to anyone who desires to join, is working to overcome the specific addictive habit of the group, and is willing to accept the program's guidelines. Programs are specific for the addictive behavior, which is why there are so many variations on the model. Millions of people worldwide participate in 12-step programs.

However, 12-step programs are not for everyone. You may object to the religious overtones of the 12-step approach or find the structure too confining. Some addictive behavior experts feel the 12-step programs, between their guidelines and frequent meetings, don't encourage people to become independent in their choices of behavior.

One group may work fine for you while another feels uncomfortable. Every group has its own dynamic and personality. Take another look at your answers to the statements earlier in this chapter. If you answered "yes" to items 2, 5, 7, and 10, you might do better in less structured approaches, like those in the following section.

The SMART Way

Established in the early 1990s, SMART Recovery is a not-for-profit organization that blends methods of cognitive behavioral therapy with scientific knowledge about addictive habits. SMART's philosophy views addictive habits as behavioral issues rather than diseases, and its goal is to teach the skills necessary to understand and change behaviors. SMART stands for Self-Management and Recovery Training.

SMART groups meet in person as well as online and are open to diverse membership. A group might have people who are changing their behaviors around alcohol use, gambling, and compulsive shopping, for example. Sometimes touted as the "Non-Twelve Step Program," SMART is widely recognized among addictive behavior specialists and organizations as a valid and effective, as well as secular (without religious or spiritual affiliation), alternative to AA-type programs.

SMART's approach emphasizes four key points (called the Four-Point Program):

1. Enhancing and maintaining motivation to abstain

2. Coping with urges

3. Problem-solving to manage thoughts, feelings, and behaviors

4. Lifestyle balance

Volunteer moderators facilitate meetings. Meetings aim to educate as well as improve skills. Most meetings are "live," the conventional sort of meeting where people gather together. Online meetings are also part of the SMART line-up, with meeting participants logging on chat rooms at specified times.

SMART gets high marks from authorities like the American Academy of Family Physicians, the American Society of Addiction Medicine, the U.S. National Institute on Drug Abuse (NIDA), and the U.S. National Institute on Alcohol Abuse and Alcoholism (NIAAA). However, SMART, too, is not for everyone. If you chose "yes" in response to items 3, 4, and 6 earlier in the chapter, you might find SMART is not a good fit for you.

Back to School

There's no better way to improve your skills than to enroll in classes that teach what you want to learn—time management, organizational skills, managing your finances, even *feng shui* to reduce the clutter in your personal environments! You might also want to learn more about specific addictive behaviors or even study subjects like psychology and yoga.

Check local community centers, community colleges, county and city agencies, and private agencies like your local Better Business Bureau and Chamber of Commerce to see what's available in your area. Some kinds of classes are low-cost or free, particularly those considered nonacademic. Consider also classes in meditation, yoga, tai chi, and qi gong. These practices calm both body and mind, giving you better clarity and easing stress.

def•i•ni•tion

Feng shui (*fung schway*) is an ancient Chinese practice of placement to achieve harmony. The principles of feng shui address the flow of life energy (called qi or chi, *chee*) through a space, such as a room or building, and the ways objects enhance or block that flow.

Employee Assistance Programs (EAPs)

Addictive behaviors have high costs in the workplace, which has led employers to offer Employee Assistance Programs (EAPs). An EAP is a benefit, sort of like medical insurance, that gives an employee access to a range of behavioral health services not usually covered under traditional medical insurance. Each individual contacts the EAP directly, and a screening therapist connects him with the appropriate services—typically providers in the local community. All services are confidential; the employer doesn't know that any employee has used the EAP. Many EAPs also provide brief intervention (typically one to three visits with an appropriate counselor or therapist).

EAPs vary widely in the kinds of services available, but nearly all have a toll-free number available 24/7 so you at least have someplace to turn in a crisis. A drawback is that EAP services are short term, intended more to get you through a crisis than to provide any kind of ongoing situation. The EAP might be a good resource for finding support groups and other services in your local community.

Weight Management Programs

We single out weight management programs because this is an area of behavior where the program can become one's lifestyle. Some weight management approaches require each participant to follow a specific eating regimen that includes purchasing food through their program.

The advantages of this approach, and one reason people experience short-term success, is that the food arrives packaged in appropriate portions and nutritional balances. The disadvantage is that people don't learn how to assess, measure, and prepare nutritious meals themselves—even when the program includes an educational component designed to teach them.

When you view this approach as you might view nicotine replacement for smoking cessation, you're on the right track. When you look at the prepared meals approach as a long-term strategy, you're creating a "solution" that doesn't integrate very well with the real world. The goal should always be for you to move toward redesigning your lifestyle to include healthy eating and exercise habits.

Although you can turn your back on your unhealthy eating habits, you can't really turn your back on eating! This is one area of addictive behavior where temptation's in your face all the time. The risk of stepping off the path of your new lifestyle is high, especially when other factors like stress and depression drop by for a visit. The support network you choose should help you develop skills to peaceably coexist with your risks for relapse. It's important to look at weight management as a lifestyle of new habits, beyond any goal of weight loss.

The Least You Need to Know

- ◆ Many forms of support are available; your challenge is to find those that are a good fit for you.

- ◆ Federal, state, and local health agencies provide a wide range of services.

- ◆ You're never too old to learn new skills.

- ◆ Your employer may offer an Employee Assistance Program (EAP) benefit that provides behavioral health services.

- ◆ The most effective weight management programs are those that guide you in making long-term lifestyle modifications.

Part 5

Out with the Old, In with the New

It's a new you—how exciting! And how scary! You know you're not the same, but do others in your life? And you know all too well how easy it could be to slide toward the old you. In your new lifestyle, you're always on guard, and that can be a pretty stressful way to live.

The chapters in Part 5 pull your fears and worries into the light of day so you can see them for what they really are and find ways to put them to rest. Chapter 16 digs below the surface of your habits to uncover the feelings that keep the pull of the old habit smoldering. Chapter 17 takes on the difficult challenge of pulling away from the people and places of your old habit. Chapter 18 explores the added stress you feel about relapsing and offers methods to keep it at a manageable level.

Chapter 16

Anger and Resentment

In This Chapter

- How your brain processes anger
- The potential harm of unresolved anger
- The many expressions of anger
- Getting a grip on your anger

Anger arises from feeling afraid and helpless. Things happen that we can't control, which could hurt us—in little ways or big ways. Our inability to control these things scares us. But we can't act scared; we can't show fear. That makes us vulnerable to even more hurt. Other people might take advantage of us in our moments of weakness—and we can't have *that*.

Or so we believe. But when it comes right down to it, anger makes us most vulnerable to that which truly will take advantage in a heartbeat: our old habits. Anger is enough of an issue on its own and can even be an addictive habit in itself. But when we're working to change our old habits for good, anger is a major risk for—and cause of—relapse.

The Roots of Anger

Anger is a natural function; it's programmed into us. We can't *not* experience anger, no matter how we try. What we can influence is how we respond to anger.

Scientists believe anger is part of the "fight or flight" survival mechanism, having the original purpose of causing us to feel, for the moment, strong ... very strong—invincibly strong, even. And right, because when we're strong and right, we take immediate action—no thinking, only action.

Early in the history of humankind, this action was all about aggression, being bigger and badder (or at least badder) than the other guy or creature. Survival was no slam dunk when every waking moment centered around eat or be eaten. The aggressive prevailed and the less aggressive ... well, let's just say they didn't.

Even though circumstances are different in our modern society, at least in the context of "guess who's coming to dinner," all that survival programming is still hard-wired into us. And when activated, that programming sets into motion a complex cascade of physical and emotional changes.

The challenge today is that what activates the anger cycle often has little to do with genuine survival threats and much more to do with behaviors we've learned over time. While we can't control what happens to us physiologically during anger, we can control the thoughts and actions that anger provokes.

The Primal Order of Anger

The *limbic system* ... does that ring a bell? No, it's not a dance you learned in the second grade. We touched on the limbic system in Chapter 2, in our discussion about the brain's pleasure pathway. Yep, now you've got it. It's the network of structures in the brain that regulates primal emotion.

def•i•ni•tion

> The **limbic system** is a network of structures and regions of the brain that regulate and process base emotions such as pleasure, pain, fear, and anger. Key components of the limbic system include the amygdala, hippocampus, hypothalamus, and parts of the prefrontal cortex. Limbic comes from a Latin term that means "edge."

The centerpiece of the limbic system, the amygdala, doesn't look much like anything important. It looks more like an almond a bit past its prime, tannish-gray in color and not quite an inch long, buried deep in the center of the brain. It registers our experiences with the outside world and encodes them for other structures of the limbic system to interpret. From the amygdala's perspective, fear and anger are one and the same. Pleasure and pain look pretty much the same as well.

One of these interpretive centers is the hippocampus, a brain structure only slightly more sophisticated than the amygdala. The amygdala sends biochemical messages to the hippocampus, which then creates an imprint—a primitive, basic form of memory. Each time the hippocampus receives the same message, it activates the imprint. By the time we're an adult, we have a substantial imprint library going.

Areas in our prefrontal cortex—the thinking part of our brain—also belong to the limbic system. They interpret the imprint and translate it into repetitive behaviors, a.k.a. habits. These behaviors engage whenever we're exposed to the imprint, sort of like tumblers in a combination lock. Over time we develop fairly complex behaviors related to anger, combinations of conditioning (remember B. F. Skinner from Chapter 9?) and cognition (thinking, reasoning, and analyzing).

Talk About It

The ability of advanced yoga practitioners to experience nirvana, an intense sense of peace and joy, has long mystified Western scientists. One theory is that the master yogi is able to use his or her conscious mind, in particular the prefrontal cortex, to stimulate the amygdala. This stimulation activates intense sensations of pleasure. This is the reverse of how the limbic system normally functions, in which the amygdala sends messages to the prefrontal cortex.

Though our limbic system and other brain structures process our experiences of and behaviors related to anger, these processes don't themselves *cause* anger. They're our responses to anger. Anger is an emotion, and like all emotions its origins are complex. Anger's intensity can be intimidating—even, or perhaps especially, when it's our own.

Your Anger Responses

Because so much of our anger responses occur without our conscious direction or even awareness, we don't have near the sense of how our anger looks as do other people in our lives. To try to see what they see, put yourself in the following situations and choose the answer that best fits.

1. If you ask people who are close to me and see me every day, they would tell you …

    a. I'm generally a happy person.

    b. I yell when I'm mad, but my anger blows over pretty fast and then, as far as I'm concerned, it's as though nothing happened.

    c. Nothing. I don't let people get close to me.

    d. They're afraid of me.

2. When something goes wrong and it's my fault, I …

    a. Blame someone else. Who says it's my fault?

    b. Try to fix it before anyone notices.

    c. Ignore the situation. Whoever finds it will take care of it.

    d. Let others know I made a mistake, apologize, and do what is necessary to correct the problem.

3. When I'm stuck in traffic for no apparent reason, I …

    a. Turn my radio to the local traffic advisory station to see how long the delay might be so I know whether to call my boss or my family to let them know I'll be late.

    b. Turn up the music, sit back, and think of pleasant things.

    c. Honk my horn and yell at the car in front of me. If everyone would do this, whatever's holding things up would get out of the way.

    d. Call my significant other to have him or her turn on the news or look on the Internet to find the source of the problem.

4. When I get to the check stand after standing in line for 20 minutes and the clerk tells me he can't do an exchange, I …

    a. Tell the people in line behind me that's an absurd policy and this is a stupid store.

    b. Ask if he can arrange for me to be next in line at the correct check stand, as I've already waited 20 minutes in this line.

    c. Throw the item on the counter and tell the clerk he can keep it and his money, too.

    d. Decide to come back another time because I have other things to do and the store right now is obviously busy.

5. Your boss calls you and a coworker into her office to announce her decision for who'll get a promotion. After telling you what a hard-working employee you are, she turns to your coworker and says, "Congratulations, you're the new supervisor!" You …

    a. Hold out your hand to your coworker and offer your congratulations, too.

    b. Say to your boss, "Are you kidding?!"

    c. Storm out of the office, yelling at the first person you encounter about what a @>#!##%!@# place this is to work.

    d. Smile, leave, and run to the bathroom where you burst into tears.

6. Your neighbor wins the lottery. When you see him on the evening news, holding up a ginormous check written for an equally ginormous sum of money, you …

    a. Start planning how you'll spend the part he'll share with you.

    b. Say out loud, "Why is it that the only people who win the lottery are the ones who don't need the money?" and throw the remote at the TV.

    c. Say out loud, "It's great to see someone win who really could use the money!" and change the channel to the show that's on next that you want to watch.

    d. Turn off the TV and stare at the dark screen.

7. The people across the street are having a party, and you notice the car of a guest is parked such that it partially blocks your driveway. You …

    a. Call the police. They didn't bother inviting you, why should you be nice to them?

    b. Bang on the door, and tell the person who answers, "Move the damn car!"

    c. Back around the car, there's still enough room for you to get out.

    d. Let the air out of the car's tires.

Talk About It

How much more grievous are the consequences of anger than the causes of it.

—Marcus Aurelius, Roman emperor

Any surprises? If 1-d, 2-a, 3-c, 4-c, 5-c, 6-b, or 7-b, were among your answers, your anger controls you in ways that others likely interpret as aggressive or violent. If 1-c, 2-c, 3-d, 4-a, 5-d, 6-d, or 7-d, you might have more issues with anger than you realize. Other responses suggest you've got a pretty good handle on situations that push your buttons, even when you do become angry.

What You Don't Know *Can* Hurt You

Unresolved, buried anger is like flooring the accelerator and the brake at the same time. Your car's not designed to rev in place, and neither is your body. Eventually something's going to blow—and sometimes in a big way.

At the first inkling of danger, the fight or flight or stress response mechanism floods your body with dozens of biochemicals that jack up your heart rate and blood pressure, divert blood flow to your muscles, and heighten your brain's ability to focus. These changes take place in the blink of an eye, though your body may stay on alert for as long as 20 minutes.

This doesn't sound so bad, at first. But if your entire day is a sequence of perceived dangers, stress hormones continually deluge your body. There's never a break. The physical consequences of this can include changes in your cells that give them increased resistance to the effects of stress hormones. It takes higher concentrations to get results. (Sound familiar?)

Steer Clear

Inappropriate anger can be a key symptom of conditions that affect the structure of the brain. Traumatic brain injury (TBI) and stroke can damage the prefrontal cortex and the brain's impulse control areas. A 2007 University of Florida study suggests long-term use of drugs, such as methamphetamine and ecstasy (MDMA), may cause the same kinds of damage.

The anger you keep bottled inside has all kinds of unpleasant effects on your body. Do you feel yourself breaking out in a sweat? Does your face turn red? Do you feel quivery or shaky inside when you're angry? These are effects of the stress hormones, cortisol and adrenaline. Persistently high levels of these hormones can cause high blood pressure (hypertension) and damage the cells that form the walls of your arteries. Over time, these kinds of changes can lead to other forms of heart disease. High blood pressure is a particular risk for stroke. When we speak of someone in a rage as "blowing a gasket," there may well be more truth in that than exaggeration!

Chronic anger is also emotionally destructive because it damages the relationships in your life. You can't establish and maintain loving, mutually supportive connections with others when you're suspicious of their motivations, believe they're treating you unfairly, or feel they're judging you. And you can't be calm within yourself when you feel agitated all the time.

The Many Faces of Anger

What does anger look like to you? Is it shouting, pushing, hitting? Is it crying, running away, avoiding people and situations that arouse anger in you? Expressions of anger don't always look like what we expect. Anger is all of these and more.

You may not even recognize anger as anger because it takes different—and, we might say, socially acceptable—forms when it surfaces. Anger may look like power, strength, bravado, ambition, determination—even caring and leadership. Anger is about control—control of situations and of other people. Because, as you remember, anger comes from fear and loss of control.

 Steer Clear

Physical violence is an extreme anger response that has serious and even dire consequences. Physical violence is never okay as a means of dealing with anger.

Everyone expresses anger in different ways, often depending on where we are and who we're with. Any of these behaviors can be signs of hidden anger bubbling below the surface of our conscious awareness:

- Procrastination of assigned tasks
- Sarcasm
- Irritability to things that don't bother other people
- Tapping our fingers
- Swirling our foot
- Jiggling or tapping our leg
- Criticism
- Complaining
- Arguing to always get the last word

Anger often lives in the past, thriving on feelings we have about things we can't change. Maybe these are things that have happened to us that we feel are unfair—an abusive childhood, being bullied in school, experiencing the death of a loved one, being passed over for an opportunity like a scholarship or a job. The events behind one's anger may go back years or even decades.

Resentment

A common witticism about resentment—feeling that someone's done something to you that you don't deserve or gotten something that's rightfully yours—is that it's like taking poison yourself and then expecting someone else to get sick. Resentment comes from unresolved anger and unmet expectations about what's fair. It targets other people and situations as the source of unfairness. Resentment thrives when you feel you've been wronged in some way, and that wrongness is the reason you perceive your life's in the toilet.

Alcoholics Anonymous considers resentment the leading obstacle to recovery because resentment keeps us anchored in the past. In resentment's grasp, we can't let go, we can't forgive, and we can't move on. Resentment has only one purpose: it holds us in the past. And the past is where all those old habits live.

When you're in the grasp of resentment, you look for opportunities for revenge rather than solutions leading to positive outcomes. It's a form of self-sabotage, really, because the only one who ends up getting hurt is you. Of course, resentment never lets you see it this way; resentment tells you it's someone else's fault.

It's Not Fair!

There's no argument here. Life's not fair. We may expect it to be, and we want it to be. Sometimes it is. But most of the time, it's not. How could it be, when we stop to think about it? What's fair to one person may not be fair to another; fairness is a very subjective experience.

Anger tends to be self-righteous. When we're angry, we feel *right*. We feel that others owe us something. Who those others are and what they owe us doesn't matter. This lets us feel powerful and in control. In this regard, anger appears to correct the balance of unfairness. It doesn't, really. But it feels that way to us at the time.

It's Not *My* Fault

Blame is a core characteristic of dysfunctional anger. *Someone* has to be at fault—and it's not going to be you! Sure, much of the time someone is at fault. But more often than not there's plenty of accountability to spread around. The problem with blame is that it puts the focus on people, not their actions. It makes everyone feel bad.

Shifting the focus to *what* happened, rather than who did it, puts the emphasis on finding a solution. Working toward shared goals pulls people together on the basis of what they have in common. Then everyone can feel good about being part of the answer.

Temper Tantrum

You're too old to throw a temper tantrum. Or are you? Think about it. When you yell, throw things, storm around, slam your hands against your desk, punch the wall, kick the chair, does this look much different from a toddler thrashing and screaming on the floor in the ice cream aisle of the grocery store? Except you probably don't have an arm wrapped around a teddy bear.

The toddler throwing a tantrum doesn't understand what she's doing; she just does it. She's tired, frustrated, bored, unhappy, and not getting what she wants. She may have learned that screaming and throwing things will get her out of situations she doesn't want to be in, like grocery shopping. Carrying her out of the store reinforces the perception that the tantrum's a successful method.

Talk About It

Anger is never without a reason, but seldom with a good one.

—Benjamin Franklin, American philosopher and inventor

As we grow up, we care more about what other people think about our actions. Our tantrums take different forms. We may give the cold shoulder or use sarcasm. When we do yell and throw things, it's usually in private. These actions are not quite as conspicuous as throwing ourselves on the floor but are just as effective. Because other people don't like them, we get what we want when we use them.

Anger, the response, becomes anger, the habit. It takes place without conscious effort. As with any other habit, once we become aware of our thoughts and actions, we can make choices about them. We can choose to yell at someone who wrongs us, or we can look for ways to make the experience positive. We can ride the wave of our anger until it dissipates, just like we surf urges related to our old habits.

Managing Your Anger

Anger, in and of itself, is neither good nor bad. It exists. The ways you respond to anger have positive and negative consequences. Those responses become problems when they're destructive. There are ways to constructively release frustration and anger so these feelings do not hurt you or others.

Even though you've got a brainful of anger imprints, you also have the ability to think before you act. The first step in overriding those imprints is to notice the behaviors you engage in when you become angry.

This is the most challenging step for most people, first, because these behaviors are so automatic and so ingrained that sometimes we can't see them until someone else points them out, and second, because confronting our own anger means facing fear and hurt. It means looking beneath the surface of our interactions with others. And it means letting go of damaging thoughts and actions that we've been carrying around with us.

Breathe

Remember the technique of focusing your attention on your breath until your thoughts calm and your body relaxes? This brings you into mindful awareness of your physical surroundings and the responses of your body. It's a great way to gain some distance on anger so you can respond with constructive, rather than destructive, behaviors.

> **Steer Clear**
>
> There's a popular perception that "venting" or "blowing off steam" by punching a pillow or throwing something across the room is a safe way to release anger. Recent studies suggest that such venting fuels, rather than subdues, the intensity of our feelings.

Anger exists in the heat of the moment. Methods like counting to 10 or waiting a full minute before responding are techniques that break the flow of your emotions, sort of like flipping a light switch off and then back on. It's simple, but effective. Use this pause for a moment of mindful reflection: what is it about the event that punches your buttons?

Does this particular person always get on your nerves, no matter what he or she says or does? Is this a situation that always raises your blood pressure?

When your answer to these two questions is "yes," you can be pretty sure it's not the situation that's causing you to feel angry. Start digging; you've got to get to the bottom of this. When you do, you might be surprised to discover it's more a molehill-to-mountain kind of thing. The true issue may not even exist anymore or may at least be something you can resolve.

Timeout

Maybe you're more familiar with putting your kids on timeout. But this is a technique that works well with adults, too. You can give yourself a timeout. Or you can arrange with the people who are close to you, the people who live with you, to call a timeout.

A timeout removes you from whatever's setting off your anger. It gives you time away from the situation or person to gather your thoughts and make conscious choices about what actions to take. You may decide, after you cool off, that the situation isn't even worth a response. Or you may be able to identify what, precisely, pushed your buttons. You can then calmly and rationally discuss this with others involved in the situation.

Take a Hike

Anger revs your body for action. So give it some! Go for a run, swim, or bike ride. Shoot some hoops. Take a brisk walk. If you can't get away when anger strikes, run in place. Do jumping jacks. At the very least, pace around your desk or up and down the hall.

Such productive expressions help dissipate the rush of hormones that floods your body when you become angry. Physical activity helps relieve the tension you feel in your body and thoughts, and you get the added benefit of sustained exercise. Plus, it gets you away from the situation so you can think through your response before making it.

Your body's anger response sends a torrent of hormones and other biochemicals surging through your system, firing up nearly every cell in your body. This call to arms has your body ready for intense physical action—fight or flight. All too often we forget the "flight" part of this equation! But the result is the same; you take action that removes you from the perceived danger. The more intense your physical effort, the more rapidly you use up all those action molecules. Your body chemistry returns to normal.

Ask Yourself: How Much Does This Really Matter?

Someone, or something, has punched your buttons. You're all fired up, right on the verge of doing your angry dance. Stop! If you just let it go, let the moment pass without responding to it, what will happen? Is your life in danger? Is someone else's life in danger? What, really, is at risk here—besides your temper and control, of course.

We tend to get so focused on not letting someone get away with something that we lose sight of what "something" actually is. What's actually at stake? If we do let that something pass, what's the worst that can happen? How much will this situation matter tomorrow, next week, next year? Odds are, not much. We'll likely not even remember it—unless our anger generates a response we regret.

Now flip the question: what's the *best* that could happen? You probably don't think about that when you're frothing at the mouth. But maybe, just maybe, you could turn the emotions of the situation into a mutually agreeable solution. That could be truly unforgettable!

Analyze This

For this exercise you need a small notebook, a pen, and four different color highlighters.

Pick *one* set of circumstances that arouses anger in you every time you encounter it, which you frequently do. Maybe it's the security receptionist who makes you show your full identification every morning when you come to work, like he's never seen you before. Maybe it's the morning traffic, the line at the grocery store when only one checker's working, the persistent notices about a bill you paid long ago. There's certainly no shortage of anger-inducing circumstances for any of us! The only challenge for this exercise is to pick only one.

In the notebook, write a description of the circumstance on the first page. Explain it as though you're telling someone who knows nothing about it. Tell what happens, who does what, how you feel, what you say and do. Now take a colored highlighter and mark all the words and phrases that are about someone else. Then take a different color and mark the words and phrases that are about you. Next use a third color to highlight all the passages that identify events within your ability to change. Finally, use the fourth color to highlight the circumstances you cannot change.

Look at the highlights that identify someone else and things you cannot change. Are these the circumstances that make you see red? Look at the highlights that identify you and what you can change. How do you feel when you read these passages? Step outside the circumstance and view it as though it's someone else's problem. What could you change, and how?

Mark the passages, and on another page in your notebook, write the changes you could make. Choose one, and the next time you encounter this circumstance, implement the change. In your notebook, write down how the experience changes. Over time, do this for all the change points you identified, and write your observations about how you feel and how the situation unfolds in your notebook.

When the Target Is on *Your* Back

We all find ourselves on the receiving end of anger, too. Someone else's angry words and actions may provoke anger in us. After all, anger coming at us is something our limbic system definitely perceives as a threat. At first this seems like a double whammy: we've got to defuse someone else's anger as well as manage our own.

Keep in mind the only behavior you can control and change is your own—your reactions and responses. When someone comes at you in anger, you can use your own behavior to keep yourself calm. Anger expects anger; this is part of the "I'm bigger and badder than you" nature of anger as a protective mechanism. When you meet someone else's anger with compassionate calm, it throws off the balance of the intended confrontation.

 Steer Clear

If someone's anger physically threatens you, protect yourself. Leave the situation. Call 911. You cannot reason with anger that's become violent. Someone else's violence is not your fault.

When someone comes at you in anger, try these responses:

◆ Say nothing as long as the other person rants and raves. Try to hear the words.

◆ If the person is swearing, calling you names, or otherwise being abusive to you, hold up your hand and say, "I want to listen to you, but I can't because your words are attacks. Please say what you have to say without attacking me."

◆ Focus on your breath to remain mindful and in the moment and to calm your own anger response.

◆ When you begin to talk, keep the volume of your voice low. Any time the other person talks over you, stop talking.

◆ Acknowledge the other person's intense feelings, but focus on the message of what he or she is saying. If it's something you've said or done that's angered the person, focus on the words or actions.

◆ If the person continues to be abusive or you feel your own anger building, say, "Clearly this is very important and very emotional. Let's take a timeout and come back to talk about it in 10 minutes." Then leave the room; take a walk outside if you can.

Anger is tough to confront, in other people as well as in yourself. Keep in mind that the issues which arouse anger are usually long-standing. Even though anger gives the perception of immediacy, these issues have accumulated over time; they're not new to either of you. You have plenty of time to address and resolve them. You don't have to deal with them right now, this very instant. Give yourself enough emotional distance to be able to focus on the issues and your feelings about them so you can talk constructively about them in ways that move toward resolution.

Forgive, Let Go, Move On

If anger's so bad for us, why hasn't evolution dulled its edge? Actually, it's given us a way to do that ourselves. Through the thousands of years of human existence, the part of the brain that thinks has gotten larger and more complex. We still have those primal survival instincts (who knows when we might need them), but we also have the ability to consciously choose how to respond when they're activated. We're smarter than our prehistoric ancestors.

You can't change what's already happened in your life. The past is just that—the past. Its actions are done; its people are gone; its events are over. You know this, of course, but still, it's hard to let go. But you can't move on until you do. The last thing you feel like doing when someone's done you wrong (for real or only in your perception) is cut him any slack. Why should you let him off the hook after he's hurt you? Because keeping him on the hook hurts you more. To forgive doesn't mean you forget. It only means you release the person and the event. Your life is ahead of you, not behind you.

The Least You Need to Know

◆ Anger is a primal emotion that arouses survival behaviors within us.

◆ Awareness and learned skills give us the ability to choose how we respond to anger.

◆ Unresolved anger or the inability to manage anger is a major risk for relapse.

◆ Moving beyond anger means letting go of perceived wrongs and forgiving people who've hurt us in the past.

Chapter 17

Breaking Ties

In This Chapter

- ◆ Balancing the old and the new
- ◆ Does your job fit you?
- ◆ There's always time to plan
- ◆ Live in the moment

Changing your life is no easy task. Maybe it could be if you lived on a deserted island and had no one to be accountable for, or to, except yourself. But you don't. Life doesn't work that way, at least not life as we know it!

Instead, you live within any number of social circles—family, work, friends, hobbies, and other interests. In many cases the people in your circles are eager to see you succeed with your changes by offering encouragement, support, and opportunities. They're willing, and able, to change the ways they interact with you and maybe even make the same kinds of changes themselves. It's wonderful when things work out that way.

Sometimes, however, the framework of your life doesn't quite support the new you. You're a different person now—the genuine article. Some, maybe many, of your life's building blocks came into existence to support the old you and now don't fit very well with your new life.

Same Life, Different Fit

For all the changing you're doing, you probably look pretty much like the same old you. You're more confident and calm, of course; you have less stress in your life with your old habit gone. And you're healthier, too, especially if you've gotten your weight down or stopped smoking or drinking. For the most part, though, if someone who's not seen you for 5 or 10 years ran into you on the street, she'd recognize you. However, you're not the same person you were back then, and you know it.

Wouldn't it be great if we could be simultaneously different and the same? If we could change a few habits, like we change the style of our furniture or wardrobe every so often, and just keep on with life the way it's always been? We work hard to get things just the way we like them, so it seems a shame to have to throw all that away and start again from scratch.

But part of what we like or used to like is what we've already thrown away: the old habit. So how much of what remains still wants to support that old habit, and how much can we adapt to fit our new lifestyle?

Out with the Old

During preparations to shed your old habit, you may have made or are now making changes to your home environment. These changes might mean:

♦ If you used to smoke, going room to room to clear away ashtrays, matches, lighters, packs of cigarettes, and the like and cleaning draperies, carpets, and furniture to remove as much of the smell of smoke as possible.

♦ If you used to overeat, going through cabinets, drawers, and the fridge, to replace unhealthy snacks with healthy ones and going through your car, your hobby room or workshop, the garage, and other places to get rid of stashed goodies.

♦ If you used to shop till you dropped, shredding your credit cards, store sale mailers, and coupons.

♦ If you used to use drugs or abuse prescription drugs, finding and destroying all drugs and paraphernalia.

♦ If you used to gamble, throwing away lottery tickets, casino tokens, and gaming coupons as well as removing all gambling sites from your computer's web favorites.

- ◆ If you're abstaining from drinking, not keeping alcohol in the house "in case guests drop by who drink."

- ◆ If you used to be a couch potato, cutting back or turning off the cable or satellite service and setting up areas to work on hobbies, read, exercise, and indulge interests other than television.

It's almost like cleaning your house to get ready for guests when you don't want them to see any evidence of the secret life of those old habits. Except that instead of stashing your secrets away in hiding places so you can retrieve them when the guests leave, you're clearing them out for good.

Steer Clear

Don't flush those drugs! Although for decades flushing was the recommended way to get rid of outdated and unwanted drugs, recent studies show that all those chemicals end up in the water sources that supply our drinking water. As well, those drugs can have adverse effects on fish who consume them and on creatures that consume the fish. Experts suggest that until there's a better solution, we should soak or crush pills and tablets and empty out capsules into a small amount of water. Then pour the mixture into a container with cat litter or used coffee grounds, seal, and throw into the garbage.

When you live alone, cleansing your environment of connections to your old habit is pretty straightforward. When you live with others, things get trickier. Others in the home may engage in some of those same old habits and are not making the same changes as you are. They may simply not understand why it's so important for you to have a clean environment that supports your changes.

In with the New

You know, of course, that giving up the old habit is only part of the change process. You're also bringing new habits into your life, habits that support a healthy, productive lifestyle. You may buy a bicycle, weight machine, or other exercise products; stock the kitchen with fruits, vegetables, and whole-grain foods; and buy books, jigsaw puzzles, and other forms of entertainment.

Though these new items replace those you've purged, they may require some other changes to your home or apartment. If you've always watched television in your living room, you may need new lamps for reading. If you've always eaten dinner on the sofa, you may want to buy a dining table and chairs. If you've taken up bicycling or tai chi, you may want to buy books and magazines about them.

Mindfulness and meditation, yoga, or other contemplative practices may now be part of your daily life. Do you have a quiet, comfortable location in your home where you can go to relax and become at peace with yourself? It doesn't need to be anything fancy, but you do need such a retreat.

People Who Need People

Compared to the relationships in your life, clearing out your home is the easy part. People are much more complex and sometimes unpredictable in their reactions. Those you count as your closest allies may actually be unhappy about your changes and sabotage your efforts or outright declare their lack of support (see Chapters 12 and 13).

> ### Talk About It
>
> A lot of people are afraid to say what they want. That's why they don't get what they want.
> —Madonna, American singer and actress

Your changes might cause others to feel uncomfortable, especially if they have the same old habits and aren't changing them. They may openly pressure you to return to your old ways or keep items (cigarettes, beer, cookies) around the house that expose you to major temptation.

You may feel pressure from other people in your life simply because they've always pressured you, but you've escaped from your feelings about it through your old habits. Now that buffer's gone, and you're left with the reality of someone else's unpleasant behaviors. You may feel you don't even know the other person, and he or she may feel the same about you.

Perhaps criticism and blame have become part of the pattern between you and your significant other. Maybe, as Chapter 13 discusses, you've established relationships based mostly or entirely on sharing the old habit. Now that the old habit's gone, nothing holds the relationship together. To figure out these things takes time, but then they sort of hit you in the face. But stay calm; you have plenty of time to reason things through and make the right decisions for the right reasons.

Heigh Ho, Heigh Ho

How goes it at work? Do your coworkers and your boss know about the changes you're making in your personal life? If so, do they support them? In what ways? You may encounter the same kinds of challenges from your coworkers and boss as you face with close friends and family. Those who shared in the old habit are likely less than thrilled that you've given it up, especially if it was the common bond between you, like taking smoke breaks together or going out for beer and pizza on Fridays.

People who encouraged you to make changes in your life are probably delighted with your progress, and even if you kept your old habit from your coworkers and boss, they're certain to notice something is different about you.

Laws and regulations help keep many temptations out of the workplace, so at least you've got a bit of a sanctuary there. Most workplaces prohibit drug and alcohol use (and may even test employees for violations for safety or security purposes); ban cigarette smoking in the building; and frown upon, if they don't outright proscribe, eating anywhere other than the lunchroom, break room, cafeteria, or off the premises.

> **Steer Clear**
>
> Gambling in the workplace can be a gray area. Though you probably can't get up a game of Texas Hold 'Em, there may be a football pool, raffle fundraiser, or other activities that involve betting.

I Love My Job!

When you enjoy your job, going to work is a big plus in your life. You feel fulfilled, connected, and productive. Positive contributions and recognition are big morale boosters, which are especially important if you're struggling at all with depression and low self-esteem in other areas of your life.

Work is an entirely different world from home or other social settings. Your work may be the setting where you can express your creative side, your analytical side, or your compassionate side. You may have passion about your work that you don't have about, or that you don't have opportunity to express in, other parts of your life. People in your personal life often are surprised when they see you in your work life.

Job Distress

However, workplace issues can create enormous stress. It seems everybody's trying to do more with less, and employees bear the brunt of this. You spend more of your waking hours at work than anyplace else. When your job's not working for you, it creates more stress than satisfaction in your life, and we don't need to tell you that the last thing you need is more stress.

So step back for a moment, and take an objective look at your job. Why do you have this particular job? How long have you been in this job? Have you had other jobs for the same employer? What are your opportunities for moving up or learning more? Do you feel you get paid what you're worth for the work you do and that your company appreciates the work you do?

Survey after survey tells us the single-most important factor in job satisfaction is the sense that our work has meaning and connects us with a larger purpose than the daily tasks we perform. Do you have such a sense about your job? And here's the million-dollar question: what's the one thing that could change in this job that would make it a job you want to keep? What you answer to this question is not nearly as important as whether you *can* answer it.

Take your time answering these questions and the additional questions that'll come to you the more you think about it. You might want to write each question at the top of a piece of paper, then jot down the thoughts that come to you. Allow this to be a free association process (remember this Freudian approach from Chapter 9?) that continues for a week. Then look at what you've written. Do you see any themes emerging?

Breaking Up Is Hard to Do

When you reach the recognition that you've got to pull away from parts of your previous life, you may feel a sense of relief. You may have worried—and rightfully so—that returning to those parts of your life would pull you back to your old habit. It's also kind of scary to put the rubber to the road, so to speak. In the beginning of your change process, all the thinking and talking about a new life that you do sounds really enchanting. Finally, you can see the way to the life you've always wanted. Now that you're on the path of that new life, the reality of your decisions can feel rather harsh.

Steer Clear

If you are experiencing emotional or physical abuse in your current situation, seek help without delay. All communities have some level of support for such circumstances. Abusive situations are the most challenging to escape and the highest risk for relapsing to your old habits. And they're dangerous, with the potential to put your health and even your life at stake.

No matter what you must do, take the time to do it in the right way. Don't rush into more major changes. Think things through. Avoid rash actions that could create hardships for you. If you can't afford to live without a job, don't quit your current one until you have a new one in place. Have another place to live lined up before you walk out of a relationship that'll put you out of your home. Make a plan, then carry it out. In the same way you've changed your behaviors around your old habit, take it one step at a time.

Leaving a Relationship

When you've tried your best to make things work and they just don't, the only option left may be to leave or ask your partner to leave. Depending on your circumstances, you may need to consider legal issues—shared property, children, joint finances, and other factors. Most communities have legal aid services that can provide you with general advice.

Leaving can be temporary or permanent. You may decide you just need some space, so you can figure out if and how you two now fit together. You might use your time apart to realize what you want in a relationship and whether each of you meets the needs of the other.

Your partner may decide to give up the old habits, too. Not to look a gift horse in the mouth here, but you need to determine whether this is a genuine desire to change or a ploy to get you to return. You might agree to stay apart until the other person follows through. As you already know, it's far more of a challenge to walk the talk than it is to talk the walk. This is the time for you to be selfish; your life is on the line, and you need to protect the progress you've made.

Take This Job and ...

You may be in your current job for a whole lot of reasons that have nothing to do with your interests or skills. It might have been the only job you could hold down when you were struggling with your old habit. Maybe it's a job you've had long enough that your employer cuts you slack. Maybe you feel loyal to the company but don't quite know why.

Earlier we asked some questions about your job. If you haven't answered them, do that before you make any decisions about your job. You want to make choices for the right reasons. If you do decide to leave your current job, do so with grace and by following all the proper procedures. Even in the worst of situations, you never know what the future holds and how other people might come back into your life. In other words, cross the bridge, but don't burn it behind you!

This could be the perfect opportunity for you to switch careers entirely. If you could have any job in the world, what would you choose? Do you have any qualifications for it already? Could you acquire the qualifications by taking classes, apprenticing, going back to school, or learning on your own? Sometimes simply expressing your interest is good enough for someone to take you on and give you a chance.

The Great Importance of Small Things

When you live in the grip of an addictive habit, the habit consumes all your experience of the world. You see, hear, taste, feel, and smell only what relates to the habit. When you break free from that grip, your experience of the world instantly changes. The cliché, stop and smell the roses, takes on profound meaning because at last, you can do just that.

In this book, we talk a lot about mindfulness—allowing your feelings to simply *be*. Instead of letting you live in your memories and your fears—in your head, as it were— or in your old habit, mindfulness pulls you into the moment. Life exists in the moment, in the details of all the little things that happen in the course of a minute, an hour, a day. These are the details that go by mostly unnoticed unless you take the time and make the effort to pay attention.

At first these details might overwhelm you. You're not used to noticing them, even though they've been there all along. But reconnecting with them is what life's all about. The details of every day give purpose and satisfaction to life. Your old habit replaced them with details of its own, and your life focused on them. Without those old habit details, you're free to again enjoy living in the moment.

Master Gardening

Nothing puts you more in the moment than nurturing a garden. It's very grounding (no pun intended) to bury your fingers in the soil, to turn the earth with your hands. Gardening is a classic *metaphor* for life, of course. But it's also a great way to immerse yourself in the details of the moment. Work-ing in the garden occupies your body and your mind. At the end of your work, you can see the progress of your efforts. The flowers and fruits that result are delayed rewards. It's a true antidote for feeling discouraged about a sense of standstill in your life.

def•i•ni•tion

A **metaphor** is a phrase or concept that creates an image as a means of explanation or understanding.

A garden reflects the attention to detail that you give it. If you work daily in your garden to keep it watered, fertilized, and cleared of weeds, your garden will flourish. You can establish a garden anywhere—in a window box, in a yard, even indoors. Plant things that smell good and look pretty, things that give you pleasure to watch grow and bloom. Every day you'll see another leaf, another bud.

Whether it's a sizeable plot of land with paths you can walk to enjoy the plantings, an arrangement of potted plants on the deck, or even a few flowers in a sunny room in your home, a garden is a place of retreat and refuge from the pressures and stresses of family, work, and just making it through the day. You might find your garden the ideal place to meditate or simply sort through your thoughts.

Oh, for a Dog's Life!

Looking for an ever-attentive ear, a sympathetic listener who never complains that the conversations are one-sided or always about you? (Who's not?) Consider adopting a cat or a dog from your local animal shelter. One of the best benefits of having a pet is unconditional love. (Alan's cat is named Dharma; we'll let you figure out the symbolism.) Your pet loves you because you're *you*. Your pet attaches no strings, no demands, and no pressures to its love for you. (Well, none beyond those related to basic care needs like food, water, shelter, and potty.)

You can talk to your pet without fear of judgment. How wonderful it is to see that attentive posture riveted on you! Having a pet also helps maintain structure in your life, a sense of schedule. You can't feel too sorry for yourself with a purring cat curled in your lap, or a dog resting its head against your foot.

Talk About It _____

Pets are our best friends for good reason. In a 2002 study, researchers at the University of New York–Buffalo suggest that talking to your dog or cat relieves stress better than talking with a partner or friend. The reason, according to study participants, is that dogs and cats don't judge what you say or do—they simply enjoy being with you.

It's hard to feel bored or lonely when you have a dog or a cat. (Less interactive pets, like fish, don't provide quite the same bond of companionship.) Pets need interaction and play—get some toys. For a dog, get a leash and collar or harness and take your canine friend out walking a few times a day even if you have a fenced yard. The exercise and companionship are good for the both of you. And dog parks are great places to meet new people.

If nothing else, buy some books or borrow some from the library and read up on your pet. Examine the many different kinds of pet foods on the market, and choose ones that offer the greatest health benefits. Caring for another living creature in this way is very satisfying.

Coulda, Woulda, Shoulda ... Get Over It!

If you had a nickel for every regret in your life, how wealthy would you be? Maybe not enough to quit your day job but perhaps enough to need the services of a financial planner? Regrets are like reverse resentments—we direct them at ourselves. And we all carry quite a stock of them. What are your three greatest regrets? Fill in the blanks:

I could've _____, but I didn't because _____.

I would've _____, but I didn't because _____.

I should've _____, but I didn't because _____.

How long have you been carrying these regrets? Many regrets are old baggage. Is there anything you can do to change these situations? Surprisingly, sometimes you can remedy a regret, particularly if it's one in which you did someone wrong. It's never to late to apologize, and doing so may not only help you move beyond your regret but also help the other person move past his or her resentment.

Most of the time, however, what's done is done and there's nothing you can change. Maybe you missed an application deadline and didn't get into the college you wanted.

Maybe your alarm clock didn't go off and you were late for an interview, costing you a job. For many things, there's often no "do-over" button in life.

And when you think about it, not all regrets are really worth regretting. As the saying goes, when one door closes, another door opens. Okay, sometimes only a window, but the point remains that other opportunities became available to you. For those three greatest regrets you just identified, what happened instead of what you had hoped or planned? Lots of good things can be said about where you are in your life, even when more road lies ahead.

Be Mindful _____

What do you do best? Are you doing it? Each morning when you get up, make a list of three things you want to do that day simply because you enjoy them and are good at them. Then do them!

Life Takes Practice

You didn't just wake up one morning to find yourself where you are in life, even though it might feel that way. You followed any number of steps, twists, and turns to get here. Now you're in a place where you can experience the journey of your life as it unfolds.

When you feel panicky, pause. There's very little, in the course of everyday events, that can't wait five minutes for you to calm yourself. The rush to act was a cornerstone of your old habit; now that's gone. Whether you're responding to the demands of others or to an unexpected urge, be clear about what you're doing and why. After all, this is _your_ life.

The Least You Need to Know

- The relationships that currently exist in your life may no longer support the changes you're making.

- You have time to evaluate the circumstances of your life and to plan further changes. Take it!

- A pet is a nonjudgmental listener who may help reduce stress and provide companionship.

- Notice and enjoy the details of life; live in the moment.

Chapter **18**

The Stress of Being at Risk All the Time

In This Chapter

- ◆ Stress affects your body and your brain
- ◆ The relationship between stress and relapse
- ◆ Down and out or wound up and worried?
- ◆ Developing your own stress-busting behaviors

You have more than enough stress in your daily life with all the pressures you face from family, work, friends, and even neighbors. Everybody wants something from you, and they want it right now (or yesterday). On top of all this, you constantly worry about being just that close to giving in when an unexpected urge strikes. You must always think about what you're doing and why you're doing it. Will you *ever* catch a break?

The short answer is yes, the pressure will eventually ease. You have a lot on your plate right now; the changes you're making in your life would be enough just by themselves. But, of course, you don't live in a vacuum, so you've got real life to contend with as well. But you're fairly new into this process, so it still requires a lot of your attention.

And we must be honest—real life might always require more attention than you're accustomed to giving to such things. Addictive habits like to sneak up on you, so you'll always need to be on the lookout for that. And the potential to slip back into the old habit will always lurk in the shadows, but you'll get better sensing that it's there and knowing what steps you need to take to stay out of its reach.

What Is Stress?

A certain amount of stress is healthy and even necessary. When you walk or run, for example, you put physical stress on your bones that stimulates bone cells to build new bone tissue, strengthening your skeleton. Too much stress can cause damage; running too hard can result in stress fractures.

Emotional stress pressures your feelings and thoughts. Your emotions exist within a different kind of stress that's more like shifting tensions to maintain balance. The levels of neurotransmitters and other biochemicals increase and decrease with your changing moods.

When you have experiences that activate primal emotions—fear, anger, pain, and pleasure—your body's fight or flight response comes into play (see Chapter 16). This fight or flight mechanism creates physical and emotional stress so you can take the appropriate action to escape danger.

Stress becomes dysfunctional when it's at such a constant level that your fight or flight mechanism never shuts down. Your mind and body are running too hard, all the time. And something's gotta give.

What Happens in Your Body

Your limbic system, a network of mostly primitive brain structures, monitors your experiences with the outside world. When it perceives any experiences putting you at risk, it sounds the alert, sending biochemical and nerve messages throughout your body. The first responders are your *adrenal glands*, which release a flood of adrenaline and cortisol.

def•i•ni•tion

Your **adrenal glands** are a pair of endocrine structures that rest one on top of each kidney. The adrenal glands produce the hormones cortisol, adrenaline, noradrenaline, aldosterone, and small amounts of testosterone.

Adrenaline (also called epinephrine) stimulates the cardiovascular system, and your heart rate, breathing rate, and blood pressure shoot up. Cortisol stimulates the release of stored sugars (glucose) and diverts it to the muscles to give your body energy (adrenaline has some role in this, too). Cortisol also shuts down nonessential functions like digestion, which is one reason you feel like puking when you've had a major scare.

What Happens in Your Brain

Your body's stress response also changes the biochemical balance in your brain. Levels of dopamine, adrenaline, and noradrenaline go up to enhance communication among brain neurons in the parts of your brain responsible for analytical reasoning. Levels of serotonin, a calming neurotransmitter, drop.

Though you become sharper with logical thinking, you won't likely remember much about the decisions you make. Because cortisol redirects glucose to your muscles, less glucose gets through to "nonessential" brain structures like the hippocampus, which forms short-term memories. Perhaps in the evolutionary design, there was no need to remember if there was a question about whether you'd even survive! At least it explains why, in times of extreme stress, people often cannot remember what happened; their hippocampus doesn't have enough energy to run memory tasks.

When Your Stress Response Gets Stuck

Scientists have many theories about why the stress response may remain active long after the perceived threat goes away. All we know for sure, however, is that sometimes the mechanism malfunctions. Instead of returning to normal levels, cortisol and adrenaline levels in the blood circulation stay high, which keeps the stress response active.

Some studies suggest people who have addictive habits are more susceptible to the effects of prolonged stress, and their levels of cortisol and adrenaline remain higher. This combination seems to increase the frequency and intensity of cravings, which may be one explanation for why, after so successfully resisting temptation for a long time, you have a particularly stressful day or week and suddenly give in. Before you know what happened, you're on the wrong side of a relapse.

Stress and Relapse

When people relapse, stress nearly always plays a leading role. Stress causes us to call on our coping skills. But our coping skills are already getting a pretty good workout, helping us stay on our path of change and a few steps ahead of relapse. We can't be watching *everything*—and don't think that old habit fails to notice.

When we can't pay as much attention to them, urges and cravings can get the upper hand on those coping skills. It's like taking four toddlers shopping and having three throw tantrums. While we're tending to the three thrashing around on the floor, the fourth is having a grand time taste-testing cookies and otherwise getting into mischief. What we really want to do is throw ourselves on the floor, too!

Getting to the bottom of what's causing us stress provides a great amount of relief. Once we know what the problem is, we can take action to change it, even if all that we change is our attitude toward the situation. Of course, we can't always change every circumstance that makes us unhappy. But just often enough to keep us thinking about it, we can. And what a difference that makes!

Complicating Factors

Studies tell us that up to two thirds of people who have addictive behaviors also have depression or anxiety. Clinicians call these *comorbidities*. Many of the problem habits we develop are attempts to either make us feel happier or make it easier for us to ignore that we're unhappy. Alan and other addictive behavior specialists refer to this as self-medicating, whether the habit is a substance like alcohol or a behavior like gambling or stress eating.

def•i•ni•tion

> **Comorbidities,** also called comorbid conditions or co-occurring disorders, are health conditions that coexist or are present at the same time. There may be direct or indirect connections among the conditions, though not always.

When these feel-good habits are the ones you've put behind you, anxiety and depressive disorders may again surface, bringing with them feelings of emptiness, sadness, hurt, guilt, fear, worry, and hopelessness. Even as much as you enjoy being the new you, these old feelings can pull you down. The symptoms of anxiety and depression are added stresses, and other stresses in your life make the symptoms worse. It becomes a cycle.

Some experts believe depression and anxiety are related conditions, with depression at one end of the spectrum and anxiety at the other. Though researchers don't yet know the exact causes and mechanisms of depression and anxiety disorders, they seem to be a blend of environmental (stressful things that happen to you) and biochemical (neurotransmitter changes that occur in your brain) causes. Genetic factors may also be at play, as both depression and anxiety tend to run in families.

Treatment for depression and anxiety may include medication as well as methods like mindfulness and meditation. Mindfulness helps increase one's awareness of his feelings (symptoms) and meditation helps a person become calm and centered within. There are many options for treatment, so work together with your health-care provider to find the ones that are best for you.

Having healthy eating habits, regularly engaging in physical activity, and participating in other activities you enjoy can further improve the way you feel. Counseling and psychotherapy are also helpful methods to acquire insights into the possible underlying causes of your symptoms.

 **Steer Clear**

Depression and anxiety disorders are not conditions one can simply power through. They result from multiple causes, including imbalances in the brain's biochemicals. Untreated, the symptoms of these disorders tend to worsen and create more stress, which increases the risk for relapse.

Beyond Blue: Depression

We tend to view being depressed as a circumstance of feeling sad or having the blues. Everyone feels down at times. But when those feelings are intense and continue for longer than a couple weeks (especially when we can't relate them to any particular experience in our lives), we could be suffering from depression.

Depression is a potentially serious health condition that often accompanies major life shifts though may occur for no apparent reason. You may've had depression all along but your addictive habit masked the symptoms. The processes of coming to grips with the old habit and sending it packing have kept you too busy to pay attention to much else. But now that you've been free of that old habit for a while, the depression is free to emerge.

How Blue Are You?

We all get the blues every now and then. But when feelings of sadness and hopelessness define your daily life, depression could be pulling you down. How many signs or symptoms of depression do you have? Choose the answer that is closest to how often you experience each.

1. I feel sad or hopeless, like I've lost something important to me and won't ever get it back.

    a. Never or rarely.

    b. Once or twice a week.

    c. Every morning when I wake up.

    d. All the time.

2. I cry for no reason.

    a. Never or rarely.

    b. Once or twice a week.

    c. At some point every day.

    d. Often enough that other people ask me what's wrong.

3. Everything, and everyone, in my daily life irritates me.

    a. Never or rarely.

    b. Once or twice a week.

    c. At some point every day.

    d. Often enough that other people ask each other what kind of mood I'm in before approaching me.

4. I don't want to do anything except lie on the couch with the curtains closed.

    a. Never or rarely.

    b. Once or twice a week.

    c. At some point every day.

    d. All the time.

5. I'm tired but I can't sleep, or all I do is sleep but I never feel rested.

    a. Never or rarely.

    b. Once or twice a week.

    c. At some point every day.

    d. All the time.

6. I feel guilty, like I've done something terribly wrong.

    a. Never or rarely.

    b. Once or twice a week.

    c. At some point every day.

    d. All the time.

7. I weigh 20 pounds more or 20 pounds less than I did this time last year.

    a. No, my weight stays pretty steady.

    b. I don't want to talk about my weight.

    c. My weight goes up and down.

    d. It's at least 20 pounds.

8. I feel numb and emotionless, like the world is passing me by and I don't care.

    a. Never or rarely.

    b. Once or twice a week.

    c. At some point every day.

    d. Pretty much all the time.

9. Activities I used to enjoy no longer interest me.

    a. Not true.

    b. Everyone gets tired of the same old stuff.

    c. I don't know, anymore, what I enjoy.

    d. What activities?

10. I wonder what purpose there is in my life.

    a. Never or rarely.

    b. Once or twice a week.

    c. At some point every day.

    d. All the time.

If four or more of your answers were "c" or "d," perhaps you should have your doctor evaluate you for clinical depression. If six or more of your answers were "b" and your answers remain the same in two or three weeks, depression is something you should consider. If most of your answers are "a," you likely have a pretty even-keeled balance in your emotional responses, and depression is probably not a concern for you.

> **Steer Clear** _____
>
> Foods high in processed carbohydrates, like cookies and chips, raise the levels of serotonin in the brain. Serotonin is a neurotransmitter that elevates mood. Some researchers believe people who crave such foods might have an imbalance of serotonin in their brain chemistry that results in mild to moderate depression. Comfort foods might truly cause them to feel better in highly stressful situations, for the short term. Other researchers believe carb cravings are symptoms of food addictions. Getting enough sleep and physical activity are other ways to boost serotonin levels.

Fear and Worry: Anxiety Disorders

We tend to feel fear and worry in situations that are unfamiliar or that we anticipate could be unpleasant, like having to speak in front of a group or having a root canal. This makes sense; these feelings are supposed to protect us from harm. Ordinarily, the emotions fade when the situation responsible for them is over.

But sometimes fear, worry, and related feelings become constant and intense, preventing us from engaging in certain activities or even interfering with all parts of life. When this happens, we may have an anxiety disorder, of which there are various kinds. Among the most common are:

- Panic disorder
- *Phobias*

def•i•ni•tion _____

> **Phobias** are excessive and unwarranted fears, such as arachnophobia (fear of spiders) or agoraphobia (fear of being in open or public places). Phobias are very common; nearly everyone has at least one. A phobia becomes a problem when it prevents us from engaging in normal activities, like going outside.

- Obsessive-compulsive disorder (OCD)
- Post-traumatic stress disorder (PTSD)

- Generalized anxiety disorder (GAD)

- Social anxiety disorder

The stress associated with the symptoms of anxiety is often very high because the intense fear and worry keep people from participating in normal, everyday activities. Untreated anxiety disorders raise the risk for relapse to old, addictive habits. Those old habits offer refuge—desperate and ultimately ineffective, but refuge nonetheless—from the discomfort of both the symptoms and the isolation that results.

Post-traumatic stress disorder (PTSD) is an especially high risk for relapse. PTSD may develop in people who have experienced a major trauma on a personal or individual level, like being in a bad car accident, being the victim of a crime, or having a life-threatening illness. Or it might result from a large scale event, like being in a war or experiencing a natural disaster. PTSD is also common in people who experienced childhood abuse, especially sexual abuse.

Symptoms of PTSD may develop a few months to even years after the trauma. People who have PTSD may react in extreme ways to sudden loud noises, may have hallucinations (see and hear things that aren't there) or flashbacks that cause them to feel they're reliving the original experience. The stress this creates is intense and often debilitating.

 Talk About It

I am in that temper that if I were under water I would scarcely kick to come to the top.
—John Keats, British poet

In the Shadow of Worry

To what extent does anxiety affect your life? Choose the answer that best fits for these questions.

1. I worry all the time, about everything.

   a. Yep, that's me, the constant worrier.

   b. Not *all* the time, and not about *every* little thing.

   c. Not really, I mostly worry about the big stuff.

   d. Nope, I don't see the point of worrying. It doesn't change anything.

2. I feel like something's majorly wrong, but I don't know what it could be.

    a. Something *is* wrong; I know it.

    b. Only after watching the news.

    c. Sometimes, but this kind of thing tends to be an intuitive sense about someone I know.

    d. No, I'm always the last to know about anything.

3. In certain situations or places, suddenly my pulse races, I can't catch my breath, I break out in a sweat, my face gets all red, and I can't get a coherent sentence to come out of my mouth.

    a. Elevators, parties, the office break room—anywhere people might notice me.

    b. If I have to speak in front of a group.

    c. Not since high school.

    d. Yeah, but I'm not one to kiss and tell!

4. I keep things, all kinds of things, in case I might need them sometime.

    a. Yep, pretty much everything. I never know when they'll stop making something I like or need, and then what am I going to do?

    b. Well, I have sentimental attachments to certain items that others think is silly, but it seems a harmless enough indulgence.

    c. It's prudent to keep receipts and sometimes an item's packaging, but that's it for me.

    d. I clear out my closets every spring.

5. I'm so afraid of certain things or places that I go out of my way to avoid them.

    a. So much so that I don't even want to see them on TV or read about them in magazines.

    b. It's not so much trouble to go out of my way.

    c. It does seem prudent to avoid certain things, like alligators, loose manhole covers, and dark stairways.

    d. Not much scares me, really.

6. I count everything I do, always do things in the same order or the same number of times, and start over if I lose count.

    a. Yes, I feel that it protects me.

    b. When it helps me keep track of details I'd otherwise forget.

    c. Only money.

    d. I'm not very good at remembering things like that.

7. I get incapacitating headaches, stomach aches, muscle pains, and other physical discomforts …

    a. All the time.

    b. Several times a week.

    c. Every now and then, mostly when I clearly have a virus.

    d. Hardly ever.

8. The amount of control I have over my daily life is about …

    a. Zilch.

    b. Thirty percent.

    c. Seventy-five percent.

    d. Pretty much full.

9. Most nights, I sleep …

    a. In short stretches, seldom longer than three hours at a time.

    b. About five hours, once I finally fall asleep.

    c. Between five and seven hours.

    d. Until the alarm clock wakes me.

10. When I'm sitting to watch television or at my desk at work, I …

    a. Can't really stay sitting for longer than a few minutes at a time.

    b. Have to get up or shift positions every few minutes or I feel like I'm going to come out of my skin.

c. I jiggle my foot or tap my fingers until someone tells me I've got to stop.

d. Stay in the same position for so long that some part of me goes numb.

If four or more of your answers are "a" or "b," anxiety seems to be a big part of your life. You might have your health-care provider evaluate you for an anxiety disorder. If six or more of your answers were "c," you might look at these questions again in two or three weeks. If your answers are the same, an anxiety disorder is possible. If most of your responses were "d," it seems you have a pretty good handle on your emotional balance and an anxiety disorder is not likely.

Your Personal Stress Triggers

Despite the common mechanisms for responding to stress, we all have our uniquely individual stress triggers. You might be able to remain perfectly calm when your boss goes on a tirade, for example, yet totally lose your cool when the guy in front of you at the checkout unloads a full cart of groceries and then announces he left his checkbook at home.

 Be Mindful _____

Holidays are especially stressful for many people. Family and others who may have little in common converge for what's often a festival of overindulgence with lots of food, drink, and other temptations. Staying on track with your new habits can be hard, especially if most people don't know about the changes you're making. Write down your action plan for resisting temptation, and carry it with you. When the stress level rises, pull it out and choose a response that fits the situation. Remember, you always have time to think before you act.

What's causing you stress in your life? Take a few minutes and list 10 situations (go ahead, include people if you want) that instantly raise your blood pressure:

1. _____

2. _____

3. _____

4. _____

5. _____

6. _____

7. _____

8. _____

9. _____

10. _____

Now look at your list. Put a star beside each situation you have some ability to change. Then put an X beside each situation that is completely beyond your ability to influence. For each star, write one thing you could do to decrease the situation's ability to cause you stress. For each X, write one way you could change your response to the situation that would lower your stress. How much of your stress can you take care of? Repeat this exercise as the items on your list change.

Your Personal Stress Busters

We have two levels of response to stress: reactive and preventive. Reactive responses are immediate and attempt to lower feelings of stress in response to a specific, limited event: someone yelling at you, feeling worried or depressed, finding yourself in a situation that's unpleasant. Reactive stress busters might include affirmations, mindful breathing, a five-minute meditation, a walk around the block or up and down a few flights of stairs, or stepping away from the situation for a few minutes.

The more specific your responses, the more effective they're likely to be. Make a list of them and the specific stress factors they target. Carry the list with you as you go through your day, and pull it out when stress starts to pile on. Practice your responses on the little stresses that crop up. This helps them to become second nature when the situation gets really tough.

Preventive stress responses are the things you can do every day to help you relax and stay calm. These responses aim to lower your overall stress threshold. They might include daily meditation, walking (alone, with a partner or friend, or with your dog), and moderate to vigorous physical exercise (biking, running, or swimming). Preventive efforts work best when you do them consistently and regularly. Create a schedule, so you remember to do them. Keep your schedule simple but specific.

In all situations of stress, try to remain mindful. Consider what might be at the root of the situation, and address that if possible. Think about what to do and say before taking any action. And it's okay to say or do nothing! Nonreaction is sometimes the best response.

The Least You Need to Know

◆ Chronic stress greatly increases the risk for relapse.

◆ Anxiety and depressive disorders, which commonly coexist with many addictive habits, both cause stress and feed from stress.

◆ Mindfulness and meditation are effective methods for reducing stress.

◆ Stress responses are reactive (immediate) and preventive.

Part 6

What Does Recovery Mean?

Recovery is just another habit, really. And what could be better? This is your new lifestyle, and you're thrilled to be living it. You sometimes fret and fuss about it, but it's where you want to be. Finally the old habit is merely a shadow, and your new habits light up your life. What matters now is that you continue to believe in yourself and your ability to press on the path you've chosen, despite occasional sidesteps and detours.

The chapters in Part 6 look at keeping the faith—and the new you. Chapter 19 encourages you to live in the moment and stay strong in your determination. Chapter 20 spotlights the joy of your new vitality. And Chapter 21 supports you in seeing and appreciating yourself for who you are and how you live your life, separate from the presence or absence of your old habit.

Chapter 19

Don't Stop Believin'

In This Chapter

◆ What shape's your attitude in?

◆ What's luck got to do with it?

◆ Talk good to yourself

◆ Dealing with criticism

"Yo, dawg, let's talk," Randy Jackson, one of the three judges on the ever-popular music talent show *American Idol*, famously says to contestants. "You sound *good*, dawg! But you've gotta keep it *real*. You've gotta *believe* in yourself!"

It's a consistent message from Jackson, himself a musician as well as a Grammy Award–winning music producer: you've got to believe in yourself if you want the audience to believe in your performance. Now you may not aspire to compete on *American Idol*, but your life is its own performance. What you believe is what you put out there. Others see it, and you see it yourself.

Does This Attitude Make My Butt Look Big?

Your attitude—*how* you say and do the things you do—says a lot about you. People who are unsure of their abilities and their self-worth often wrap themselves in a mantle of bravado (you might call it something, um, more colloquial). They act like (a) they know absolutely everything or (b) they absolutely don't care about anything. Neither, of course, is true.

> **Talk About It** _____
>
> I was always looking outside myself for strength and confidence, but it comes from within. It is there all the time.
>
> —Anna Freud, psychoanalyst and Sigmund Freud's daughter

Your attitude is a blend of your personality (who you are) and your experiences (what you learn). It projects your beliefs and your emotions. And other people tend to respond to your attitude in kind. If you're defiant and hostile, the other person may flip defiance and hostility right back at you. Or, in a work setting, the person take an authoritarian tone because you come across as unsure, insecure, and confrontational. People might even tell you you've got a bad attitude.

A positive attitude is confident and assured. You get the point across that you're serious and that you also believe in your knowledge and abilities. At the same time, you respect other people. A positive attitude is crucial when it comes to making changes because it projects your belief that you can succeed. Other people then believe you can succeed, which encourages and reinforces your behaviors. As B. F. Skinner's research so convincingly demonstrated (see Chapter 9), rewarding very small changes lays the path to entire new behaviors.

As You Believe, So You Are

Which comes first: the attitude or the behavior? Like the chicken and the egg, you could argue for either, but in the end, it doesn't much matter because one doesn't exist without the other. Most psychologists believe that although it's important to understand how you feel and why, changing the way you behave can change the way you feel.

Motivational coaches emphasize: to be what you want to be, envision it and practice it. At first you might feel awkward and uncomfortable, like you're putting on a false front, but all you're doing is letting out the real you that's been buried for so long.

All the World's a Stage

The cornerstone of many bad habits is the desire and effort to please other people. Such patterns start naturally in childhood, where praise and reward are important for development and learning. Praise comes easily when you're a baby—for a while, all you have to do is smile and everyone around you falls all over themselves telling you how cute and good you are. So you smile more, and even laugh and clap your hands. Yo, dawg, you're keepin' it *real* and your audience is lovin' it!

Life quickly gets more complex, though. To just lie there and show your drooly gums is not enough. You've got to sit up and hold that oversized baby head of yours all by yourself and then figure out how to roll yourself onto all fours. The biggest cheers come with those first wobbly steps. After that, everyone wants you to do what they want you to do. Walk over here; sit right there; eat this; take your nap. You learn, well before you're two years old, that the things you want in life come by doing what makes other people happy.

Under ideal circumstances, this arrangement remains a balance that helps you grow into yourself, so to speak, to learn how to say and do the things that make you happy—safely and confidently. Few of us have the advantage of the ideal; we do the best we can with what we have. If a structure of encouragement and support wasn't the hallmark of your earlier life, you have plenty of time—and a lot more skills—to build it now. This time, the person most important to please is you.

Some People Have All the Luck

It sure seems like some people—*other* people—get all the lucky breaks, doesn't it? Those folks are the ones who walk into a store and get the last one of what they're looking for, rather than a sign that says, "Sorry, sold out!" Those folks have packages get to their destinations a day earlier than scheduled, get bumped to first class when they fly, and find parking spaces in the free zone. The lucky ones get sunny days when they plan barbecues; their computers never crash; and they always have cell signals, even in elevators and parking garages.

How is it that they're so lucky? Is some cosmic force opening doors for them? Maybe, sometimes. But mostly, people who seem to have extraordinarily good luck work very hard at the little things that then become big opportunities. They're open to change rather than needing to be in control. Luck, by itself, isn't the ticket to success at anything. The lottery winner who spends through thousands and even millions of dollars to end up flat broke is sadly common. Is it good luck … bad luck … or simply a path of decisions?

Bemoaning someone else's "dumb luck" is part of that whole fairness chip that sometimes lands on your shoulder. Shake it off! Live in the moment, and such things no longer matter. Do the best that you can to shape the daily events of your life, as they unfold, to be what you want them to be. Adjust and adapt when you need to.

> ### Talk About It _____
>
> My mother drew a distinction between achievement and success. She said that achievement is the knowledge that you have studied and worked hard and done the best that is in you. Success is being praised by others, and that's nice, too, but not as important or satisfying. Always aim for achievement.
>
> —Helen Hayes, American actress

When things don't go the way you want them to go—when bad luck rears its head—learn what you can from the situation and move on. Remember, you can't change the past—not the small stuff, not the big stuff. And you might be surprised how quickly you, too, seem to have the lucky breaks coming your way. Of course, when it's your good luck, there's nothing dumb about it!

Everyone has "off" days and times when nothing seems to go right. This is just part of life. It doesn't mean you've failed; it only means you're having an off day. Tomorrow will be different. Look ahead, not behind.

Self-Fulfilling Prophecies

Self-talk is all the stuff you say to yourself when you're alone in your car, in the shower, or otherwise deep in your own head. What do you say to yourself? When you've struggled with a problem habit, your self-talk tends to get negative. You tell yourself all about what a loser you are (you're not!) and how you can't do anything right (not true!).

So try this: when you're by yourself, speak your thoughts out loud. Just let them come out; don't try to change them. Listen to yourself as though you're listening to someone else who's talking to you. How do you feel about what you are saying? Do this for a few days and get a sense of the pattern of your thoughts.

Then turn what you say around. If you're beating yourself up for something you didn't do, talk about something you did do. It doesn't matter what it was—could be "I took the dog for a walk" or "I washed three loads of laundry." Make a conscious effort to listen to the thoughts in your head and recast them in this way.

Now take a little leap of faith: remember something you didn't do especially well, and envision yourself doing it so absolutely right that other people stop to notice. Again, it doesn't matter what it is. Maybe you burned the burgers at the family barbecue. So see yourself, in your mind's eye, grilling every burger to absolute perfection. Maybe you made too many typos in the report you submitted. So see yourself hitting every key right—and fast, too; you might as well go for it all.

Talk About It

> If a man is called to be a street sweeper, he should sweep streets even as Michelangelo painted, or Beethoven composed music, or Shakespeare wrote poetry. He should sweep streets so well that all the hosts of heaven and earth will pause to say, here lived a great street sweeper that did his job well.
>
> —Martin Luther King Jr., American civil rights leader and Nobel Peace laureate

Whenever you find yourself stuck in negative self-talk—talking bad about yourself—turn it around. It may take a lot of practice, and sometimes you'll struggle to find the positive in a bad situation. But overall, the more you can shift your outlook to focus on what you do well, the more you'll do well.

Try Something Different

The great thing about trying something you've never done before is that you have no history, memorable or forgettable, about it. You've probably got vague expectations, but because you've never done whatever it is, you don't really know what to expect.

Perhaps you've always wanted to ice skate, ride a train across the country, groom dogs, swim in the ocean, read the 10 greatest novels ever written, or maybe even write the next Great American Novel yourself. Perhaps you'd like to go back to school to complete a degree or to take an entirely different course of study, like music or art, mathematics or archeology. Maybe you want only to take a two-hour walk by yourself, go to the movies or a ballgame alone on a weekday afternoon, or listen to National Public Radio in your car.

So what's stopping you? You've probably got all kinds of reasons, and some of them are probably valid. But many of them are obstacles you place in your own way. Can't go back to school because you work full time? See what evening and weekend classes are available. Taking watercolor classes seems too frivolous, a waste of time? Says who?

We may set aside our personal dreams because they're not practical or find that somewhere along the line we simply lost touch with those dreams. Maybe someone else told you your dreams were silly or impossible for you to achieve. But such dreams nourish your soul and satisfy the inner you. That's what you were trying to do with that old habit. Don't you think it's far more positive to try something you've always wanted to do? We do!

Motivation and Goals

Motivation is the drive you feel within yourself to accomplish, achieve, or obtain something you want. Sometimes outside factors influence your motivation, like a desire to please someone who's important to you. Sometimes motivation is intangible; you don't really know why you want something, you know only that you do. Goals are the steps you plan that move you toward accomplishment and achievement. You can measure goals.

Goals can be big: I want a Master's degree in history … to win the Memorial Day Marathon … to live in Hawaii. Goals can be small: I want to read Anne Tyler's latest novel … to get to work 10 minutes early … to write a letter to my sister. Goals become more tangible when a sense of time is attached to them: I want a Master's degree in history by the time I'm 28 years old. I want to write a letter to my sister tonight after dinner.

When goals are big, like a degree in history, set smaller "step" goals to help you make progress. To get that degree in history, maybe you need to take one evening class a week. Maybe you need to put together a budget so you can save enough money to quit your job and go to school full time.

Break down your goals into steps that are manageable, even if those steps seem impossibly small right now. When you're looking at four years of college, it can seem like an eternity. How can you ever do that? But one class a week starts to whittle away, and before long eternity isn't quite so far away.

Habits hate motivation, plans, and goals. Such an orientation in your life requires thought, intent, and focused action. There's no autopilot. It doesn't matter how simple or elaborate your plan is; it matters only that you have one. And you can change your plan as you go along; nothing's carved in stone.

Practice

Practice is the foundation for success in many endeavors, perhaps none so noticeable as athletics. Athletes may spend hours each day repeating the same moves, strokes, or techniques. To watch, you might think it's the same thing, over and over, and it already looks about as good as it can get. So why keep doing it?

Be Mindful _____

Practicing skills is more than rote repetition. It's important to keep your focus on what you're doing, to be aware of your thoughts and actions.

The essence of practice is to keep doing what you do *right*. This reinforces the skill and you get better and better at it. If you're doing something the wrong way and you keep making the same mistakes, you only get better at making those mistakes. Sometimes it helps to have someone else observe what you're doing and give you feedback about it. Sometimes you need to break down whatever you're doing into smaller steps, practice each step until you get it down, and then put all the steps together.

Nothing Personal, But ...

No matter how well-intended and graciously delivered, criticism feels personal. Under the best of circumstances, you leave the experience knowing what you did wrong, how to do it right, and where to find the information or acquire the skills you need. It's still personal, but you feel good about yourself and your ability to do better. It's another step ahead (and sometimes a leap) on your learning curve.

Unfortunately, giving criticism constructively is not something many people do well. Most people are abysmal at it. Whatever's happened, whatever it is you've done (or not done), has affected someone else. Maybe they've taken heat because of it or had to scramble to cover for your mistake. Further, now the other person has to confront you about your mistake—not exactly a pleasant prospect. All kinds of emotions come into play, and before you know it, you're in the middle of "You Done Me Wrong!"

Effective criticism zeroes in on specific behaviors from a perspective of identifying actions, consequences, and solutions. Consider the following criticisms about an employee's interaction with a customer.

(a) "Are you some kind of idiot or what? You can't talk to customers that way! I ought to dock your paycheck for every customer you chase away!"

(b) "When Mrs. Robinson asked where the Slime-B-Gone was on the shelf, you said to her, 'Lady, we haven't carried that worthless product for years!' She was insulted. A more appropriate response would've been to say, 'We don't carry Slime-B-Gone anymore, but we do have Slime-Away and Slime-No-More. Would you like to try one of those products?' Or you could have paged me, and together we could have helped Mrs. Robinson find a product to meet her needs."

No one likes to feel belittled. With a boss like the one who gave the (a) response, it's little wonder the employee treated the customer the same way. This model applies to all kinds of situations, not only work. When someone does something that makes you unhappy or hurts your feelings, focus on behaviors (words and actions) and how they make you feel, rather than making personal attacks that make the other person feel as bad as you do.

Be Mindful

Criticism should improve skills to correct mistakes, not attach blame or demean. Giving constructive criticism is itself a skill that requires practice. Turn negative criticism around by shifting the focus. When you're on the receiving end of criticism that makes you feel bad about yourself, think through the situation and try to identify the specific attitudes, words, and actions at the core of the criticism. How can you improve these specific behaviors?

Even when the person criticizing you doesn't start from such a point, you can bring the dialogue to it by paraphrasing what the person is saying. Move the situation away from blame and shame. Identify the problem, and offer a solution. It's not easy; you, too, want to match attitude with attitude, especially when the other person is confrontational or angry. But you can be the one who takes the mindful approach and turns the situation around.

Um ... My Mistake

We all make mistakes: little ones no one knows about but us, bigger ones that take a group effort to fix, and even monstrous ones, from which no recovery seems possible. But appearances can be deceiving. Sometimes the only, and most appropriate, fix is to move on, and that often turns out to be the best solution.

Living in the grip of an addictive habit compresses our perspective. We tend to expect the worst whenever things don't go quite right. We've developed this approach from the constant need to provide whatever our old habit demanded—a cigarette, a drink, an hour at the poker table—because without it we were in crisis. We came to live on the line of worst-case thinking.

Though this approach can help us feel prepared for a full range of possible outcomes in a situation, more often it shoots us straight to the worst case, without even looking at other options. When you make a mistake at work, for example, and your worst-case framework is in place, you panic and fear you'll be fired! On top of everything else, anticipation of the worst case creates great, and mostly unnecessary, stress.

A more productive, positive approach is to pull back from the situation so you can see it for what it actually is. Nearly all mistakes have boundaries that contain them. What are the boundaries of *this* mistake? What are the probable consequences of the mistake? Not the *possible* consequences—that could well be an endless list. But what's most likely to happen? What are the possible remedies? (This is always a shorter list.) What would it take to implement them? Can you do it yourself, or do you need help or additional expertise?

Most important, cultivate the ability to laugh at yourself! Humor is often a great way to defuse difficult situations, and many mistakes are funny, once you get over yourself.

I'm Sorry

Apologizing is hard for many of us. It's tough enough to make a mistake or be wrong about something because mistakes make us feel defensive. If you've lived most of your life in the world of the worst-case scenario, you may feel a sense of panic or desperation. You may worry that you're setting yourself up to take a fall.

I'm sorry: two words that speak volumes. They're the only two words you need to use, most of the time, when you've made a mistake. You don't usually need to go into lengthy explanations or descriptions about what you did and why. If you know what happened and how it happened, so do others. An apology accepts responsibility (not blame), acknowledges and respects the feelings of others, and positions you to be part of the solution rather than part of the problem.

If "I'm sorry" feels awkward for you to say, then practice saying it. Apologizing is a learned skill, just like other forms of communication. Say the words out loud when you're standing in the shower, driving in your car, or walking your dog. The more familiar the feel and sound of the words, the more easily you'll be able to call on them when you need them.

> **Steer Clear**
>
> Sometimes you might feel cornered into making an apology when you really don't believe you're at fault or have done anything that requires an apology. This kind of apology may backfire if your tone is defensive. Resist the desire to follow "I'm sorry" with "but ...." That isn't an apology at all, but rather an attempt to explain why, from your perspective, there's no need for you to apologize. You'll get further with an honest, "Let's talk about this."

The New, Self-Confident You

You're orchestrating the biggest change ever, the redesign of your life. How exciting! For the first time in a long time, you're in charge of your daily activities, from when you get up in the morning to when you go to bed at night.

You, afraid of change? Of course you are. But look what you're doing anyway! Your confidence in your own abilities grows with each positive experience, with each success, small or large. You're living mindfully, with awareness of your thoughts, feelings, and actions.

Grow Your Strengths

Without your old habit to cloud the view, your many strengths are beginning to show. Do you see them? Sometimes it's difficult for us to recognize our own strengths, especially the ones that come easily. It doesn't seem, somehow, that they count as much when we don't have to work at them. But of course they do, and sometimes the strengths we don't notice in ourselves are our greatest strengths.

> **Be Mindful**
>
> Give a helping hand: volunteer in your community. When you shift your focus from your problems and worries to helping other people find solutions for theirs, you rise above the details of your own life.

What are some of your strengths? Do you listen well, navigate through traffic like you've got built-in sonar, balance your checkbook in your head, swim the length of the pool underwater, say the right things at the right times? Strengths come in many shapes and forms. List 10 strengths you have that you feel are most important:

1. _____
2. _____
3. _____
4. _____
5. _____
6. _____
7. _____
8. _____
9. _____
10. _____

If you're having trouble coming up with 10, just think about the things you do well or the things you like to do. If you're not used to thinking about how good you are at doing certain things, it feels awkward to try to highlight your own abilities in this way. But if you don't know your strengths and abilities, how will anyone else figure them out? A key part of self-confidence, of believing in yourself, is knowing what you do well and taking pride in your capabilities.

Reward Yourself

Once upon a time, and maybe for quite a long time, your primary source of reward was your old habit. It was your treat when you did well, and your retreat when things got rough. But this was a false sense of value; your old habit was no reward, really. True rewards make you feel good about yourself.

What are your favorite self-rewards? List 10 ways to treat yourself that support your new path and make you feel good:

1. _____
2. _____
3. _____

4. _____

5. _____

6. _____

7. _____

8. _____

9. _____

10. _____

Did 10 rewards come easily to you? Great! Did you get to six or seven and run out of ideas? That's great, too! You're growing and learning. More ideas will come to you, and you'll come back to finish the list. Now that you see your favorite rewards on paper, find ways to use at least three of them each day. Feel free to add to your list; there are no limits to the good things you can do for yourself.

The Least You Need to Know

◆ The reactions of other people play important roles in shaping our behaviors and beliefs about ourselves.

◆ Luck is neither good nor bad, but rather the ways we use the circumstances that arise in our lives.

◆ When you try something different, something you've never done before, you have the great advantage of starting fresh, without expectations from yourself or from others.

◆ Goals and practice help you to live in the moment, aware of your choices and decisions.

Chapter 20

Feel It

In This Chapter

- ◆ To your good health
- ◆ Eating well
- ◆ The joy of exercise
- ◆ Indulge your inner child

While your old habit was in control, it consumed your passion for life. It led you to believe that it *was* your passion … but now you know better. Gone are the extremes that once marked your life, the excessive highs and the dreadful lows. In their place, a steady vitality keeps you enjoying life on a pretty even keel.

Do you feel like a new person these days? You should! You've worked hard to get here, where you are today. And the future looks bright and promising. It's okay to look ahead to that future, which maybe you've been afraid to do for a while. You probably want to begin making plans, and you should. You've got a lot of living to look forward to.

It's exciting to be living a lifestyle where *you* determine what you're going to do and when you're going to do it, rather than having to structure every waking hour around draining demands. So what kinds of things are you doing to nourish and support your new vitality?

Long Live the New You!

An all-consuming habit causes you to set aside all kinds of matters you'd otherwise give close attention. With only so many waking hours in the day and that old habit staking claim to most of them, there wasn't much time left over for taking care of you. Maybe you've put off routine doctor, dentist, and optometrist visits because you just haven't had the time or because you didn't want to have yet one more person tell you how bad your habit was. Maybe you already have health problems related to your old habit, and you don't want to hear any more about it or you don't really know what to do. It's hard to deal with health issues, no matter the state of your life, and you've certainly had plenty on your plate.

Many addictive habits aren't very good for a person's health. They have, as doctors say, adverse consequences. Smoking, including exposure to secondhand smoke, is the leading cause of heart disease, lung disease, and numerous cancers. Excessive alcohol consumption damages the liver and nervous system and is a factor in some kinds of cancer.

> **Steer Clear**
>
> Although treatments are available for HIV/AIDS, this infection currently has no cure. Some forms of hepatitis are curable, and others are not.

The health risks of using various illicit drugs may include infectious diseases such as HIV/AIDS and hepatitis, both life-threatening infections commonly spread through sharing needles and through contact with bodily fluids such as occurs with sex. Changes to cardiovascular function (heart, lungs, and blood vessels) can also affect various organs and body systems. Even nonsubstance-related habits often interfere with the amount of sleep one gets, depriving the body of much needed rest for its natural recovery processes.

Some health concerns begin to get better or even go away as soon as a person stops the old habit, and they continue to improve the longer one follows the path of his new lifestyle. Lung cells begin to repair themselves within hours of stopping smoking, for example. Other health problems may linger or have caused long-term or even permanent damage to the body.

You may be putting off a comprehensive health exam from your regular health-care provider because you don't want to have to explain all that you've been through in overcoming old habits. Or you might worry that the doctor will blame you for whatever health issues you have. Put these worries aside. Your health-care provider wants to help you make the best of your health, and part of your new lifestyle is taking care of yourself. Your health is a big piece of that picture.

But if you do have health problems, they're likely treatable. And the earlier you get started, the more likely—and the more quickly—the treatment will improve your health situation. There are also many simple ways that you can take control of your general health and well-being that will improve your health and leave you feeling better.

Nourish Your Body, Soothe Your Soul

Your body requires nourishment to maintain all those functions that carry you through the day. You may have done alright with nutritional eating all along, or maybe you've got some catching up to do to get your body back in nutritional balance. If the old habit you bid good-bye to had to do with eating, the food choices you make—what, how much, when, and where you eat—are particularly important.

To pick up a few pounds (sometimes quite a few, to your dismay) is common as your new lifestyle takes hold. You may be eating more as a means of managing other cravings. Food activates your brain's pleasure pathways. Now that those pathways are less cluttered because your old habit's out of the way, food may have a greater effect on how you feel.

When the level of sugar (glucose) in your bloodstream goes up in the hours immediately after a snack or a meal, your brain responds by releasing serotonin. This brain chemical makes it easier for brain cells to send messages about how good you feel, giving you a sense of calmness and satisfaction. Comfort foods—like macaroni and cheese, chocolate cake, and apple pie—are especially high in carbs. It's no illusion: you truly do feel better, in the short term, after you eat comfort foods.

Steer Clear

Cigarette smoking dulls both the sense of taste and the sense of smell, giving the perception that smoking is a way to keep one's weight down. The myth of this arises from the weight gain many people experience when they stop smoking. When a person can taste and smell her food, she's inclined to eat more. Eating also is a way to manage urges. Learning to distinguish between the craving for a "feel good" hit and hunger helps one make appropriate choices when it comes to eating.

You might be eating more now because you again have an appetite. Many addictive habits are so demanding of your attention that you don't feel like eating or don't want to take the time to eat. The environment of gambling locations like casinos, for example, is designed to cocoon people in a sense of timelessness. With no clocks, no windows, and the same level of lighting 24/7, a person loses track of day and night. The normal routines he'd otherwise follow, like eating and sleeping, fall by the wayside. The same often happens with habits like compulsive shopping or video gaming.

Even as your life begins its return to normal, you may struggle with eating. Making nutritious food choices is a skill you learn, and if you haven't been tuned in, you may feel confused and uncertain when you go grocery shopping or eat out. Many good sources of information about nutrition are available in libraries and on the Internet. Your health-care provider may also have specific recommendations for you that address any special nutritional needs you may have.

Good Foods Are Good for You

Food packaging labels contain standardized nutritional information to help you make choices that are good for you. Labels tell you:

◆ How much is one serving—by weight, number of pieces, or other measure.

◆ The number of calories in a serving size.

◆ The measure of key nutrients—carbohydrate, protein, fat—in a serving size.

◆ The measure of certain minerals and vitamins in a serving size.

Your body needs a variety of foods to meet its nutritional needs. Health experts recommend that fats are no more than a third of what you eat. It's hard to go wrong eating fruits and vegetables, which provide lots of vitamins and minerals.

All foods provide energy for your body; carbohydrates are the fastest source of energy. Proteins help build and maintain muscle and are essential for many cell functions. Fats, despite the bad rap they get, are necessary to get vitamins and other nutrients into your bloodstream so your body can use them. And no matter what you eat, if you eat too much of it, your body will store the extra calories as body fat (your body's idea of an energy savings account).

The U.S. Department of Agriculture provides information and resources for the latest dietary guidelines and nutritional planning on its website, www.mypyramid.gov.

Enough, Already!

Most of us don't have all that much trouble picking out the foods that are better for us. We pretty much know that a steady diet of hot dogs, potato chips, and ice cream doesn't do us much good. And fortunately, we soon get bored with the same old thing, day in and day out, so such a diet doesn't stay steady for long.

The issue isn't so much what we eat as how much of it we eat. The amount that nutritionists or package labels say is a serving size and what we put on our plates as a serving size are sometimes vastly different quantities of food. When did you last grill a 3-ounce steak? Yet that's the serving size. And that bottle of soda? Check the label; it could contain three or more servings.

If you're not used to paying this kind of attention to what you eat, you might measure serving sizes for a while to get a sense for what they look like on your plate. You don't have to invest in fancy scales and all that; just read labels. If the package contains three servings, divide it into thirds and have one third. A serving of meat (beef, pork, chicken, fish) is 3 ounces; that's about the size of a deck of cards or the palm of your hand. When it comes to snacks like chips and nuts, a handful is about one serving— no scooping to your fingertips or spilling over.

You don't think this looks like enough food to satisfy you? Try it for a week. Eat a variety of different foods with each meal, and make sure you're getting your full calorie count over the day. Chew your food instead of gulping it down! Enjoy the flavors and textures of what you eat. Sit at the table when you eat, especially if you often eat alone, so eating is your only focus.

Be Mindful

Eat regular meals at about the same time each day. The convention in the United States is three meals a day—breakfast, lunch, and supper (or dinner, depending on what region of the country you live in). Nutritionists recommend you evenly divide your day's dietary requirements among the three meals to keep your energy level fairly constant. Extra activity may raise your calorie needs, so match what you eat with what you do. Healthy snacks between meals—like fruits, veggies, and whole grains—give you extra energy and calm hunger attacks.

Get Moving!

It may seem that no matter where you turn these days, someone's talking up the benefits of regular physical exercise. From doctors to talk show hosts to infomercials, everyone has a sure-fire way to get you fit and trim. Some suggestions are sound, while others sound too good to be true. The bottom line is: fitness is your body at its best. And the best way to get and stay fit is to move your body every day. Walk, run, bike, swim, dance—whatever gets your heart pumping and your lungs expanding.

Every cell in your body loves exercise. Like flowers to the sun, cells open themselves to the energy of activity. Scientists don't know exactly how it happens, but they do know that cells function more efficiently when the body is active. Physical activity also increases the levels of natural chemicals, like serotonin and *endorphins*, in your brain that activate your pleasure pathways.

def•i•ni•tion

Endorphins are a family of natural neurotransmitters that bind with opiate receptors in your brain. Your body releases endorphins in response to intense stress or pain. Intense physical exercise also seems to release endorphins, which is what some health experts believe accounts for the euphoria that may follow playing a tennis match or running a marathon. There are no synthetic (fake) endorphins; only your body can produce these biochemicals.

Regular physical exercise builds muscle mass and causes your body to draw energy from fat, which is its storage system. Though it seems like a paradox, the more active you are, the more energy you have. But rather than the frenzied sort of energy you got from your old habit, this is a steady, reliable, and predictable energy. And the more you make physical activity a regular part of your day, the more you want to have that activity. With exercise, though, this is a good thing because it tells you your body is returning to a normal state of functioning.

Put on Those Walking Shoes

If it's been a while since you've been very active, you might feel particularly out of shape. Many of those undesirable habits don't exactly encourage you to run marathons! Relax … you don't need to. Health experts say that walking 45 to 60 minutes a day, every day or at least most days, is enough to keep your heart and lungs strong and well. More aerobically intense exercise—longer durations of activities that push your heart rate and breathing—further improves your cardiovascular capacity.

Start walking 10 or 15 minutes at a time. Stop to catch your breath if you become winded or to rest your legs if they really start to complain, but keep going until you complete those 10 or 15 minutes. You might not go very far at first, but you'll be surprised at how quickly you improve to go further and faster. Work yourself up to walking 45 minutes at a time each week day, with a 60-minute walk on a weekend day. Before long that 60 minutes will be a breeze as well as a break from everything else in your life.

Exercise Helps You Stand Strong Against Urges

Physical exercise is a great way to relieve stress. All the worries and anxieties you accumulate over the day or the week can leave you feeling tense and irritable. Working your body more intensely two or three times a week brings your thoughts to a steady state of calmness so you're better able to manage urges and cravings.

Engaging in activities is, for many people, an effective method for dealing with cravings. Taking a walk or a bike ride engages both your body and your mind. Your body produces enough feel good biochemicals to placate your pleasure pathways. Focusing on what you're doing increases your mindfulness, so you're living in the moment instead of in your head.

Practices that combine physical activity with meditation can give you the best of both worlds. These include yoga, tai chi, and qi gong.

The Structure of Your Life

Maybe you're one of those people who naturally loves order—everything in its place, a place for every thing. Maybe you're the kind of person who knows precisely where something is even if someone else looking for it wouldn't have a clue where even to start. Or maybe you're somewhere in-between.

For all their dependence on routine, addictive habits don't much like structure. The routine of habits is mindless; it runs its course without direction from you. Structure is mindful; it puts you in control. You know what you're doing because you've made the choice to do it, although it may not feel that way when the alarm clock goes off in the morning. You make conscious, aware decisions about what you do and when you do it. Structure provides purpose in your life and puts your best interests front and center.

Your Daily Routine

Work and family tend to establish daily routines for many people. When you have to be somewhere at a certain time for a certain amount of time, much of your schedule revolves around that. Even though you might feel these demands are out of your control, you're still the one making the decisions.

Set your alarm clock to give yourself enough time to get showered and dressed without rushing and to have a decent breakfast. Similarly, give yourself enough room at the end of the day to relax and wind down before it's time for bed.

If work or family is not part of your daily routine, you still need to have structure to your day. Plan activities to fill your time. Set days or times for cleaning, grocery shopping, working in the yard, washing your car. If you find yourself with an abundance of free time, check into volunteering. Or consider going back to school or taking up a hobby that interests you.

Though you don't want to cram every minute of the day with some sort of activity, it's important to stay busy. Having enough to occupy your mind helps keep you focused on the here and now, narrowing the gap for stray thoughts about that old habit to wiggle their way into your consciousness. You're a valuable member of your community with lots to offer—put yourself out there!

> **Talk About It**
>
> Even the most tedious chore becomes endurable as you parade through each day convinced that every task, no matter how menial or boring, brings you closer to fulfilling your dreams.
>
> —Augustine "Og" Mandino, American inspirational author

Get Enough Sleep

As you're settling into your life, you may find you want to sleep longer than you used to. You could finally be getting enough sleep. Your body needs sleep to restore itself, and when your old habit was in control, it didn't much care about that. Now that you're in charge, you can give your body the rest it requires.

Though a person can get by with as little as five hours of sleep a night (and this is enough for some people), most adults need that eight hours of pillow time to feel refreshed and ready for the new day. Some people need even more; up to 10 hours of sleep a night could be normal for you.

> **Be Mindful**
>
> To have dreams about your old habit is not uncommon. You might dream you're engaged in the habit again, or you may have urges related to the old habit appear in your dreams. You may wake up in a panic and wonder whether you've actually done something, like had a cigarette or a drink. If you're having a craving when you wake up, go right to your coping skills—surf the urge, do a breath meditation, whatever you usually do to calm yourself. Like any other urge, this one, too, will pass.

Lack of sleep causes all sorts of problems, not the least of which is feeling tired and cranky. Without enough sleep, every little thing that bothers you feels more intense: aches and pains hurt more, everyday hassles are more stressful, and it's harder for you to focus and concentrate.

Sleep experts offer these tips for making sure you get the sleep your body needs:

- Go to bed at about the same time each night, and get up at about the same time each morning.

- Start winding down about 30 to 45 minutes before bedtime so your mind and your body can begin to relax.

- Sleep in a dark, quiet bedroom that's a comfortable temperature for you.

- If you wake up at night and can't fall back asleep within 20 minutes, get up and go into another room. Read, listen to music, or even watch a little television until you feel relaxed enough to go back to bed.

- Get up when your alarm clock goes off, even if you feel you want to snooze a bit longer.

You can get used to not having enough sleep, but your body doesn't really adjust. Eventually that sleep debt comes due. You may get sick because chronic lack of sleep weakens your immune system and lowers your resistance to viruses and other infections. Or you may simply crash for an entire weekend, sleeping until your body feels replenished.

"You" Time

What do you do that's only for you? It's easy to find your day so filled with work, family, and related activities that the day's over before you know it and you're too exhausted to even think about doing anything but tumbling into bed.

Sure, it's important to stay occupied. But it's also important to make sure that some of what occupies you are things you do simply because you enjoy them.

What do you do for fun? Take a trip back in time. What was your favorite thing to do when you were 10 years old? Ride your bike? Climb trees? Read a book? Lie on your back in the grass and pick out animal shapes in the clouds? At age 10, you still had both feet in the world of childhood, even as your awareness of a bigger world was dawning. Life was about having fun, even in school.

 Be Mindful _____

When was the last time you indulged your inner child? Take a field trip to a toy store! Maybe you'd like to build with Legos, do jigsaw puzzles, work with modeling clay, fly remote-control airplanes, or have a model train set.

The older we get, the more our lives fill with things we have to do. We have to study; we have to work; we have to clean the bathroom. Responsibilities, even when we enjoy them, tend to take over, and we forget about the joy of simply having fun.

It's great to take vacations to exotic places and experience new adventures. If you can do this and it refreshes you, good for you. But you can have fun sitting at home doing jigsaw puzzles, gardening, or playing Frisbee with the dog. Fun is what you like to do, with no strings attached. Like when you were 10 and did things just because. What are five things you'd like to do just because they're fun?

1. _____

2. _____

3. _____

4. _____

5. _____

Now, what keeps you from doing any of them? What would it take to do each of them? Make it so! At the very least, set aside a certain time every day that is yours and yours alone. You can plan things to do during this time or just see what you feel like doing. You can't be 10 again (sorry). But you can return the sense of joy to your life that you had when you could choose to do things only because you wanted to do them.

The New, Improved You

There's no time like the present to go back to school, take up a hobby, or pursue a long-delayed interest. These are all ways to improve yourself and engage in healthy, positive interactions with other people in settings that support, rather than challenge, your new lifestyle.

You might decide this is a good time for a career change and focus your educational efforts on learning new skills. You might follow your heart and take watercolor lessons or learn to play the drums or the piano or another musical instrument that calls to you. Whatever it is you choose to do, it's an investment in your most valuable resource: you.

The Least You Need to Know

- ◆ It's important to take care of any health issues you might have neglected while your old habit was in charge.

- ◆ Good nutrition and regular exercise help heal your body and allow you to feel good about yourself.

- ◆ Structure in your daily life makes it harder for old habits to come back.

- ◆ Get enough sleep every night, and make time for the things that interest you.

Chapter 21

Getting Unstuck

In This Chapter

- Separating you from your habit
- How your memories help you configure your future
- How much does your old habit define who you are now?
- Finding your comfort zone

You've come a long way with the changes you're making. But will you ever reach the point where that old habit is simply something that was once part of your life but is no longer, like braces on your teeth when you were 14 years old? Your teeth are straight now. You have a beautiful smile. Can't you just say the same about your life? You don't smile at someone and then say, "Oh, but I used to wear braces."

So must you always and forever define yourself by the habit you're working so hard to leave behind? Opinions on this vary and continue to evolve as we learn more about the functions of the brain and how addictive behaviors develop. We conclude our book with a look at what it means to define yourself neither by your old habit's presence nor by its absence but simply by … you.

Here's to letting your old habits join the company of your old braces!

You Are Not Your Habit!

At the start of your journey of change, acknowledging the hold of your old habit was crucial to being able to break free from it. You needed to tell yourself, and you needed to tell other people who could support you along the way.

Now that you've made it this far, you just want to get on with living. You may not care to tell other people what you've been through. You may be so far beyond your old self that you don't want to continually remind yourself of how you used to be, either.

Labels are great for giving you a general idea about what's inside when you can't otherwise tell for sure. We like labels; they're like sound bites. They give us just enough information to make snap decisions. The problem with labels is that they only summarize what's inside, and even that's subjective. You've got to put together your experiences beyond the label to understand the contents.

Say you're looking at a jar of peach mango salsa. You know from the label that what's inside is a spicy sauce made with peaches and mangos. The fine print might tell you the names of the spices and other ingredients. But you don't know whether the salsa's tangy, sweet, peppery, chunky, or pulpy. You've got to open the jar and take a taste to find that out.

But you're not a jar of salsa! It's hard to get a sense for what's behind the label when the label applies to a person. How do you get beyond something like "alcoholic" or "smoker" or "gambler"? Putting "ex" or "former" or even "recovering" in front of the label doesn't do much to enlighten anyone. You still know nothing more about the person, only about the habit.

There's a certain comfort in labels because they suggest definition and structure. Some people label themselves and remain on track with their lifestyle changes by always reminding themselves, and others, where they've come from. They're able to succeed in transforming their lives through their determination to not go back to where they've been.

Other people want to break free entirely. They don't want the quality they share in common with others to be their old habit. They find it more difficult to truly move ahead in their lives when the focus remains on where they've been rather than where they're going.

There are no absolute answers when it comes to what works best for *you*. Wherever you are along this continuum, just remember: habits are learned behaviors. No matter what labels you or anyone else uses, you are not your habit!

Photographs and Memories

New research suggests the way you remember your past influences your ability to imagine your future. In the January 2008 article, "Age-Related Changes in Simulation of Future Events," published in the journal *Psychological Science*, researchers at Harvard University studying memory loss in older adults reported a strong connection between the ability to recall snippets of memories—called internal episodic details—and the ability to create an imaginary future.

In the study, older people who excelled at such memory recall also could vividly create imaginary images. Those who struggled to remember the details of past experiences also struggled to imagine events that had not yet occurred. This mental process requires the brain to sift through episodic memories, pull out specific details, and reassemble the details into new, imagined events.

Such research suggests that to construct an image of who you want to be, you must start with fragments of remembered details of experiences you've already had. Your hippocampus stores, and your prefrontal cortex interprets, episodic memories. And both of these brain structures belong to the brain's pleasure pathway (see Chapter 2).

> **Be Mindful**
>
> Much of daydreaming is a way to escape the boredom of the moment. But you can use daydreaming in a constructive, mindful way by focusing on seeing yourself the way you want to be. It's not a bad thing to spend 15 minutes or so every day watching yourself on the big screen of your imagination!

The Harvard study wasn't looking specifically at memory and addictive behaviors. But what's interesting about its findings when it comes to changing addictive habits is the strong correlations the study confirms between what you can remember and what you can project—how your brain bridges your past and your future.

Alan and other addictive behavior specialists know that your ability to envision yourself living a life free from your addictive habit is crucial to your ability to do just that. So if you work to remember the events of your old habit, always reminding yourself of where you've been, how does that shape your ability to see a future without that habit? We don't know for certain, but research such as the Harvard study seems to give a big push to approaches that emphasize focus on the future.

We don't entirely know how the processes of memory work. But many scientists now believe that rather than endlessly storing memories as was once the accepted understanding, the hippocampus instead dumps off older, uncalled-upon episodic memories to other parts of the brain (probably segments of the prefrontal lobe). The hippocampus then stores new episodic memories in their place, somewhat like the way a computer hard drive works.

If this is the case, then it might be that the more you focus on replaying the memories of new experiences—your new lifestyle—then eventually your hippocampus will clear out those older memories that have to do with your old habit. The prospect that this is indeed how episodic memory functions is exciting and raises hope that you might be able to free yourself from old habits.

Talk About It

It's a poor sort of memory that only works backwards.
—Lewis Carroll, English author

There's still much to learn about memory and the brain, of course. Research continues to probe these functions and bears watching over the coming years. What scientists learn is certain to change the ways we think about the brain and likely to change the ways we approach addictive habits.

Let Me Introduce My Ex ...

Some people talk about being always in recovery but never recovered. They worry that they just can't seem to escape their old habits. Instead, those old habits continue to define who they are, even after the habits have been missing in action. Will you always be an ex-this or a former that? Certainly your old habit will always be a part of your past, and because of that, a part of you. Unlike those braces that gave you grief for a few years and vanished without a trace when their job was done, habits leave residue as evidence of their passage. The extent to which that old habit will continue to influence your present and your future, no one can really say.

There's a growing shift toward looking at behavior as a continuum, with addictive habits at one end and mindful behaviors at the other. We move back and forth along this continuum throughout our lives. Some people live their entire lives in the middle or at the mindful end of the continuum, never quite experiencing the struggle and harm of addictive habits in themselves or even in family or friends. That's hard to imagine, we know, but it happens!

You, of course, know all about that other end of the continuum. It still feels fresh and new—even exhilarating, at times—to be sliding around in the center and even at the mindful end. It's great, isn't it? You're probably guarding, more at some times than at others, against slipping back to the old habits end. But with the knowledge and skills you have now to help you deal with cravings and urges, you're in pretty good shape to live in the mindful behaviors neighborhood.

Be Mindful

As you become more confident about your ability to resist temptations and surf your urges, stay mindful about your thoughts and actions. You've made great progress—keep moving forward!

And you know, now, that a slip isn't the end of the world. It's not even the end of anything. And it's not the start of anything, either. You're not necessarily headed toward a full relapse, if you draw on what you've learned and pull yourself back on track. Certainly the risk for relapse is there. But now you have a new awareness and new mindful strategies that are what you need to deal with it.

Will you forever carry with you the risk of relapse? Well, probably, at least in some form. Those pathways in your brain may fade to nearly nothing, but it seems they nonetheless remain at the ready to reactivate should you fall off track and into a relapse. The best we understand relapse, you're more vulnerable to the habit because you've already experienced it, and you might also be more vulnerable to other addictive habits.

But you now also carry with you a virtual toolbox of knowledge and skills. You're living mindfully, so not much sneaks up on you these days. You know how to deflect many of the temptations that cross your path, sending them scurrying away. You're taking care of yourself. You eat nutritionally, exercise and meditate daily, and are actively engaged in interests you enjoy. You're as prepared as you can be.

Talk About It

Remember always that you not only have the right to be an individual, you have an obligation to be one.

—Eleanor Roosevelt, human rights activist and wife of U.S. President Franklin D. Roosevelt

I Don't Do That Anymore

Juanita had been smoke free for 11 years, long enough that she no longer thought of herself as an ex-smoker. Occasionally the smell of cigarette smoke aroused a faint craving, but she seldom had to move beyond her mental mantra, "I don't smoke."

Traveling on business, she attended a dinner party at the home of a company exec. Many people were smoking in the house, so she stepped out onto the patio for some fresh air. She felt a tap on her shoulder and turned around to see Peter, an old friend from college who worked for the same company but in a different city. They talked for a few minutes, then Peter reached into his jacket pocket. "Smoke?" he asked.

Juanita hesitated only long enough for Peter to pull out a lighter from his other pocket. "Sure," she said. *It's only one cigarette*, she told herself. Over the course of the evening, however, that one became five. It was great to see her, Peter said as they finally parted ways, just like old times. Juanita was very angry with herself, so angry that when she got back to her hotel, she stopped in the lounge and bought a pack of KOOLs. Just like old times, indeed!

Later, Juanita told a friend that she didn't know quite what had happened with Peter. When he offered her a cigarette, she got flustered and confused. Though she'd kept in touch with him through the years, their contact was by phone and e-mail, and he didn't know she wasn't smoking anymore.

Even though Juanita had faced the same challenge countless times before with other people and held her ground, she lost her bearings with Peter. It was as if she was in college again when they were all so broke they shared cigarettes as their one indulgence. After not more than a brief moment's hesitation, she acted automatically.

No matter how far you remove yourself from the people and places of your old habit, eventually you're going to run into someone who urges you to indulge. It might be someone from your past or someone you've just met. And no matter how often you've practiced, there will be times when it's hard to turn down an offer that once was second nature. That's where you'll need to apply the information and skills you've learned.

> ## Talk About It
>
> A true friend knows your weaknesses but shows you your strengths; feels your fears but fortifies your faith; sees your anxieties but frees your spirit; recognizes your disabilities but emphasizes your possibilities.
>
> —William Arthur Ward, American educator and writer

Countering Cues

Juanita had prepared herself for the party. She knew people would be smoking and drinking, and she knew how to call on her mantras (see Chapter 7) and SOBER meditation (see Chapter 12). She just didn't expect to see Peter there. Too many elements of their encounter were like the old days, activating a cascade of cues. By the time Juanita realized what had happened, she felt trapped in her lapse. The abstinence violation effect kicked in, and she lost control.

It's impossible to practice for every potential scenario where you might encounter triggers for your cravings. The most important action you can take in an unexpected crisis is to listen to the tiny whisper telling you to stop. You may choose to go ahead with your lapse; after all, you're an adult and you can do that. But odds are, that single hesitation will be enough for you to activate your relapse resistance plan instead.

If what you try first doesn't quite do it for you, reach back into your skill set and pull out something else. By now you have more coping skills than any situation has temptations. And remember, nothing is forcing you to stay in a situation that causes you to feel uncomfortable. You wouldn't hesitate to run were the building on fire, and you should feel no less protective about your new lifestyle.

 **Talk About It**

Between stimulus and response there is a space. In that space is our power to choose our response. In our response lies our growth and our freedom.

—Viktor Frankl, Austrian psychiatrist and Holocaust survivor

No Judgment

It's so neat and clean to simply say, "no thanks" to an offer that comes from a person who doesn't know you once shared the old habit. This is the approach someone who never had the habit uses, without even thinking about it. There's no judgment attached; you're not criticizing the other person for his or her choices. It's a decision that affects only you. It has no further meaning. You wouldn't hesitate to say "no thanks" to going to see a movie that doesn't interest you, would you? For the person who hasn't ever had an addictive habit, it's just this straightforward.

But you're not such a person. You've been through so much with your addictive habit, and even with it behind you now, your experiences with it still influence how you think. You wonder what's really behind the offer and what the other person will think of you after you respond.

Keep in mind that most of the time, the other person isn't trying to prey on a weakness in you but is instead feeding his or her own PIG (see Chapter 7). Maybe the other person feels selfish about not offering to share the habit! You don't know what someone else's motivations might be. But you do know your PIG is sound asleep, and you know how to keep it that way even if the other person's PIG is awake and hungry.

Of course, you know this was once your turf, too. Maybe you're afraid—or you believe—the other person knows this about you. But this belief, like your cravings, lives *within* you, not in the other person or any outside circumstances. You can decide what to do about how you feel and act accordingly.

def•i•ni•tion

The **broken record** is a technique for standing your ground in the face of confrontational or manipulative behaviors that are attempting to get you to do something. You repeat your response, "no thanks," over and over.

You've got the power, because you know more. You can become a *broken record*, repeating your polite refusal over and over until the other person gives up. You can turn and walk away; you can even, if you choose, confront the person about his or her own bad habit. (Although, as you know from your own experiences, it's not likely to influence the situation in ways that are good for you.) Whatever your response, you have time to think it through and make the choice that is right for you.

Mind Your Shoulds and Wants

Be sure, as you continue on your path of change, that you have a good balance between the shoulds and the wants in your life. When we get caught up in all the things we should do, especially all the efforts to stay on the path of change, we lose sight of the real reasons for embarking on this new lifestyle.

Where is your balance of "shoulds" and "wants" right now? Do you have enough "wants" happening in your daily life that you feel content? If not, take a look at what you're doing with your time, and make more room for the activities that bring you joy.

The Rest of Your Life Awaits

No matter how long you wait, no matter how much you fuss and worry, your past isn't going to change. It is what it is, and no amount of regret or remorse will bring you a "do over." The button you can push now is "move forward." So push it with everything you've got! *Life is life* … and yours awaits! Your entire future lies ahead of you; it's an open path waiting for you to chart its course.

The Least You Need to Know

◆ You always have time to stop and think before making a choice or a decision.

◆ You have many techniques and skills for coping; feel free to use any or all of them as the situation requires.

◆ As researchers continue to learn more about how the brain functions, our understanding about addictive habits continues to evolve.

◆ You can say "no" to temptations, whether they arise from people or situations, without making any statements of judgment.

Glossary

12-step program   A recovery approach that requires participants to follow specific procedures to remain "clean" from addictive behaviors. The original 12-step program was Alcoholics Anonymous, founded in 1935.

80/20 rule   Holds that in general, 80 percent of results come from 20 percent of your effort. The amount of additional effort necessary to achieve 100 percent of results is generally so excessive as to not be worthwhile. The 80/20 rule is also called the Pareto principle, after the Italian economist Vilfredo Pareto (1848-1925) who first made the observation that 80 percent of income in Italy went to 20 percent of the population.

abstinence   The complete stopping of a behavior.

abstinence-violation effect (AVE)   A predictable and common reaction to a return to an old habit, marked by intense feelings of guilt, shame, and hopelessness.

addiction, addictive behavior   A pattern of behavior in which one continues to engage even when the result is harmful to him in some way.

adrenal glands   A pair of endocrine structures that rest one on top of each kidney. The adrenal glands produce the hormones cortisol, adrenaline, noradrenaline, aldosterone, and small amounts of testosterone.

affirmation   A positive statement of intent or truth.

amygdala   An almond-shaped structure in the core of the brain that receives and decodes primal emotions, such as fear and desire, and establishes conditioned responses to them.

anxiety   Feelings of fear, uncertainty, tension, apprehension, and worry that are more intense than the situation warrants or that occur without an apparent reason.

avatar   An icon that represents a user in a virtual community. It can be a character (as in computer role-playing games), a symbol, or words (as in screen names). The term comes from the ancient Sanskrit word *avatara*, meaning "incarnation."

aversion   Creating a negative association or sense of unpleasantness around an undesirable habit.

avoidance   Removing the temptations of the old habit from one's environment or removing oneself from temptations.

behavior   A thought, emotion, or action.

benzodiazepines   A class of medications that treats anxiety, muscle spasms, and sleep disorders. Benzodiazepines can cause dependency.

bipolar disorder   A psychiatric condition of extremes in emotions and behaviors, with depression at one end of the spectrum and mania at the other. The extremes are usually cyclic.

broken record   A technique for standing one's ground in the face of confrontational or manipulative behaviors that are attempting to get someone to do something. He repeats his response, "no thanks," over and over.

bruxism   The medical term for teeth grinding. In children, bruxism often appears during teething and then goes away; in adults, bruxism may be a stress response.

bupropion   An antidepressant medication that reduces the cravings associated with ending addictive habits. Bupropion trade name products available for such use in the United States include Zyban and Wellbutrin.

chronic relapse disease   A way of looking at addictive behaviors as conditions of remission and relapse, with symptoms that wax and wane though the condition itself does not entirely go away.

codependency   An entrenched pattern of enabling behaviors in partnerships and family relationships in which one person has an intense emotional need to control and care for another.

cold turkey   Suddenly and completely quitting a behavior.

comorbidities   Also called comorbid conditions or co-occurring disorders, these are health conditions that coexist or are present at the same time. There may be direct or indirect connections among the conditions, though not always.

conditioned response   A learned association between a cue and a behavior that have no natural connection between them.

cognition   The processes of thought, logic, and reasoning that occur within the brain.

cognitive behavioral therapy (CBT)   A treatment approach within psychology based on learning to recognize a person's personal high-risk situations and developing behaviors to respond to them.

compulsion   A repeated, uncontrolled pattern of behavior intended to make unpleasant thoughts or feelings go away. See also *obsessive-compulsive disorder* (*OCD*).

coping skills   Behaviors people learn and practice so they can make choices in high-risk situations that prevent lapsing or relapsing.

craving   An intense feeling of desire for an experience.

cue   An event that triggers a behavior.

cutting   Intentional self-injury as a means of attempting to cope with intensely emotional or stressful situations.

decision matrix   A model for evaluating the consequences, positive and negative, of a choice.

dependence   A physical or emotional need for a substance or behavior.

depression   A clinical disorder in which one feels intensely sad, hopeless, and worthless (has low self-esteem). Health experts believe that imbalances of brain neurotransmitters cause most depression.

dichotomy   When two things are mutually exclusive; they exist in an either/or context.

disulfiram   Best known by its trade name Antabuse, a medication that blocks the metabolism of alcohol. Drinking alcohol while taking disulfiram causes extremely unpleasant symptoms.

dopamine   A key neurotransmitter in the brain associated with perceptions of pleasure, desire, elevated mood, and motivation.

dual diagnosis   The presence of at least one underlying psychiatric condition in addition to an addictive habit. Often, a person may have multiple underlying psychiatric conditions as well as multiple addictive habits.

eating disorders   Addictive behaviors involving abnormal food consumption. Common eating disorders include anorexia nervosa, bulimia, bingeing, and overeating.

enabling   To engage in a pattern of behavior that implicitly or explicitly supports another person's damaging habits.

endorphins   A family of natural neurotransmitters that bind with opiate receptors in the brain. The body releases endorphins in response to intense stress or pain. Intense physical exercise also seems to release endorphins.

evidence-based approaches   Methods and techniques tested through conventional scientific research and demonstrated to be effective for specific purposes.

feng shui   An ancient Chinese practice of placement to achieve harmony.

free association   The process of talking or writing about whatever comes to mind, without interpretation or judgment.

generalized anxiety disorder (GAD)   A clinical disorder in which a person feels so intensely fearful and stressed that he's unable to function in his daily life. Health experts believe that imbalances of brain neurotransmitters cause most GAD.

habit   A learned pattern of behavior that results in automatic, or unconscious, thought, emotion, or action.

harm reduction   A structured approach to minimizing the risks of potentially dangerous habits, such as drinking or substance abuse.

hippocampus   A structure of the inner brain that stores intense, pleasurable memories.

hoarding   A compulsive habit of keeping items most people throw away, such as magazines and newspapers, junk mail, catalogs, parts (electronic, automotive, mechanical, etc.), and clothes that are worn out or don't fit. The accumulations often overrun living spaces.

hypothalamus   A brain structure at the top of the brainstem that regulates nerve and chemical signals from the brain to the body that have to do with survival and basic pleasure (notably eating, drinking, and sex).

instinct   An inherent or inborn (not learned or acquired) pattern of behavior.

interpersonal risks   Emotions and feelings that arise from one's relationships with other people, particularly conflicts.

intrapersonal risks   Emotions and feelings that arise from within a person. They are risks for lapse and relapse because they tempt one to return to his old habit to make himself feel better.

lapse   A single episode of engaging in an old habit.

limbic system   A network of structures deep within the brain, including the pleasure pathway, that integrate memory, emotion, learning, and motivation.

magical thinking   A perception that events, thoughts, or actions share connections when there is no true relationship.

mania   An extremely elevated state of mood, often characterized by high energy, impulsive actions, racing thoughts, and easy distractability.

mantra   A brief saying or set of sounds one repeats, often in meditation or prayer, to focus one's mind and energy.

meditation   A practice of focusing the mind as a method for increasing nonjudgmental awareness.

memory   The storage of learned knowledge and experiences.

metaphor   A phrase or concept that creates an image as a means of explanation or understanding.

methadone   A synthetic narcotic used in replacement therapy to treat heroin addiction.

mindfulness   A state of focused and intentional awareness.

naltrexone   A medication that blocks the sense of euphoria that comes with drinking alcohol and taking some other drugs.

negative reinforcement   A consequence that's unpleasant enough to discourage repetition of the behavior. Compare with *positive reinforcement*.

neuron   A nerve cell.

neuroreceptor   A specialized molecule on a neuron's axon that receives (binds with) the neurotransmitter.

neurotransmitter   A chemical messenger (a molecule) that enables communication among neurons.

nicotine   The addictive chemical in tobacco.

nicotine replacement   Products that contain nicotine that are used to help with smoking cessation.

nucleus accumbens   A brain structure that determines how many dopamine receptors brain neurons have (and thus how good those neurons can make a person feel) and is believed to be the bridge between emotion and reason, playing a key role in motivation.

obsession   A pattern of unpleasant thoughts or feelings that persistently occurs in response to specific triggers. See also *obsessive-compulsive disorder* (*OCD*).

obsessive-compulsive disorder (OCD)   A mental health condition in which a person has uncontrolled, repeated unpleasant thoughts or feelings (obsessions) and engages in uncontrolled, repeated behaviors (compulsions) to try to make the thoughts or feelings go away.

pathway   A functional network of communication that neurons establish in the brain to rapidly transmit repeated information and messages.

PET scan   Short for positron-emission tomography scan; a highly sophisticated imaging procedure that uses radioisotopes to create images of activity in the brain and other organs and structures.

phobia   An excessive and unwarranted fear, such as arachnophobia (fear of spiders) or agoraphobia (fear of being in open or public places).

placebo effect   A much studied phenomenon in which people experience the same result from an inactive substance or procedure as from an active or "real" one. Placebo testing is an important part of clinical research.

positive reinforcement   A consequence that feels good enough to encourage repetition of the behavior. Compare with *negative reinforcement*.

post-acute withdrawal syndrome (PAWS)   Symptoms, ranging from irritability and restlessness to palpitations and nightmares, that most people experience randomly during the first two years following the quit of an addictive habit.

post-traumatic stress syndrome (PTSD)   An anxiety disorder that develops after an experience that is physically or emotionally threatening. Symptoms include flashbacks or reliving the experience, nightmares, irritability, outbursts, and avoiding circumstances that evoke memories of the traumatic experience.

prefrontal cortex   A segment of the front of the brain that's responsible for selective attention, learning, motivation, planning, intellect, short-term memory, and interpreting mood and emotion.

principle of good enough (POGE)   Defines a decision-making approach that gets a new computer application into use with minimum frills. POGE assumes work to modify, expand, and correct the application will continue after it's in use and that the application will continue to evolve.

Problem of Immediate Gratification (PIG)   The behaviors we've developed to instantly satisfy the appetite of our cravings and urges.

procrastination   Putting off tasks and responsibilities.

psychoanalysis   A method for treating emotional and psychological symptoms by uncovering and interpreting unconscious feelings and thoughts. Austrian physician and psychologist Sigmund Freud is widely acknowledged as the father of psychoanalysis.

psychotherapy   A treatment approach in which a psychologist helps a person gain insight and understanding into thoughts and behaviors that create dysfunction in his or her life. The goal is to make changes that improve the person's ability to function and participate in the activities of daily life.

qi gong   A traditional Chinese medicine (TCM) method that combines movement and meditation.

quit   To end an addictive habit.

recovery   The process of quitting an addictive habit.

relapse   Periods of time of the return to an old habit.

relapse prevention plan   A personal, specific plan for meeting challenges to one's change efforts.

remission   Periods of time of following the new habit.

ritual   Compulsive repetition of specific behaviors. Rituals are often associated with obsessive-compulsive disorders.

selective attention   The ability to choose to focus on specific details at the exclusion of others.

SSRIs   Short for selective serotonin reuptake inhibitors; a class of antidepressants. Long-term use of SSRIs may cause dependency.

Stages of Change   A widely accepted model, developed by psychologists Carlo DiClemente, Ph.D., and James Prochaska, Ph.D., that summarizes the six steps an individual goes through when making a change. These steps are precontemplation, contemplation, preparation, action, maintenance, and termination or relapse.

status quo   A Latin term that means "state in which." In common use, we use the phrase to mean the situation as it currently exists.

stream of consciousness writing   A method of writing your thoughts as they come to you without concern for grammar, structure, or punctuation.

stress   Pressures we experience that affect us physically and emotionally.

substitution   Replacing an undesirable habit with a more desirable one.

support system   A network of people and resources that provide encouragement for a person as he's making changes.

symptoms   Subjective experiences of feelings and sensations. An acute symptom arises suddenly, is typically intense, and is of short, predictable duration. A chronic symptom develops over time, usually is less intense than an acute symptom, and continues indefinitely.

syndrome   A set of symptoms and signs that consistently occur together.

tai chi   A martial art that uses slow, graceful movements to focus and integrate the energy of the body and the mind.

talk therapy   See *psychoanalysis.*

tapering   A quit process of gradually cutting back on the undesired habit.

tolerance   The brain's diminished response to persistent stimulation.

trichotillomania   Compulsive behavior of pulling the hair, sometimes pulling it out.

trigger   The circumstance—which may be a person, place, event, experience, stressor, or other factor—that activates a habit.

urge   The intent to act on a craving.

varenicline   A non-nicotine medication to help with smoking cessation that works by blocking nicotine's effect in the brain.

ventral tegmental area (VTA)   A collective of specialized neurons near the base of the brain, just above the brainstem, which produces significant amounts of the feel-good neurotransmitter dopamine.

visualization   A relaxation technique of holding a particular image in one's thoughts and focusing on the supportive or pleasant feelings the image evokes.

withdrawal   Symptoms—physical, cognitive, and emotional—that occur when quitting an addictive habit.

yoga   From an ancient Sanskrit word that means "to yoke," a mind-body practice that combines poses (body positions) and meditation.

Resources

Looking for additional information? Here are some resources to steer you in the direction of your interests.

Web-Based Resources

www.aap.org   The website of the American Academy of Pediatrics, the accreditation board for pediatricians in the United States, features a public education section with articles about children's health and behavior.

www.affirmationplanet.com   This website posts a new affirmation every day.

www.alcoholics-anonymous.org   This website for Alcoholics Anonymous (AA), the original 12-step program, provides information about alcohol abuse and links to locate AA meetings around the world.

www.americanheart.org   Smoking is the leading cause of heart disease. The American Heart Association provides online articles and print material about the health consequences of smoking as well as resources for smoking cessation. The AHA website also has information for healthy eating and exercise.

www.caron.org   A not-for-profit organization, Caron provides treatment programs and resources for chemical dependencies.

www.debtorsanonymous.org   Debtors Anonymous (DA) applies the 12-step model to compulsive shopping and spending. This website provides information, resources, and links to locate DA meetings.

www.dhamma.org   This website features S. N. Goenka teachings of Vipassana meditation, authentic to the tradition of this ancient heritage. The website also offers informational articles and discussions as well as listings of classes worldwide, which are taught at no charge.

www.eatingdisorderfoundation.org   The Eating Disorders Foundation is a not-for-profit organization that provides education, advocacy, resources, and support for people who have eating disorders.

www.eatingdisordersanonymous.org   Eating Disorders Anonymous (EDA) applies the 12-step model to eating disorders. This website provides educational articles, resources, and links to locate local EDA meetings.

www.gamblersanonymous.org   Gamblers Anonymous (GA) applies the 12-step model to compulsive gambling. This website features information, resources, and links to locate GA meetings.

www.hazelden.org   The Hazelden Foundation is a not-for-profit organization providing help for people who have alcohol and other substance dependencies.

www.kidshealth.org   The Nemours Foundation operates this website. Three divisions tailor health content for specific audiences: kids, teens, and parents. Articles tackle topics of current interest including drugs, alcohol, smoking, sexual health, steroid use, eating disorders, cutting (self-injury), self-esteem, and food and fitness.

www.lungusa.org   Smoking is the leading cause of lung disease. The American Lung Association provides online articles about the health consequences of smoking and resources for smoking cessation. The ALA sponsors the free online smoking cessation program, Freedom from Smoking.

www.mayoclinic.org   The health information website of the Mayo Clinic provides in-depth articles about health topics including addictions, smoking cessation, eating disorders, sexual obsession, and other compulsive behavior conditions.

www.medhelp.org   This website is a collection of online support groups and forums for a broad range of health topics. Several dozen physicians, psychologists, and other health-care professionals from various medical centers participate in the forums to answer questions and provide information.

www.meditationcenter.com   This website provides instruction in basic meditation techniques for mindfulness, relaxation, stress reduction, centering, and healing.

www.na.org   Narcotics Anonymous (NA) follows the 12-step model of recovery from substance abuse. This website provides access to informational literature and links to locate NA meetings worldwide.

www.oa.org   Overeaters Anonymous (OA) applies the 12-step recovery model to compulsive eating. The OA website features resources and support as well as links to locate OA meetings.

www.ocfoundation.org   The Obsessive-Compulsive Foundation provides information and resources for people who have obsessive-compulsive disorders.

www.ocfoundation.org/hoarding   This website focuses on compulsive hoarding and hoarding disorders, providing informational articles and links to support groups.

www.sexaa.org   Sex Addicts Anonymous (SAA) applies the 12-step model of recovery to sexual addictions. The SAA website features educational information, resources, and links to locate local meetings.

www.umassmed.edu/Content.aspx?id=41252&linkidentifier=id&itemid=41252
This unwieldy web address takes you to the website with an equally unwieldy moniker, The University of Massachusetts Medical School Center for Mindfulness in Medicine, Health Care, and Society. It's worth the care in keyboarding … UMass is the home base of mindfulness guru Jon Kabat-Zinn.

www.webmd.com   This general health and wellness website offers articles and suggestions about various addictive habits.

Books and Publications

Adamson, Eve, and Gayle Williamson. *The Complete Idiot's Guide Dream Dictionary*. Indianapolis: Alpha Books, 2007.

Baer, Ruth A., ed. *Mindfulness-Based Treatment Approaches: Clinician's Guide to Evidence Base and Applications*. Burlington, MA: Academic Press, 2005.

Benson, April Lane, ed. *I Shop, Therefore I Am: Compulsive Buying and the Search for Self*. New York: Jason Aronson Publishers, Inc., 2000.

Blumenthal, Noah. *You're Addicted to You: Why It's So Hard to Change—and What You Can Do About It*. San Francisco: Berrett-Koehler Publishers, Inc., 2007.

Brach, Tara, Ph.D. *Radical Acceptance: Embracing Your Life with the Heart of a Buddha.* New York: Bantam Books, 2003.

Brick, John, Ph.D., and Carlton K. Erickson, Ph.D. *Drugs, the Brain, and Behavior: The Pharmacology of Abuse and Dependence.* Binghamton, New York: The Haworth Medical Press, Inc., 1998.

Carnes, Patrick J., Ph.D. *Out of the Shadows: Understanding Sexual Addiction* (third edition). Center City, MN: Hazelden, 2001.

Daley, Dennis C., and G. Alan Marlatt. *Overcoming Your Alcohol or Drug Problem: Effective Recovery Strategies Therapist Guide* (second edition). New York: Oxford University Press, Inc., 2006.

———. *Overcoming Your Alcohol or Drug Problem: Effective Recovery Strategies Workbook* (second edition). New York: Oxford University Press, Inc., 2006.

Danowski, Debbie, Ph.D., and Pedro Lazaro, M.D. *Why Can't I Stop Eating? Recognizing, Understanding, and Overcoming Food Addiction.* Center City, MN: Hazelden, 2000.

DiClemente, Carlo C. *Addiction and Change: How Addictions Develop and Addicted People Recover.* New York: The Guilford Press, 2003.

Dimeff, Linda, et al. *Brief Alcohol Screening and Intervention for College Students (BASICS): A Harm Reduction Approach.* New York: The Guilford Press, 1999.

Dodes, Lance, M.D. *The Heart of Addiction: A New Approach to Understanding and Managing Alcoholism and Other Addictive Behaviors.* New York: HarperCollins Publishers, 2002.

Donovan, Dennis M., and G. Alan Marlatt, eds. *Assessment of Addictive Behaviors, Second Edition.* New York: The Guilford Press, 2005.

DuPont, Robert L., M.D. *The Selfish Brain: Learning from Addiction.* Center City, MN: Hazelden, 2000.

Erickson, Carlton K. *The Science of Addiction: From Neurobiology to Treatment.* New York: W. W. Norton & Company, Inc., 2007.

Glickman, Marshall. *Beyond the Breath: Extraordinary Mindfulness Through Whole-Body Vipanassana Meditation.* Boston: Periplus Editions (HK) Ltd., 2002.

Grant, Jon E., J.D., M.D., and S. W. Kim, M.D. *Stop Me Because I Can't Stop Myself: Taking Control of Impulsive Behavior.* New York: McGraw-Hill, 2004.

Griffiths, Mark. *Gambling and Gaming Addictions in Adolescence.* Oxford: Blackwell Publishers, 2002.

Gunaratana, Bhante Henepola. *Mindfulness in Plain English: Updated and Expanded Edition.* Somerville, MA: Wisdom Publications, 2002.

Gwinnell, Esther, M.D., and Christine A. Adamec. *The Encyclopedia of Addictions and Addictive Behaviors.* New York: Facts on File, 2005.

Hetherington, Ian. *Realizing Change: Vipassana Meditation in Action.* Onalaska, Washington: Pariyatti Publishing, 2003.

Hoffman, John, and Susan Froemke. *Addiction: Why Can't They Just Stop?* New York: Rodale, Inc., 2007.

Ihnen, Anne, MA, LMHC, and Carolyn Flynn. *The Complete Idiot's Guide to Mindfulness.* Indianapolis: Alpha Books, 2008.

Kabat-Zinn, Jon. *Arriving at Your Own Door: 108 Lessons in Mindfulness.* New York: Hyperion Books, 2007.

———. *Full Catastrophe Living: Using the Wisdom of Your Body and Mind to Face Stress, Pain, and Illness.* New York: Dell Publishing, 1990.

———. *Mindfulness for Beginners* (audiobook). Louisville, CO: Sounds True, 2006.

———. *Wherever You Go There You Are: Mindfulness Meditation in Everyday Life (Tenth Anniversary Edition).* New York: Hyperion Books, 2005.

Katherine, Anne. *When Misery is Company: End Self-Sabotage and Become Content.* Center City, MN: Hazelden, 2004.

Koob, George F., and Michel Le Moal. *Neurobiology of Addiction.* Burlington, MA: Academic Press, 2006.

LaMarr, June, and G. Alan Marlatt. *Canoe Journey: Life's Journey.* Center City, MN: Hazelden Press, 2007.

Lancelot, Marilyn. *Gripped by Gambling.* Tucson, AZ: Wheatmark, 2007.

Marlatt, G. Alan, and Dennis M. Donovan, eds. *Relapse Prevention: Maintenance Strategies in the Treatment of Addictive Behaviors, Second Edition.* New York: The Guilford Press, 2005.

McQuaid, John R., Ph.D., and Paula E. Carmona, R.N., M.S.N. *Peaceful Mind: Using Mindfulness and Cognitive Behavioral Psychology to Overcome Depression.* Oakland, CA: New Harbinger Publications, Inc., 2004.

McQuillan, Susan, M.S., R.D. *Breaking the Bonds of Food Addiction*. Indianapolis: Alpha Books, 2004.

Miller, William R., and Kathleen M. Carroll, eds. *Rethinking Substance Abuse: What the Science Shows and What We Should Do About It*. New York: The Guilford Press, 2006.

Moran, Victoria. *Fat, Broke, and Lonely No More! Your Personal Solution to Overeating, Overspending, and Looking for Love in All the Wrong Places*. New York: HarperOne, 2007.

Newport, John, Ph.D. *The Wellness-Recovery Connection: Charting Your Pathway to Optimal Health While Recovering from Alcoholism and Drug Addiction*. Deerfield Beach, FL: Health Communications, Inc., 2004.

Prochaska, James O., Ph.D., John C. Norcross, Ph.D., and Carlo C. DiClemente, Ph.D. *Changing for Good: A Revolutionary Six-Stage Program for Overcoming Bad Habits and Moving Your Life Positively Forward*. New York: Collins, 2007.

Robinson, Bryan E., Ph.D. *Chained to the Desk: A Guidebook for Workaholics, Their Partners and Children, and the Clinicians Who Treat Them*. New York: New York University Press, 2007.

Siegel, Daniel J. *The Mindful Brain: Reflection and Attunement in the Cultivation of Well-Being*. New York: W. W. Norton & Company, Inc., 2007.

Steketee, Gail, and Randy O. Frost. *Compulsive Hoarding and Acquiring: Therapist Guide*. New York: Oxford University Press, Inc., 2007.

———. *Compulsive Hoarding and Acquiring: Workbook*. New York: Oxford University Press, Inc., 2007.

Thich Nhat Hanh. *The Miracle of Mindfulness* (second edition). Boston: Beacon Press, 1999.

———. *Peace is Every Step: The Path of Mindfulness in Everyday Life*. New York: Bantam Books, 1991.

Thombs, Dennis L. *Introduction to Addictive Behaviors, Third Edition*. New York: The Guilford Press, 2006.

Tolin, David F., Randy O. Frost, and Gail Steketee. *Buried in Treasures: Help for Compulsive Acquiring, Saving, and Hoarding*. New York: Oxford University Press, Inc., 2007.

Tucker, Jalie A., Dennis M. Donovan, and G. Alan Marlatt. *Changing Addictive Behavior: Bridging Clinical and Public Health Strategies*. New York: The Guilford Press, 2001.

Turner, V. J. *Secret Scars: Uncovering and Understanding the Addiction of Self-Injury*. Center City, MN: Hazelden, 2002.

Velasquez, Mary Marden, et al. *Group Treatment for Substance Abuse: A Stages-of-Change Therapy Manual*. New York: The Guilford Press, 2001.

Weiss, Andrew. *Beginning Mindfulness: Learning the Way of Awareness*. Novato, CA: New World Library, 2004.

Willard, Nancy E. *Cyber-Safe Kids, Cyber-Savvy Teens: Helping Young People Learn to Use the Internet Safely and Responsibly*. San Francisco: Jossey-Bass, 2007.

Witkiewitz, Katie, and G. Alan Marlatt, eds. *Therapist's Guide to Evidence-Based Relapse Prevention*. Burlington, MA: Academic Press, 2007.

Wright, Judith. *The Soft Addiction Solution: Break Free of the Seemingly Harmless Habits that Keep You from the Life You Want*. New York: Jeremy P. Tarcher/Penguin, 2006.

Affirmations

Affirmations are more than simply "feel-good" slogans. Affirmations are statements that describe your ideal self in tangible, positive, present-tense words. What you believe, you are. Affirmations help you express what you believe about yourself.

To get you started, we've written 31 general affirmations that you can use or adapt, once a day for a month. Affirmations are most effective when you say or read them to yourself throughout the day. Think about each word and how its meaning applies to you today.

Daily Affirmations

I am worthy of love, from myself and from others.

Today's experiences are gifts through which I learn and grow.

I like who I see when I look in the mirror.

What I say in kindness to another person, I say in kindness to myself.

I am strong.

My opinion matters.

I can say "no."

I am a beautiful person, inside and out.

I do my best, and it's good enough.

Today is only one day, and I can handle anything for only one day.

I am reliable.

I make a difference.

I, and I alone, control my thoughts and my actions.

I am my ideal self.

I tell the truth.

I respect my body.

I know a lot, and I use what I know to better myself, my family and friends, and my community.

I am fun to be with.

I am a good person.

I forgive myself.

I express my thoughts and feelings in ways that honor the thoughts and feelings of those who are listening to me.

I am calm and centered within myself.

I make only promises I can keep.

I trust myself.

I make choices and decisions that support the lifestyle I want to live.

I accept the help others offer me.

I am at peace with myself.

I cherish this day and appreciate that I am able to experience it.

I am patient with myself.

I bring goodness and joy into the lives of others.

I am resilient.

My Personal Affirmations

Use this space to write your own affirmations. When you write your affirmations, use language that is positive, direct, and personal ("I"). Write in the present tense, as though what you're saying is already happening.

Index

S

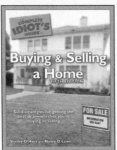
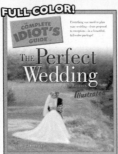

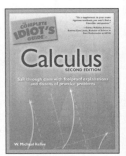